国际财务报告简明教程

主编 蒋 涌 陈健铭

郑州大学出版社

图书在版编目(CIP)数据

国际财务报告简明教程/蒋涌,陈健铭主编. — 郑州:郑州大学出版社,2023.6
ISBN 978-7-5645-9220-2

Ⅰ.①国… Ⅱ.①蒋…②陈… Ⅲ.①国际会计准则-教材 Ⅳ.①F233.1

中国版本图书馆 CIP 数据核字(2022)第 207500 号

国际财务报告简明教程
GUOJI CAIWU BAOGAO JIANMING JIAOCHENG

策划编辑	孙理达	封面设计	苏永生
责任编辑	丁忠华	版式设计	苏永生
责任校对	孙 泓	责任监制	李瑞卿
出版发行	郑州大学出版社	地　　址	郑州市大学路40号(450052)
出 版 人	孙保营	网　　址	http://www.zzup.cn
经　　销	全国新华书店	发行电话	0371-66966070
印　　刷	郑州印之星印务有限公司		
开　　本	787 mm×1 092 mm　1 / 16		
印　　张	17.25	字　　数	411 千字
版　　次	2023 年 6 月第 1 版	印　　次	2023 年 6 月第 1 次印刷
书　　号	ISBN 978-7-5645-9220-2	定　　价	58.00 元

本书如有印装质量问题,请与本社联系调换。

作者名单

主　编

蒋　涌　陈健铭

副主编

王美宁　蔡　欢

作者简介

主编简介：

蒋涌，广东外语外贸大学国际商务英语学院教授，博士后，副院长。主要研究领域：公司财务、国际财务报告准则。获广东外语外贸大学"青年教学十佳"、首届MBA教学奖、"我最喜欢的MBA老师"以及全美国际教育协会"国际交流贡献奖"等奖励。近年来，发表论文近20篇，其中核心论文近10篇，国际发表8篇。参编教材2部，获得教学成果奖2项。主持国家社科基金项目1项，教育部项目1项，省级项目4项，参与国家级（含省部级）项目4项。

陈健铭，广东外语外贸大学业界教授，国际注册会计师（ACCA）、英国皇家管理注册会计师（CIMA）、全球特许管理会计师（CGMA）、英国特许证券投资分析师（CISI）以及美国管理会计师（CMA），曾任香港某全球咨询公司财务总监，现任某教育公司总裁。教学和研究方向为企业财务管理和国际会计准则。2019年，受ACCA伦敦代表处邀请为全球ACCA会员讲授IFRS 16 Leases国际财务报告准则——租赁对企业财务报表的影响。

副主编简介：

王美宁，1992年毕业于广州外国语学院专门用途英语专业，获学士学位。2004年毕业于英国中央兰开夏大学，获工商管理硕士学位。2010—2011年，澳大利亚昆士兰大学访问学者。1992年至今任教于广东外语外贸大学国际商务英语学院，教研和科研方向：财务会计和管理会计，主持教育部产学合作协同育人CGMA课程体系下高水平师资建设项目。

蔡欢，广东外语外贸大学国际商务英语学院副教授，美国密苏里大学会计学硕士，澳门科技大学在读博士。曾主持教育部项目并参与多项国家级及省级项目，发表国内外核心期刊数篇。研究方向包括财务会计、公司金融与供应链管理。

内容提要

本书对《国际财务报告准则》(IFRS)的内容进行了深入浅出的剖析和详解。IFRS 为企业的财务人员提供了实务的工作参考,同时也规范了企业人员的实务工作。通过学习本书,您可以快速且高效地收获财务知识和财务技能;参照本书,您能迅速地积累财务理论知识,并结合工作实务,将理论用于实践。本书同时也为相关财务背景的学员提供了便捷的学习机会,本书详细且周密地对每一条准则做出了注解,并给出案例,最终做到让大众更方便地理解每一条准则的意义和用途,更有利地促进会计财务人员通过各项会计专业资格考试(ACCA、CGMA)等。本书覆盖的 IAS、IFRS 包括:IAS 2、IAS 8、IAS 10、IAS 12、IAS 16、IAS 20、IAS 21、IAS 23、IAS 32、IAS 33、IAS 36、IAS 37、IAS 38、IAS 40、IAS 41、IFRS 5、IFRS 7、IFRS 9、IFRS 15、IFRS 16。

前 言

习近平总书记多次强调,精心构建对外话语体系,增强对外话语的创造力、感召力、公信力,讲好中国故事,传播好中国声音,阐释好中国特色。高等教育必须培养通晓国际商业语言,了解中国企业实际的国际化商务人才。《国际财务报告准则》(IFRS)就是商业企业的国际通用话语体系,全球100多个国家的公司在准备财务报告的时候都已采用《国际财务报告准则》(IFRS),还有很多国家正处于向 IFRS 转换的过程中,其重要性日益彰显。撰写一本解释国际财务报告准则的主要内容、介绍准则在实务中具体应用的书,就显得尤有必要。一方面,随着我国有越来越多的企业在海外上市,利用国际财务报告准则编制的财务报表将逐渐成为国际上认可的报表,企业的会计及有关人员需要了解与掌握国际财务报告准则;另一方面,中国会计准则体系与国际财务报告准则逐渐趋同,学习国际财务报告准则有助于其掌握我国会计准则的思想与内容,推动我国会计准则的实施与应用;此外,我国的会计教育日益出现国际化的趋势,目前已经有越来越多的高校开设了 ACCA、CIMA、CGA 等国际会计资格证书特色方向班,主要讲授如何根据国际财务报告准则来编制财务报表,这些学生需要一套关于国际财务报告准则的参考用书。

目前已出版的关于国际财务报告准则解读方面的相关书籍不多,主要集中在翻译准则的原文,或者对原文本身进行解释。总体来看,现有教材和书籍难度较大,高深且难以理解,大多数不适合本科生的课程教学,市场亟需难度适合并且配以实际范例解释的教材。本教材对目前仍有效的国际会计准则的常用项的适用范围和主要内容、确认和计量,以及列报和披露等进行解读,并配合示例使读者能够全面认识和理解国际财务报告准则。

本教材的特点与优势包括:第一,易读性和时代性。贴近年轻学生读者的学习习惯,配合移动学习,以轻松的方式展示准则的内容;第二,引入丰富的实例,用深入浅出的框架式方法分解准则,配以企业示例,阐释其应用的领域;第三,整合了学术、业界和海外专家研究成果,各取所长,共同打造。因此,本书的出版必然迎合上述读者的需求,满足众多本科院校对此类教材的需要,并为对《国际财务报告准则》(IFRS)感兴趣的有关人士提供一本实用的参考用书。

本教程是省级教学团队"广东外语外贸大学 CIMA 全英教学团队"集体智慧的结晶,特别感谢团队的业界教授陈健铭老师,他对教程内容的无私奉献使本书更具实效性和实践价值。在编写过程中,本教程还借鉴了国内外专家的学术成果,获得广东省质量工程教学团队专项基金、国家级一流本科专业建设点(国际商务)的特别资助,得到了学院郭桂杭院长、彭玲玲副院长的大力支持。在此,向这些老师一并表示真诚的感谢。

限于水平和时间,本书难免存在错误和不妥之处,敬请读者批评指正。

《国际财务报告简明教程》编写组

2022年8月于广州白云山麓

Contents

Chapter 1　Inventories 1
    1.1　*Definition of Inventories* 2
    1.2　*Initial Measurement* 2
    1.3　*Subsequent Measurement* 6
    1.4　*Reasons Why Costs Are Higher Than NRV* 7
    1.5　*Reversal of Write-Down of Inventories* 8
    1.6　*Cost Formulae Example* 9
    1.7　*Consistency Requirement—Different Cost Formulas for Inventories* 13

Chapter 2　Tangible Non-Current Assets 14
    2.1　*IAS 16 PP & E Cost Accounting* 14
    2.2　*IAS 16 PP & E Depreciation Accounting* 27
    2.3　*IAS 40 Investment Property* 33
    2.4　*IAS 23 Borrowing Costs* 44

Chapter 3　Intangible Assets 53
    3.1　*Recognition and Amortisation* 54
    3.2　*Goodwill：IFRS 3 Business Combinations* 70

Chapter 4　Impairment of Assets 72
    4.1　*Different Standards Dealing with Impairment* 72
    4.2　*Definitions* 73
    4.3　*Identifying a Potentially Impaired Asset* 75
    4.4　*Common Impairment Indicators in Different Industries* 78
    4.5　*Accounting Entries* 78
    4.6　*Cash-Generating Units (CGUs)* 78
    4.7　*Examples of CGUs* 79
    4.8　*Considerations to Determine a CGU* 79
    4.9　*Practical Examples to Determine a CGU* 79

4.10	*Impairment Test for CGU*	82
4.11	*Allocated Goodwill*	83
4.12	*"Consistency" Rule*	84
4.13	*Impairment Reversal for an Individual Asset*	85

Chapter 5 Revenue 89

5.1	*Scope*	89
5.2	*Key Definitions*	90
5.3	*Five-Step Model [COPAR]*	92
5.4	*IFRS 15 Five Steps in Detail*	94
5.5	*Incremental Costs of Obtaining a Contract (Contract Costs)*	117
5.6	*Common Types of Transactions*	119
5.7	*Presentation*	127
5.8	*Disclosure*	127
5.9	*Contract in Progress*	127

Chapter 6 Non-Current Assets Held for Sale and Discontinued Operations 138

6.1	*Objective*	139
6.2	*Scope*	139
6.3	*Definitions*	140
6.4	*Classification of Non-current Assets (or Disposal Groups) as Held for Sale*	140
6.5	*Non-Current Assets to Be Abandoned*	143
6.6	*Initial Measurement of Non-Current Assets Held for Sale*	144
6.7	*Subsequent Measurement*	145
6.8	*Impairment Reversal*	145
6.9	*Ceases to Be Held for Sale*	146
6.10	*Accounting Treatment When the Sale Is Expected to Be Beyond One Year*	147
6.11	*Presentation of a Non-Current Asset or Disposal Group Classified as Held for Sale*	148
6.12	*Additional Disclosures*	149
6.13	*Presenting Discontinued Operations*	150

Chapter 7   IFRS 16 Leases   154
- 7.1   Definitions and Scope of a Lease   154
- 7.2   Lessee's Accounting   156
- 7.3   Lessee's Accounting in Detail: Right-of-Use Assets   163
- 7.4   Lease Identification   165
- 7.5   Recognition Exemptions   175
- 7.6   Sale and Leaseback Transactions   177

Chapter 8   IAS 37 & IAS 10   183
- 8.1   Provisions   183
- 8.2   Contingent Liabilities   194
- 8.3   Contingent Assets   195
- 8.4   Adjusting Event   197
- 8.5   Non-Adjusting Event   198

Chapter 9   IAS 33 Earnings Per Share (EPS)   201
- 9.1   Objective   202
- 9.2   Scope   202
- 9.3   Definitions   202
- 9.4   Basic Earnings Per Share (EPS)   203
- 9.5   Treatment of Preference Dividends   205
- 9.6   Practical Steps to Calculate the Weighted Average Number of Shares Outstanding   207
- 9.7   Effects on EPS of Changes in Capital Structure   209
- 9.8   Diluted EPS   216
- 9.9   Alternative EPS Figures   225
- 9.10   Significance of Earnings Per Share   226

Chapter 10   IAS 8 Accounting Policies, Changes in Accounting Estimates and Errors   227
- 10.1   Key Definitions   228
- 10.2   Selection and Application of Accounting Policies   229
- 10.3   Consistency of Accounting Policies   229
- 10.4   Change in Accounting Policy   230
- 10.5   Retrospective Application   230

10.6	*Disclosures*	233
10.7	*Comparability*	233
10.8	*Changes in Accounting Estimates*	234
10.9	*Prospective Adjustments*	234
10.10	*Consistency and Comparability*	235
10.11	*Disclosure*	235
10.12	*Correction of Accounting Errors*	236
10.13	*Disclosure*	237
Chapter 11	**Taxation**	239
11.1	*Key Definitions*	241
11.2	*Accounting Treatment for Corporation Tax*	241
11.3	*Underpayment of Corporation Tax*	242
11.4	*Over Payment of Corporation Tax*	242
11.5	*Payment to the Tax Authority*	242
11.6	*Tax Rates or Tax Laws Which Are Enacted or Substantively Enacted*	243
11.7	*Trading Losses Carried Back*	243
11.8	*Trial Balance Where the Under or Over Provision of Corporation Tax Is Shown*	244
11.9	*Tax Directly in Equity*	245
11.10	*Deferred Tax*	246
11.11	*Deferred Tax Liabilities*	250
11.12	*Deferred Tax Assets*	250
11.13	*Difference Between Temporary/Timing Difference and Permanent Differences*	252
11.14	*Deferred Tax Implications for Specific Items*	252
11.15	*Components in Deferred Tax*	258
11.16	*Changes in the Tax Rate in the Deferred Tax Calculation*	259
11.17	*Discounting for Deferred Tax*	259
11.18	*Presentation in P/L*	260
11.19	*The Reason to Calculate the Deferred Tax*	261
11.20	*Presentation of Current Tax and Deferred Tax*	263
References		264

Chapter 1

Inventories

IAS 2 Inventories

Topic outline:

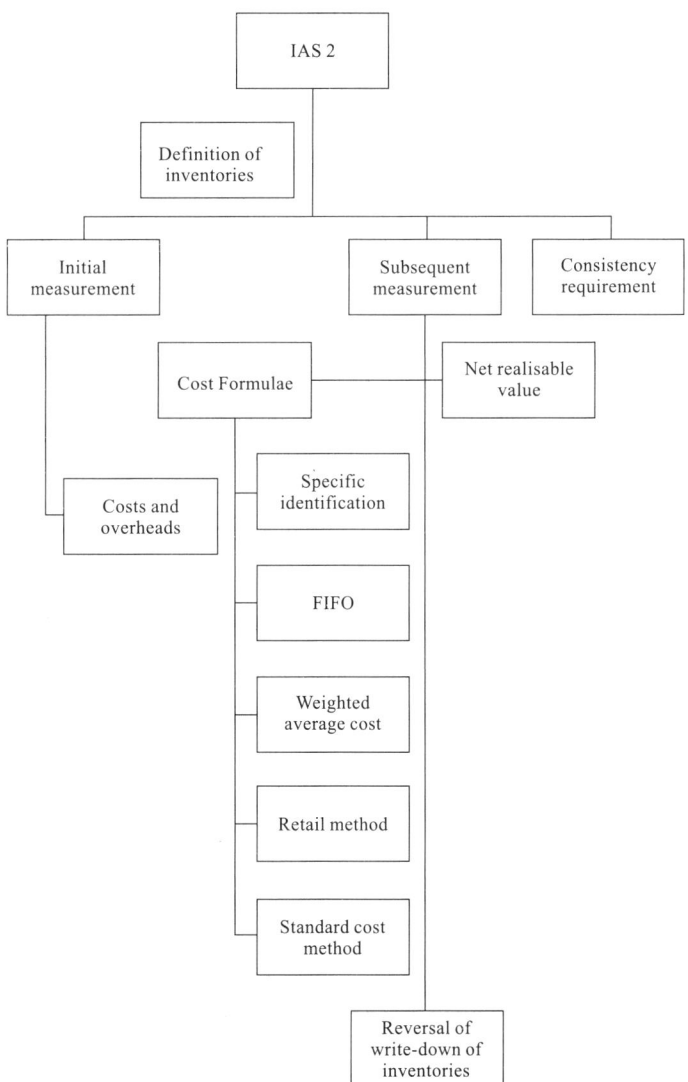

1.1 Definition of Inventories

No.	Easy Rules
1	**Inventories are assets:** 1. Held for sale in the ordinary course of business. For instance, bottles of water in the supermarket to be sold to customers. 2. In the production process for sale, i.e. work in progress or partly-finished inventories. For instance, partly-finished cars at the automotive manufacturing plant. 3. In the form of materials or supplies to be consumed in the production process or in the rendering of services. For instance, ingredients or materials such as flour, sugar, salt, baking powder and milk for breadmaking within a bakery. (IAS 2:para.6-8)

1.2 Initial Measurement

No.	Easy Rules
1	The following items should be included in the inventories costs. **Purchase Costs:** • Initial purchase price. However, the trade discount on sale (such as 30% off) should be excluded from the initial purchase price; rebates such as the refund received from the seller if the business purchases goods exceeding a certain amount should also be excluded from the initial purchase price. • Import duties or value added taxes not recoverable from tax authorities when importing inventories from other countries. • Transportation or carriage inwards costs. • Handling costs the business pays to move inventories into the production line. • Any other cost directly attributable to the acquisition of finished goods, services and materials such as specific storage, insurance costs and specific packaging costs for inventories purchased. For instance, certain unique biological assets need special storage before they are further processed in the next production stage, to make sure the temperature is minus 150 Celsius; Jewellery may also incur specific packaging costs such as the acquisition of beautiful velvet gift boxes.

No.	Easy Rules
2	**Conversion Costs:** • Labour costs and overheads expenses. • Variable and fixed production overheads incurred in converting materials into finished goods. For instance, electricity, other utility costs, factory rents as well as property taxes.
3	**Costs Should not be Included in Inventories According to IAS 2** • Abnormal wastage of materials, labour, or other production costs such as machine breakdown repair expenses. • General storage costs incurred not specifically for purchased inventories such as general rent expenses in the warehouse. • Administrative overhead not incurred to bring inventories to their present location, and costs such as security guard salary and CCTV. • Selling costs to sell those inventories such as salespersons' salaries and wages, commissions, payroll taxes and advertising costs. (IAS 2:para. 10–16)

Example:

Jackson Ltd has the following costs for the acquired inventories:

	$
Purchase price of materials	1,000
5% trade discount	50
	950
Import duty at 10%	95
Direct labour costs	100
Allocation of fixed production overhead	30
General storage costs (after inventories are complete)	20
Advertising costs	10
Specific storage costs (before inventories are passed to the next production stage)	15
Total costs	1,220

Note: 20% of the materials above were wasted because of an abnormal machine breakdown.

Required: Calculate the total costs to be included in inventories.

Answer:

		$
	Purchase price of materials (exclude the abnormal wastage net of trade discount): ($1,000 – $50)×(1–20%)	760
	Import duty at 10% (revised) 10% × $760 (above)	76
	Direct labour costs	100
	Allocation of fixed production overhead	30
	Specific storage costs	15
	Total costs to be included in inventories	981

Allocation of Overheads:

No.	**Easy Rules**
1	Examples of variable production overheads expenses include electricity expenses and machine maintenance costs. Examples of fixed production overheads expenses include machine depreciation and rent costs. Variable production overheads expenses should be allocated based on the actual use of production facilities. Fixed production overheads expenses should be allocated based on the normal capacity of the department. Because by doing so, low production or idle plant will not result in a higher fixed overhead allocation to each unit.
2	However, if the production is abnormally high during the period, the fixed production overhead allocated to each unit needs to be reduced to avoid inventories being stated at more than cost.
3	Normal capacity is the average level of capacity after considering the loss of capacity of planned maintenance and the customers' demand. For instance, the capacity level for the business in year one was to produce 1,000 units of products and 1,200 units of products in year two; normal capacity is therefore 1,100 units of product (dividing the total 2,200 units by two years).

No.	Easy Rules
4	The overheads should be charged or absorbed to inventories according to actual resources needed. For instance, according to IAS 2, the absorption costing method should be used to charge the overhead absorption rate into products using different bases, such as machine or labour hours. Suppose the fixed production overheads per labour hour is $ 0.05 and the product production requires 100 hours. Therefore, the fixed production overheads costs charged to the product should be $ 5 ($ 0.05/hour×100 hours used). (IAS 2: para. 13-14)

Example:

A business produces inventory B in the manufacturing department. The variable production overheads incurred was $ 3,000 whereas the fixed production overheads costs were $ 2,000. The normal capacity of the department is 100,000 hours.

Situation 1: Suppose the actual capacity of the department was to be 80,000 hours used during the period. Calculate the total production costs of inventory B.

First, let's calculate the production overhead absorption rate. This is achieved by dividing costs by capacity:

$$\frac{\text{Variable production overhead}}{\text{Actual capacity}} + \frac{\text{Fixed production overhead}}{\text{Normal capacity}} *$$

$$= \frac{\$ 3,000}{80,000 \text{ hours}} + \frac{\$ 2,000}{100,000 \text{ hours}}$$

$$= \$ 0.0375/\text{hour} + \$ 0.02/\text{hour}$$

$$= \$ 0.0575/\text{hour}$$

Dr	Finished goods $ 0.0575/hour×80,000 hours	$ 4,600
Cr	Costs of sales	$ 4,600

* The reason normal capacity is used when calculating the fixed production overheads per hour is to avoid overstating the inventories costs due to low production level. In this case, the actual capacity is lower than normal, i.e. 80% of capacity has been utilised. If the fixed overheads costs calculation were to be based on actual capacity, i.e. if we divided $ 2,000 by 80,000 hours, equalling $ 0.025/hour, this would result in a higher inventory cost and this is not allowed.

From the above calculation, total fixed production overhead expenses should be $ 2,000 with only $ 1,600 ($ 0.02/hour × 80,000 hours) being charged to products. Therefore, the remaining $ 400 fixed production overheads expenses are not absorbed. The unallocated $ 400 should be charged to costs:

Dr	Costs of sales	$ 400
Cr	Production overheads	$ 400

Situation 2: Suppose the actual capacity of the department was to be 110,000 hours used, calculate the total production costs of inventory B.

$$\underline{\text{Variable production overhead}} \quad + \quad \underline{\text{Fixed production overhead}}$$
$$\text{Actual capacity} ** \quad\quad\quad \text{Actual capacity} ***$$

$$= \frac{\$\ 3,000}{110,000 \text{ hours}} \quad + \quad \frac{\$\ 2,000}{110,000 \text{ hours}}$$

$$= \$\ 0.027/\text{hour} \quad + \quad \$\ 0.018/\text{hour}$$

$$= \$\ 0.045/\text{hour}$$

(rounded to three decimal places)

Dr	Finished goods $ 0.045/hour×110,000 hours	$ 4,950
Cr	Costs of sales	$ 4,950

** For variable production overheads, the overhead absorption rate calculation should be based on the actual capacity.

*** For fixed production overheads, if the production level is abnormally high during this year, i.e. the actual capacity of 110,000 hours is greater than the normal capacity, in order not to overstate inventories costs, the actual capacity (the higher figure) should be used.

This is because if the normal capacity were used in the calculation, the fixed production overheads per hour would be $ 0.02/hour and if we absorbed $ 0.02/hour to the actual capacity of 110,000 hours, this would leave us $ 2,200 total fixed production overhead costs, more than the $ 2,000 actually incurred. The fixed production overhead costs would not change irrespective of the changes in production volume.

1.3 Subsequent Measurement

No.	Easy Rules
1	Total inventories costs are calculated by multiplying the volume and their value. According to IAS 2, total inventories value should be the lower of costs and net realisable value. (IAS 2: para. 9)

Example:

B&G Ltd. has the following items of inventories:

Items	Cost	Net realisable value (NRV) *
A	$ 100	$ 80
B	$ 250	$ 350
C	$ 300	$ 290

* Net realisable value (NRV) is calculated by using the inventory expected selling price and to subtract the costs to complete and sell the inventory, such as advertising and commission fees.

The cost of each item of inventory is determined by the original purchase costs, conversion and other costs mentioned above. In later studies, we will also see examples where costs could be calculated using other methods.

For each item of inventory, the value is determined as follows:

Items	Cost	Net realisable value (NRV) *	Lower of cost and NRV
A	$ 100	$ 80	$ 80
B	$ 250	$ 350	$ 250
C	$ 300	$ 290	$ 290
		In total =	$ 620

* The value of individual inventory items is determined by the lower of cost OR net realisable value, and the total inventories value is determined by the lower of cost AND net realisable value.

1.4 *Reasons Why Costs Are Higher Than NRV*

No.	Easy Rules
1	The reason for the inventory net realisable value being lower than its original cost is that the inventory will be sold at a loss. For instance, obsolete or damaged inventory would result in a lower net sales revenue than its costs. The net realisable value is a management estimate and therefore, some businesses may try to overstate it to avoid recognising any inventories losses.

No.	Easy Rules
2	Below are common ways this is done: • Hiding the actual selling price by issuing invoices late to customers; • Overstating the estimated selling price of those inventories which does not agree with its past sales; • Excluding additional costs to complete the inventories. For instance, if the stock is returned by the customer, there might be additional repair costs or packaging costs to turn the stock into a resalable condition again. • Understating selling expenses such as advertising and commission fees. This could be detected by analysing and comparing the selling expense to sales revenue ratio to confirm whether this is reasonable.

1.5 Reversal of Write-Down of Inventories

No.	Easy Rules
1	The amount of any reversal of any write-down of inventories, arising from an increase in NRV, is recognised as a reduction in the amount of inventories recognised as an expense in the period in which the reversal occurs. (IAS 2: para. 34)

Example:

At the end of the first year, the cost of the inventory item A is $ 15 and its net realisable value is $ 12.

At the end of the second year, the cost of the inventory item A is still $ 15 but its net realisable value is revised to $ 18.

Required: Accounting entry.

Answer:

The first year:

Dr	Costs of sales	$ 3
Cr	Inventory	$ 3

The second year:

Dr	Inventory	$ 3
Cr	Costs of sales	$ 3

1.6 Cost Formulae Example

Let's apply these methods based on the following example:

Case: Paw & Simon Ltd. has recorded the following inventory movements:

Date	Transaction	Value
1st January	Purchased inventory A	$ 100
1st February	Purchased inventory B	$ 120
1st March	Sold the inventory	

Method 1: Specific Identification Method:

(IAS 2: para. 23-24)

This method is suitable for businesses selling high value or a small number of easily-distinguishable inventories. Examples include selling jewellery, high value limited edition cars, handicrafts, ships and aircraft. Suppose the selling price of inventory A is $ 500. The cost of inventory A is $ 100 per the original record. Therefore, the profit from the sale is $ 400 ($ 500 selling price and minus $ 100 costs).

We can argue that this method makes sense because the selling price of inventory A should be matched the cost of inventory A. We should not use the cost of inventory B to match with inventory A's selling price. The inventory cost flow matches its physical flow. However, think about what happens if the business sells lots of items, let's say thousands of items of inventories. It may not be practical for businesses to correctly measure their actual cost flow because this will significantly increase the management cost. A disadvantage of this method is that the profit may somehow be manipulated by the management if similar inventory items are purchased with different prices.

Method 2: First In, First Out (FIFO) Method:

(IAS 2: para. 25)

This is different from the above method because the cost of inventory measured does not agree with its physical flow. It assumes the inventory purchased first should be sold first, and therefore, the cost of the inventory sold should be matched with the inventory cost purchased first. Let's look at how this method applies to the above example:

Date	Transaction	Value
1st January	Purchased inventory A	$ 100
1st February	Purchased inventory B	$ 120
1st March	Sold the inventory	Cost = $ 100 *

* This method assumes that inventories are very similar in nature. The cost is $ 100 in this case because the inventory A was purchased earlier than the inventory B, hence when the inventory is sold, the inventory A cost should be used.

This method is logical to businesses selling perishable items such as food and flowers, because older items deteriorate if they are not sold first. In a period when there is inflation, i. e. the purchase price increases over time, this method may yield a higher profit compared to other methods. The reason is when the old item of inventory is sold, its low cost is recognised in the statement of profit or loss, and therefore it gives a higher profit.

A disadvantage of this method is that the business increases its management costs because the business needs to identify each batch of inventories separately.

Another disadvantage is that the cost and revenue of the inventory do not accord. From the above example, the selling price of the inventory is now $ 500, and this selling price should match its latest cost of $ 120 instead of $ 100. However, if the cost of $ 120 is used in this case, this is called the "Last in, first out (LIFO)" method, and this is not allowed in most countries including the UK, China, Singapore as well as International Accounting Standard. However, this is allowed in the United States of America.

Method 3: Cumulative or Continuous Weighted Average Cost (AVCO) Method:

(IAS 2: para. 27)

The cumulative or continuous weighted average cost method assumes that the new cost of inventory is recalculated each time a new purchase is made.

Date	Transaction	Value
1st January	Purchased inventory A	$ 100
1st February	Purchased inventory B	$ 120
1st March	Sold the inventory	Cost = $\dfrac{\$ 100 + \$ 120}{1 + 1 *}$ = $ 110

* The denominator is two, because one item of each inventory A and B was purchased. However, if we change the scenario to three items of inventory A and five items of inventory B:

Date	Transaction	Value
1st January	Purchased 3 items of inventory A, each @ $ 100	$ 300
1st February	Purchased 5 items of inventory B, each @ $ 120	$ 600
1st March	Sold the inventory	Cost $= \dfrac{\$\ 900}{3+5} = \$\ 112.5$

This method works in a perpetual inventory system. The perpetual inventory system means the cost of the inventory is determined both when it is purchased and when it is sold. This is different from the periodic inventory system explained below. The double entry to record the transaction is as follows:

1. When inventories were purchased:

Dr	Inventory (A and B: $ 100+ $ 120)	$ 220
Cr	Cash or payable	$ 220

2. Recognise their costs when inventories are sold:

The inventories costs of $ 220 match against their selling revenue, and profits are therefore calculated. Businesses do not need to identify different batches of inventories separately using this method. However, the downside of this method is that since the average inventory cost is calculated, this value is entirely different from the actual cost. In the above case, inventory A or B was purchased at $ 100 and $ 120, but the average price for the inventory is calculated as $ 110 using this method.

Method 4: Periodic Weighted Average Cost Method:

(IAS 2: para. 27)

Method three works well in the perpetual inventory system and method four works well in the periodic inventory system. The periodic inventory system means the inventory cost can only be known at the end of the period, i.e. at the end of each month, quarter or even the year end after the inventory count takes place. This means that when the business acquiresinventories, inventories costs are included in the "purchases" account, and the purchases account is then used to calculate the total costs of sales when the number of unsold inventories is known. The value of each item of unsold inventory is calculated using this method. The average cost of each unsold inventory is calculated by dividing the total opening inventories and purchased inventories costs into the number of opening and purchased inventories during the period.

From the above example, the cost of each item of unsold inventory is calculated as ($100 + $120) / (1+1) = $110. This value happens to be the same as we have seen in method three, but this value would be different under these two systems if more transactions were to take place. The following journal entries would be recorded using this method:

1. When inventories were purchased:

Dr	Purchases	$220
Cr	Cash or payable	$220

2. There will be no costs to be recognised when inventories are sold.
3. At the end of the accounting period, when the inventory count takes place, the unsold inventory volume is one unit (let's say), the closing inventory value is calculated as one unit multiplied by $110/unit which gives us $110 in total. The following entry would be made:

Dr	Inventory (closing inventory)	$110
Cr	Costs of sales	$110

If we combine these into the costs of sales calculation in the statement of profit or loss:

Opening inventories	0
Purchases	$220
Closing inventories	$(110)
Total costs of sales	$110

The inventory control may be weak if the periodic system is used, i.e. total inventories sold will only rely on the inventory counting records at the end of the period. Therefore, some items of inventory may have been stolen during the period but the business may not notice this.

Other Methods:
- The retail method may be used by retailers or wholesalers where inventory value is determined by using their sales value and subtracting the appropriate gross margin. Let's say the selling price of inventory A is $10, the gross margin is 40%; therefore, its cost is 60% multiplied by the selling price of $10, which gives us $6.
- The standard costs method is also widely used by manufacturing businesses where the direct material, labour and other cost elements are standardised. The business sets the predetermined costs for those elements, and accounts for the changes of those costs during the year.

1.7 Consistency Requirement—Different Cost Formulas for Inventories

No.	Easy Rules
1	IAS 2 provides that an entity should use the same cost formula for all inventories having similar nature and use to the entity. For inventories with different nature or use, for instance, certain commodities used in one business segment and the same type of commodities used in another business segment, different cost formulas may be justified. A difference in geographical location of inventories and in the respective tax rules are not sufficient to justify the use of different cost formulas. (IAS 2: para. 25)

Chapter 2

Tangible Non-Current Assets

IAS 16 PP &E Property, Plant and Equipment

2.1 *IAS 16 PP &E Cost Accounting*

Topic outline:

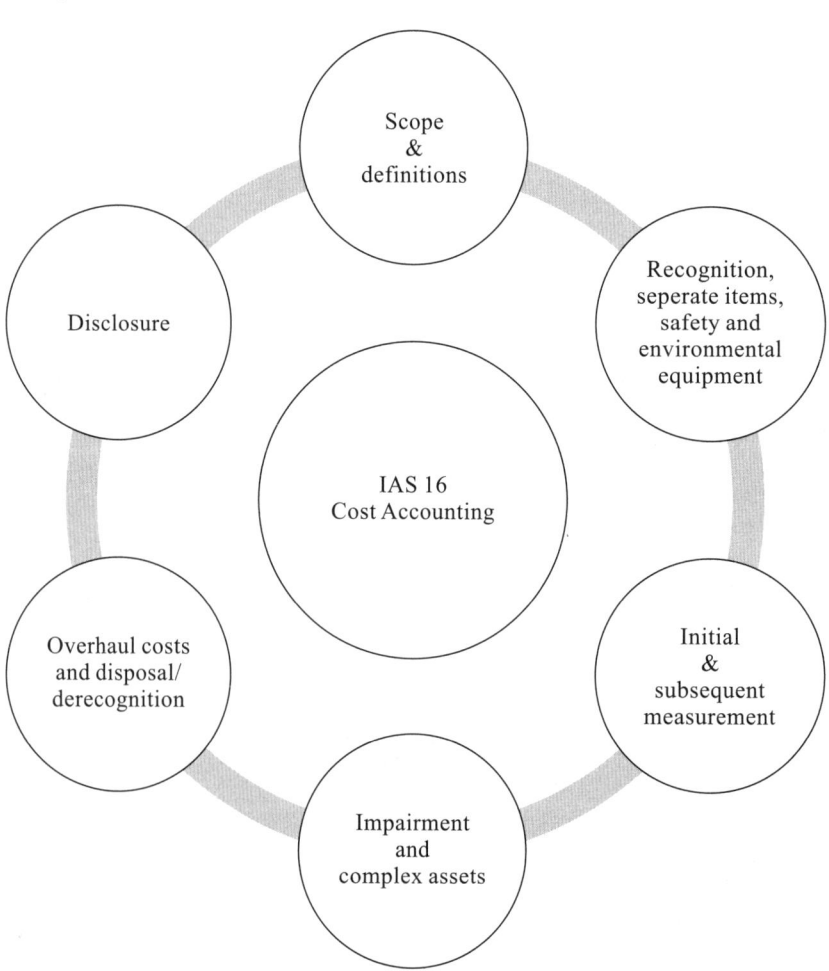

2.1.1　Scope

No.	Easy Rules
1	IAS 16 also applies to bearer biological assets such as grape vines (measured at accumulated cost until maturity and then subject to depreciation and impairment charges.) (IAS 16：para. 2–5)

2.1.2　Definitions

No.	Easy Rules
1	**PP&E**： ● Held for： 　-use in production； 　-supply of goods or services； 　-rental to others； 　-administrative purposes. ● For more than one period.
2	**Cost**： ● Cash/cash equivalents ● Fair value of other consideration
3	**Residual value**：this is the net amount expected to collect.
4	**Entity specific value**：present value of continuing to use the PP&E.
5	**Fair value**：per IFRS 13. For PP&E such as land, it normally refers to as market value
6	**Carrying amount**：Cost-Accumulated depreciation-Accumulated impairment loss
7	**Impairment loss**：Carrying value > Recoverable amount (IAS 16：para. 6)

2.1.3　Recognition

No.	Easy Rules
1	The cost of an item of property, plant and equipment shall be recognised as an asset if, and only if： a) **it is probable that future economic benefits associated with the item will flow to the entity；and** b) the cost of the item can be measured reliably. (IAS 16：para. 7)

2.1.4 Separate items

No.	Easy Rules
1	Smaller parts/components: expense
2	Major parts/components: PP&E
3	Very large and specialised items such as ship/aircraft, different parts have different useful lives (different depreciation applies)
4	In determining whether the value is small or major, IAS 16 does not specifically gives us guidance on this area. However, we could base our conclusion on the aggregate value of the item for this, for instance, if each item of part is worth at $5, individually, it is not material to the account. However, if there are 1 million parts, total/aggregate value is therefore $5m, then it might be material to the account, hence we could treat this as major part. (IAS 16: para. 44)

2.1.5 Safety and environmental equipment

No.	Easy Rules
1	Items of property, plant and equipment may be acquired for safety or environmental reasons. (IAS 16: para. 11)

Example 1:

AA company installed the filter equipment to comply with the safety and environmental law of the machine. The carrying value of the machine was $10 million, the cost of the filter equipment was $3million. The filter equipment did not directly increase its future economic benefit because this is for compliance reason.

Required: Accounting treatment.

Answer: We should capitalise the $3 million as part of PP&E because the item is necessary for AA company to obtain future economic benefits from its machine, i.e. to produce products.

Dr	PP&E		$3m
Cr	Cash		$3m

Example 2:

The recoverable amount of the machine after the filter was installed was $12 million.

Required: Accounting treatment.

Answer: We should perform the impairment review test for the machine by comparing its carrying value with the recoverable amount. If the carrying value of the machine is higher than its recoverable amount, the impairment loss should be recognised and this is according to the IAS 36 Impairment of Assets.

In this case, the original assets plus the safety equipment gives us the total value of $ 13 million and this is greater than its recoverable amount, hence the impairment loss of $ 1m should be recognised.

Dr	Impairment expense	$ 1m
Cr	PP&E	$ 1m

2.1.6 Initial measurement

No.	Easy Rules
1	**Capital expenditure: acquisition or improve PP&E costs (Capitalise as PP&E)** • Purchase price, includes any import duties paid, but excludes any trade discount and reclaimable sales tax paid. • Directly attributable costs of bringing the asset to working condition for its intended use, for example: -The cost of site preparation, i.e. levelling the floor of the factory so the machine can be installed -Initial delivery and handling costs -Installation and assembly costs -Professional fees (costs of lawyers, architects, engineers) -Costs of testing whether the asset is working properly, after deducting the net proceeds from selling samples produced when testing equipment (see the Test Co example later) -Staff costs arising directly from the construction or acquisition of the asset • Dismantling costs
2	**Revenue expenditure: maintain PP&E for trading purposes (Expense in P/L)** • Operations expenses that are incidental to the construction or development of the item (incidental income being recognised into the P/L: see the Inci Co example later) • Administration and other general overhead costs • Start-up and similar pre-production costs (such as pre testing costs) • Initial operating losses before the asset reaches planned performances • Staff training costs • Maintenance and repair expenses **Note:** For self constructed assets, abnormal costs should be expensed. (IAS 16: para. 16-22)

2.1.7 Components of costs

Example: Test Co: Directly attributable costs

Test Co incurred $100,000 testing expenses to test the machine to ensure it functions properly. A few samples of products were produced during the testing process and the net proceeds from selling these sample products are $10,000.

Required: Identify the total testing costs to be capitalised as PP&E.

Answer: $90,000.

The directly attributable costs (testing costs) should deduct the net proceeds from selling any items produced when bringing the asset to its location and condition.

(IAS 16: para. 16)

Example: Inci Co: Income and related expenses operations

Inci Co develops a building and rent it to the employees as apartments. The building is partly finished and Inci Co rents part of the space in the building to the employees and it incurs electricity and maintenance costs. Inci Co gets rental income from employees also and the car park income.

Required: Accounting treatment for the incidental costs and income.

Answer: The incidental costs and income should be recognised in the statement of profit or loss. This is because income and related expenses of operations that are incidental to the construction or development of an item of PP&E should be recognised in the profit or loss. These costs and income are not necessary for the building to be completed.

Integrated example 1 on initial measurement:

Company A incurred the following costs regarding an item of its new PP&E:

	$
Purchase price including VAT of 14% (the VAT is refundable)	570,000
Import duties not refundable	100,000
Installation costs	30,000
Transportation costs-fuel	45,000
Staff party to celebrate the acquisition of the PP&E & staff training costs	14,000
Administrative expenses	12,000
Testing to ensure plant fully operational before start of production	10,980
Proceeds from sale of samples during testing	13,000
Advertising fee	50,000
Initial operating losses due to relocation to another place	35,000
Estimated costs of dismantling/removal costs at the end of its useful life (future costs discounted at 10% discount rate)	27,020

Answer:

	$
Purchase price including VAT of 14% 570,000/114%	500,000
Import duties not refundable	100,000
Installation costs	30,000
Transportation costs-fuel	45,000
Staff party to celebrate the acquisition of the PP&E and staff training costs	-
Administrative expenses	-
Testing to ensure plant fully operational before start of production	10,980
Minus: Proceeds from sale of samples during testing	(13,000)
Advertising fee	-
Initial operating losses due to relocation to another place	-
Estimated costs of dismantling/removal costs at the end of its useful life (future costs discounted at 10% discount rate)	27,020 (present value)
Total value of PP&E to be capitalised	700,000

Note:

The refundable VAT would go into the Dr side, i.e. to debit the VAT liability account. If the VAT is not refundable, it should be capitalised as an item of PP&E.

The dismantling costs would need to be unwound at the end of each year per IAS 37 Provisions, Contingent Liabilities and Contingent Assets, the next year finance costs would be $ 27,020×10% = $ 2,702

Dr	Finance costs	$ 2,702
Cr	Provision	$ 2,702

2.1.8 Subsequent expenditure

No.	Easy Rules
1	Same rules applied to the subsequent measurement as in initial measurement (capital and revenue expenditure)
2	Subsequent expenditure on replacement/renew: • Expenditure in replacing/renewing the item of PP&E should be capitalised. • The old item of PP&E should be derecognised, with the balancing figure going into the profit or loss. (IAS 16: para. 12-14)

Example: Old item replacement

Company A spent $ 100 million in replacing the item of PP&E in the production process. The carrying value of the old item of PP&E in the process was $ 50 million (its costs were $ 80 million and the accumulated depreciation were $ 30 million).

Required: Accounting treatment.

Answer:

Replace the new item of PP&E:

Dr	PP&E	$ 100m
Cr	Cash	$ 100m

Old item of PP&E:

Dr	Accumulated depreciation	$ 30m
Dr	Expense	$ 50m
Cr	Cost	$ 80m

2.1.9 Exchange of assets

No.	Easy Rules
1	This is where an entity exchanges the item of PP&E with another item of PP&E or inventories/cash. Same principles would be applied in IAS 38 Intangible Assets (depreciation should be replaced with amortisation in IAS 38).

No.	Easy Rules
2	The cost of such an item of property, plant and equipment is measured at fair value unless (a) the exchange transaction lacks commercial substance or (b) the fair value of neither the asset received nor the asset given up is reliably measurable. The acquired item is measured in this way even if an entity cannot immediately derecognise the asset given up. If the acquired item is not measured at fair value, its cost is measured at the carrying amount of the asset given up. (IAS 16: para. 24)

Example:

Company A exchanges an item of the PP&E (cost is $ 60 million and the accumulated depreciation were $ 40 million, and the fair value at the date of exchange is $ 15 million) with another item of PP&E with the fair value being $ 15 million. Company A also needs to pay the cash of $ 3 million. The transaction has commercial substance.

Required: Accounting entries.

Answer:

	Dr	New asset (fair value of the new asset) $ 15m + $ 3m	$ 18m
	Cr	Cash	$ 3m
	Cr	Old asset (PP&E) at cost	$ 60m
	Dr	Accumulated depreciation	$ 40m
	Dr	(balancing figure) loss on exchange	$ 5m

Special situation: (very rare!)

No.	Easy Rules
1	If the transaction lacks commercial substance, i.e. after the entity exchange, there will be no changes to the entity's future benefits. Alternatively, the fair value difference of the assets being exchanged is not material/significant [for instance, asset A (fair value is $ 100m) exchanged for asset B (fair value is $ 99.9m)], and in this case, no profit or loss should be recognised. (IAS 16: para. 24)

Example:

Company A exchanges an item of the PP&E with the carrying value being $ 100 million and fair value being $ 120 million with the item of the new PP&E (fair value is $ 80 million and the company A needs to pay additional $ 40 million cash).

Required: Accounting entry.

Answer: In this case, after the exchange has taken place, the fair value of the asset would not change, i.e. before the exchange, the fair value of the old asset is $ 120 million. After the exchange, the new asset fair value is $ 80 million plus the cash paid of $ 40 million and in total, $ 120 million.

In this case:

Dr	Cash	$ 40m
Dr	New PP&E *	$ 60m
Cr	Old PP&E (carrying value)	$ 100m

* balancing figure is $ 60m because the transaction has no commercial substance.

2.1.10 Subsequent measurement

No.	Easy Rules
1	**Accounting policies**: • Policy one: Cost model (Cost-accumulated depreciation and impairment losses) • Policy two: Revaluation model (Revalued amount-new depreciation)
2	A change in the above policy does not require retrospective adjustment per IAS 8 Accounting Policies, Changes in Accounting Estimates and Errors. (IAS 16: para. 30-31)

2.1.11 Revaluations

No.	Easy Rules
1	Whole class of assets should be revalued and the revaluation should be done at the same time.
2	Frequency of valuation depends on fair value volatility.
3	New depreciation is based on the revalued amount (because the revalued amount is the new cost of PP&E).
4	Revaluation gain goes to revaluation surplus not retained earnings.
5	Excess depreciation may be transferred from revaluation reserve to retained earnings by entities so they wish to. (IAS 16: para. 34-42)

2.1.12 Accounting for revaluation

Dr Cost (Revalued amount-Original Cost)
Dr Accumulated depreciation (Remove all of them)
Cr Revaluation reserve (in statement of financial position, statement of changes in equity and other comprehensive income)

2.1.13 Reversing a previous decrease in value

Dr Cost (New value-old value)
Dr Accumulated depreciation
Cr Revaluation reserve (in statement of financial position, statement of changes in equity and other comprehensive income)

2.1.14 Revaluation decrease

Dr Revaluation surplus (in statement of financial position, statement of changes in equity and other comprehensive income)
Cr PP&E (New value-Old value)
Dr Accumulated depreciation (Remove it)
Dr Impairment expense (balancing figure)

2.1.15 Revaluation and depreciation

Excess depreciation:

Dr Revaluation reserve (in statement of financial position and statement of changes in equity but not in other comprehensive income)
Cr Retained earnings

2.1.16 Depreciation

No.	Easy Rules
1	**Review the useful life/depreciation method:** • Change in accounting estimate-applies prospective adjustment method; • Depreciation method should be reviewed at lease at each financial year end. (IAS 16: para. 61)

2.1.17 Impairment of carrying amounts of non-current assets

No.	Easy Rules
1	If the carrying value of the PP&E is higher than its recoverable amount, the impairment loss should be recognised per IAS 36 Impairment of assets.
2	The revaluation increase should be recognised as income to the extent that it reverses an impairment loss expense. This should adjust any decrease in depreciation expense as a result of the impairment loss being recognised. (IAS 16:para.63)

Example:

The cost of an item of the PP&E is $10,000 and the accumulated depreciation were $3,000 (suppose each year, the depreciation expense charged was $520). As at the current Financial Statements year end, the recoverable amount of the PP&E is now $6,000.

Required: Accounting entries.

Answer:

Dr	Accumulated depreciation	$3,000
Cr	Cost ($10,000 - $6,000)	$4,000
Dr	Impairment loss	$1,000

Example of reversal of impairment loss:

Continuing with the previous example, the cost of the asset is $6,000. During the year, $500 of depreciation expenses were charged. As at the year end, the PP&E is now revalued to $20,000.

Required: Accounting entries.

Answer:

Dr	Cost ($20,000 - $6,000)	$14,000
Dr	Accumulated depreciation	$500
Cr	Impairment loss *	$980
Cr	Revaluation reserve * *	$13,520

* Previously recognised impairment loss-saved depreciation expense: $1,000 - $(520-500)

* * Both in equity and OCI as the balancing figure

The revaluation increase should be recognised as income to the extent that it reverses an impairment loss expense. This should adjust any decrease in depreciation expense as a result of the impairment loss being recognised.

(IAS 16: para. 63)

2.1.18 Complex assets

No.	Easy Rules
1	Different parts should be depreciated separately. (IAS 16: para. 43)

2.1.19 Overhauls

No.	Easy Rules
1	Overhauls costs should be capitalised as a part of PP&E. (IAS 16: SIC 23)

2.1.20 Retirement (not use the PP&E anymore) and disposals

Accounting entries for normal disposal:

Step 1: Decrease the cost account:

Dr Disposal account

Cr Cost

Step 2: Remove accumulated depreciation:

Dr Accumulated depreciation

Cr Disposal account

Step 3: Recognise bank/receivable:

Dr Bank/Receivable

Cr Disposal account

Accounting entries for part exchange:

Step 1: decrease the cost account:

Dr Disposal account

Cr PP&E at Cost

Step 2: remove accumulated depreciation:

Dr Accumulated depreciation

Cr Disposal account

Step 3: Recognise part exchange allowance/trade in price:

Dr PP&E at cost

Cr Disposal account

Step 4: Additional cash to pay the PP&E:

Dr PP&E at cost
Cr Cash/Payable

2.1.21 Disposal of a revalued asset

This would be the same as the above journals. One additional journal should be made:
Dr Revaluation reserve
Cr Retained earnings

2.1.22 Derecognition

No.	Easy Rules
1	The carrying amount of an item of property, plant and equipment shall be derecognised: (a) on disposal; or (b) when no future economic benefits are expected from its use or disposal. The gain on disposal of the PP&E should be separately presented on the face of the P/L but not mixed with revenue.
2	But we need to determine whether this meets the criteria for the sale of PP&E in accordance with IFRS 15 Revenue from Contracts with Customers. For instance, if the probability to get the payment from the buyer from the sale of the PP&E is remote, no gain on disposal should be recognised. (IAS 16: para 67-71)

2.1.23 Disclosure

1	• Cost • Depreciation methods • Useful lives • Accumulated depreciation • Reconciliations from additions/disposals etc. • Revalued assets including who; when and the valuation figures. (IAS 16: para. 73)

2.2 IAS 16 *PP & E Depreciation Accounting*

Topic outline:

```
┌─────────────────────────────┐
│   Depreciation Accounting   │
└─────────────────────────────┘
         │
         ├── Key definitions
         │
         ├── Residual value
         │
         ├── Useful life
         │
         ├── Depreciation methods
         │
         └── Disclosure
```

(IAS 16: para. 43–66)

2.2.1 Key definitions

No.	Easy Rules
1	Depreciable amount = $\dfrac{\text{Historical cost / Substituted Cost (Revalued amount)} - \text{Residual Value}}{\text{Years/number of units expected to obtain}}$
2	This is based on accruals concept or marching principle, i.e. to match the benefits earned from using the PP&E with the costs that the entity thinks it might incur.
3	The depreciation expense here is just an "accounting depreciation" and this is not "economic depreciation or actual depreciation". Therefore, a change in depreciation methods is a change in accounting estimate, the current and future years' Financial Statements would be affected. This is known as a prospective adjustment.

2.2.2 Residual value

No.	Easy Rules
1	If the residual value is significant, it must be estimated at the date of purchase or in any subsequent revaluation.
2	Net residual value = Gross residual value−expected costs of disposal
3	The value of the PP&E after fully depreciated can either be: 1. Residual value (if the residual value is available) 2. Nil (if the residual value is not available)

2.2.3 Useful life

No.	Easy Rules
1	**Consider the following factors:** • Expected physical wear and tear (This depends on number of shifts or the entity's repair and maintenance programmes) • Obsolescence (such as changes in technological factors and market demand) • Legal or other limits on the use of the assets (An example could be the length of a related lease, i.e. in the lease contract, it states the asset can only be used for 5 years, however, it is likely that the lessee would exercise the option to extend the lease contract to another 3 years, therefore, the asset should be depreciated over 8 years.)

2.2.4 Depreciation methods

1. Straight line method:

Depreciation expense $= \dfrac{\text{Cost}-\text{Residual Value}}{\text{Years}}$

This method assumes that depreciation expense would be the same in each financial year.

2. Reducing balance method:

Depreciation expense $=$ Carrying value×depreciation rate

This method assumes that more depreciation expenses would be provided in earlier years than in subsequent years.

3. Sum-of-digit method:

Step 1: Plus all the years together such as $5+4+3+2+1=15$;

Step 2: Depreciate the asset at 5/15, then 4/15, 3/15, 2/15, 1/15 year at the depreciable amount (Cost−Residual Value).

4. Machine hour method:

$$\text{Depreciation expense} = \frac{\text{Cost} - \text{Residual Value}}{\text{Machine hours}}$$

This method assumes the depreciation expense would be more if more machine hours are used and would be less if less machine hours are used.

Example:

The business acquired a van for $ 17,000 and its expected useful life is five 5 years. It is expected to be sold at the end of the fifth year for $ 2,000. Usage over the five years is expected to be as follows:

Year one	200 days
Year two	100 days
Year three	100 days
Year four	150 days
Year five	50 days

Required: Calculate the depreciation charge each year under:

1. The straight line method;
2. The reducing balance method using a rate of 40%;
3. The machine hour method;
4. The sum of the digits method.

Answer:

1. The straight line method:

$$\text{Depreciation each year} = \frac{\$ 17,000 - \$ 2,000}{5 \text{ years}} = \$ 3,000$$

2. The reducing balance method:

Years $	Depreciation	Accumulated depreciation	Carrying value
Cost	-	-	17,000
1	6,800	6,800	10,200
2	4,080	10,880	6,120
3	2,448	13,328	3,672
4	1,469	14,797	2,203
5	203	15,000	2,000

3. The machine hour method:

Total usage days = 200+100+100+150+50 = 600 (days)

Depreciation per day = $\frac{\$17,000-\$2,000}{600 \text{ days}}$ = \$25/day

Years	Usage in days	Depreciation \$ (days× \$ 25/day)
1	200	5,000
2	100	2,500
3	100	2,500
4	150	3,750
5	50	1,250
		15,000

4. The sum of the digits method:

To add up the years of useful life:

5+4+3+2+1=15

The total depreciable amount (\$ 17,000- \$ 2,000= \$ 15,000) is allocated as follows:

Years	Depreciation	\$
1	15,000×5/15	5,000
2	15,000×4/15	4,000
3	15,000×3/15	3,000
4	15,000×2/15	2,000
5	15,000×1/15	1,000
		15,000

Two methods:

No.	Easy Rules
1	**Method 1: Full in the year of acquisition and none in the year of disposal** This means that a full year depreciation expense is charged irrespective when the asset was acquired, for instance, even though the asset was acquired on 15th March in the first year, we do not charge 9 months and 15 days depreciation expenses, but instead, we charge the full 12 months depreciation expenses. However, in the year of disposal, we do not charge depreciation expense for this. Therefore, more depreciation expense in the year of acquisition and less in the year of disposal and the effects would cancel each other out.
2	**Method 2: Proportional method** This means that a full year depreciation expense is charged irrespective when the asset was acquired, for instance, even though the asset was acquired on 15th March in the first year, we do charge 9 months and 15 days depreciation expenses instead of the full 12 months depreciation expenses.

Example:

A business has a machine costing $15,000 on 1 April 20×6. The machine is depreciated over five years with no residual value. On 1 February 20×8, the machine is sold for $1,000.

Required: Calculate the profit or loss on disposal under two depreciation methods.

Answer:

Method 1: Full in the year of acquisition and none in the year of disposal:

	Cost 1 April 20×6	$15,000
	−Accumulated depreciation $15,000/5 years×2 years	$(6,000)
	Carrying value on 1 February 20×8	$9,000
	Sold	$1,000
	Loss on disposal	$(8,000)

Method 2：Proportional method：

Cost 1 April 20×6	$ 15,000
−Accumulated depreciation From 1 April 20×6−1 February 20×8 = 22 months $ 15,000/5 years / 12 months×22 months	$ (5,500)
Carrying value on 1 February 20×8	$ 9,500
Sold	$ 1,000
Loss on disposal	$ (8,500)

Accounting entries：

	Method one			Method two	
Dr	Disposal	$ 15,000	**Dr**	Disposal	$ 15,000
Cr	PP&E at cost	$ 15,000	**Cr**	PP&E at cost	$ 15,000
Dr	Accumulated depreciation	$ 6,000	**Dr**	Accumulated depreciation	$ 5,500
Cr	Disposal	$ 6,000	**Cr**	Disposal	$ 5,500
Dr	Cash	$ 1,000	**Dr**	Cash	$ 1,000
Cr	Disposal	$ 1,000	**Cr**	Disposal	$ 1,000

2.2.5 Disclosure

No.	Easy Rules
1	• Deprecation methods • Useful lives • Total depreciation for the year • Cost and accumulated depreciation

2.3 IAS 40 *Investment Property*

Topic outline:

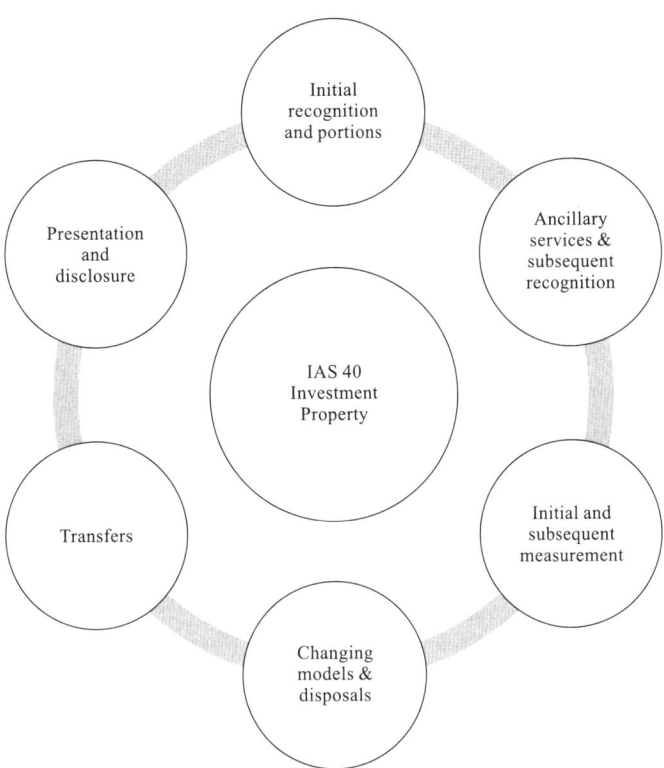

2.3.1 Initial recognition

No.	Easy Rules
1	**Investment property (the property can be land or/and a building or part of a building)** 1. The property is held for investment purposes: • Held for rentals to others; or • Held for capital appreciation. 2. It is probable that the future economic benefits that are associated with the investment property will flow to the entity; 3. The cost can be reliably measured. <div style="text-align:right">(IAS 40: para. 16)</div>

No.	Easy Rules
2	Note: Owner-occupied properties are not investment properties: • Use in production or supply of goods or services (IAS 16 PP&E) • Administrative purposes (IAS 16 PP&E) Sale in ordinary course of business (IAS 2 Inventories) (IAS 40:para. 9)

Examples of items are investment properties	Examples of items not investment properties
• Land held for undetermined use • Land held for long term capital appreciation rather than short term sale in the ordinary course of business • A building leased out under an operating lease (from the lessor's perspective) • Property being constructed for future use as investment property • A building held by parent and leased to subsidiary. To parent individual account: investment property. To group account: PP&E (IAS 16)	• Property occupied by employees (whether or not employees pay rent at market rates) • Property leased out under finance lease (from the lessor's perspective) • Owner occupied property • Property intended to be inventories • Constructed/developed on behalf of third party (IFRS 15 Revenue from Contracts with Customers)

(IAS 40:para. 8)

2.3.2 Portions

No.	Easy Rules
1	If portion can be sold separately or leased out separately, the business should account for them separately, i. e. one portion under investment property and another portion under other standards such as IAS 16 PP&E or IAS 2 Inventories.
2	If portions can not be sold separately/leased out separately, then the property is investment property only if an insignificant portion is owner occupied. (IAS 40:para. 10)

Example of portions:

A business has a 2,000 square metres wide office space held for rentals. However, inside the office space, there is a room with 20 square metres being used by the business for administrative purposes, i. e. to store goods.

Required: Should the business treat the entire 2,000 square metres wide office space as the investment property or PP&E under IAS 16?

Answer: We should treat this as the investment property. Although we did use the 20 square metres room ourselves, however, the portion is insignificant compared to the 2,000 square metres wide office space. In this example, we are not told whether 2,000 square metres wide office space can be further divided into different small areas to be rented out. Therefore, we should account for the entire space as investment property because this is held by the business for investment purposes, i.e. for rental payments.

2.3.3 Ancillary services

No.	Easy Rules
1	The business entity may provide add services to occupants. • If services are insignificant to the arrangement, the business should treat the property as investment property; • If services are significant to the arrangement, the business should treat the property as owner occupied properties and this is accounted for under IAS 16.
2	In some cases, an entity provides ancillary services to the occupants of a property it holds. An entity treats such a property as investment property if the services are insignificant to the arrangement as a whole. An example is when the owner of an office building provides security and maintenance services to the lessees who occupy the building and the business income generated does not primarily depend on this service. In other cases, the services provided are significant. For example, if an entity owns and manages a hotel, services provided to guests are significant to the arrangement as a whole and the business income generated primarily depends on this service. Therefore, an owner-managed hotel is owner-occupied property, rather than investment property. (IAS 40. Para. 11 and 12)

2.3.4 Subsequent recognition

No.	Easy Rules
1	**Principle**: we need to evaluate the recognition criteria (investment purposes; probable future economic benefits; reliably measurable expenses) every time when costs are incurred.
2	However, **day to day service costs** (described as repairs and maintenance of the property) such as labour and consumables costs should not be capitalised as investment properties, we should charge them into the **statement of profit or loss**.

2.3.5　Initial measurement

No.	Easy Rules
1	**Costs include:** • Purchase price, but excluding any trade discount. • Directly attributable costs of bringing the asset to working condition for its intended use, e.g.: 　-The cost of site preparation 　-Professional fees (lawyers, architects, engineers) 　-Property transfer taxes 　-Staff costs arising directly from the construction or acquisition of the asset
2	**Costs exclude:** a) start-up costs (unless they are necessary to bring the property to the condition necessary for it to be capable of operating in the manner intended by management), b) operating losses incurred before the investment property achieves the planned level of occupancy, or c) abnormal amounts of wasted material, labour or other resources incurred in constructing or developing the property. <div align="right">(IAS 40:para. 20-23)</div>

2.3.6　Accounting entry for initial measurement

No.	Easy Rules
1	**Dr** Investment property at cost * **Cr** Cash * Fair value model should be applied, unless the fair value for the investment property cannot be determined, we should use cost model. An example of where the fair value of the property can not be determined is when there are few recent transactions, price quotations are not current or observed transaction prices indicate that the seller was forced to sell. <div align="right">(IAS 40:para. 53)</div>

2.3.7 Subsequent measurement

No.	Easy Rules
1	**Accounting policies:** **Policy 1:** The fair value model; **Policy 2:** The cost model.
2	**Note:** Either the policy 1 or 2 is chosen by the business, it should be applied to ALL (not each class) investment properties.
3	**Policy 1: Fair value model:** • Gains or losses from the changes in investment property fair value goes into the statement of profit or loss. • No depreciation expenses should be recognised. • Rental payments received from the lessee would increase the cash and rental income account.
4	The fair value of investment property excludes prepaid or accrued operating lease income, because the entity recognises it as a separate liability or asset. (IAS 40. para. 50)

Example:

The business has two investment properties: A and B.

Investment property A is held to earn capital gain and investment property B is let out to others to earn rental income. The carrying value of property A is $ 1 million and as at the year-end, a qualified valuer values this property to be $ 1.5 million.

During the year the business earns $ 0.3 million from letting out investment property B.

Required: Accounting entries.

Answer:

Investment property A:

Dr	Investment property ($ 1.5m– $ 1m)	$ 0.5m
Cr	Income (P/L)	$ 0.5m

Investment property B:

Dr	Cash or rent receivables	$ 0.3m * *
Cr	Income (P/L)	$ 0.3m

* * The fair value of investment property excludes prepaid or accrued operating lease income, because the entity recognises it as a separate liability or asset.

(IAS 40. para. 50)

2.3.8 Additional notes on fair value

No.	Easy Rules
1	If a business finds a buyer who is willing to pay extra and the business is over eager to sell, the price that the buyer pays is not the fair price (value).
2	If a business has financial troubles and it therefore sells the property at a very low price. The sale is a forced sale, and the price is not fair.
3	An entity should not double count assets: equipment such as lifts, air-conditioning and furniture is often an integral part of a building and the value of those assets should have been included in the fair value of investment properties, and we should not separately account for them as PP&E.
4	After the initial recognition of investment property, the lessee should use the fair value as the value of the right-of-user asset per IFRS 16 Leases if the fair value model is adopted. However, if the cost model is used, the right-of-use asset should be valued at cost per IAS 16 (cost minus accumulated depreciation and impairment losses).
	Policy 2: Cost model: The carrying value of the investment property = Cost – Accumulated depreciation and impairment losses. No residual value should be included in the depreciation expense calculation. If possible, the range of estimates within which fair value is highly likely to lie. (IAS 40: para. 78)

Example: fair value and cost model

A business acquired a property for $ 1 million at the year start. The land element is $ 400,000 and the building element is $ 600,000 with the expected useful life of 50 years.

As at the current year end, the fair value of the property has risen up to $ 1.1 million according to the local property indices.

Required: Accounting entries for the investment property under cost and fair value model.

Answer:
Initial acquisition:

Dr	Investment property	$ 1m
Cr	Bank	$ 1m

1. Cost model:
Depreciation expense = $ 600,000/50 years = $ 12,000

Dr	Depreciation expense	$ 12,000
Cr	Investment property	$ 12,000

We should also disclose the fair value of the investment property at $ 1.1 million in the disclosure note.

2. Fair value model:

Dr	Investment property ($ 1.1m – $ 1m)	$ 0.1m
Cr	Gain (P/L)	$ 0.1m

2.3.9 Changing models

1	Entities can change from one model (fair value model to cost model) to another. However, a change from fair value model to cost model is highly unlikely to result in a more appropriate presentation. (IAS 40: para. 31)

2.3.10 Transfers

This occurs when there is a change in asset use.

At date of transfer, if the investment property is carried at fair value model:

No.	Easy Rules
1	**Situation 1: From investment property to PP&E or inventories:** **Rule:** The fair value of the investment property at the date of transfer should be used as a deemed cost of PP&E or inventories.

Example:

Instead of holding the property for capital appreciation, the business now determines to use the property on its own. The fair value at the date of transfer of the property is $80 million.

Answer:

Dr	PP&E	$80m
Cr	Investment property	$80m

If the business decides to sell the property, i.e. it now becomes inventories, the accounting entry is as follows:

Dr	Inventories	$80m
Cr	Investment property	$80m

No.	Easy Rules
2	**Situation 2: From PP&E to investment property:** **Rules:** Fair value > Carrying value: balancing figure goes to revaluation reserve Fair value < Carrying value: balancing figure goes to the impairment loss expense

Example: Fair value > Carrying value

Fair value of the PP&E is $80 million with carrying value being $50 million at the date of transfer.

Required: Accounting entries.

Answer:

Dr	Investment property	$80m
Cr	PP&E at carrying value	$50m
Cr	Revaluation Reserve	$30m

The revaluation reserve would be transferred to retained earnings on disposal.

Example:

Fair value of the PP&E is $50 million with carrying value being $80 million at the date of transfer.

Required: Accounting entries.

Answer:

Dr	Investment property	$ 50m
Cr	PP&E at carrying value	$ 80m
Dr	Impairment expense	$ 30m

No.	Easy Rules
3	**Situation 3: From inventories to investment properties**: **Rule**: The difference goes into statement of profit or loss.

Example:

The carrying value of the inventory is $ 50 million. At this date, the business determines to change its use, i.e. to hold it for capital appreciation. The fair value of the investment property is $ 100 million.

Required: Accounting entries.

Answer:

Dr	Investment property	$ 100m
Cr	Inventory	$ 50m
Cr	Gain (P/L)	$ 50m

At date of transfer, if the investment property is measured using cost model:

No.	Easy Rules
1	When an entity uses the cost model, transfers between investment property, owner-occupied property and inventories do not change the carrying amount of the property transferred and they do not change the cost of that property for measurement or disclosure purposes (IAS 40: para. 59)

Example:

The carrying value of the inventory is $ 30 million and the business determines to holding it for capital appreciation. At the date of transfer, the fair value is $ 50 million.

Answer:

Dr	Investment property	$ 30m
Cr	Inventory (carrying value)	$ 30m

2.3.11 Disposals

No.	Easy Rules
1	Just like the sale of PP&E, gains or losses from disposal go into the statement of profit or loss. (IAS 40:para.69)
2	If there is revaluation reserve (transfer), we should reclassify the revaluation reserve to retained earnings if the property is disposed of. (IAS 40:para.62)

Example:

The carrying value of the investment property is $ 30 million and the business sold it for $ 35 million.

The cumulated revaluation reserve of the investment property is $ 2 million.

Required: Accounting entries.

Answer:

Sale:

Dr	Bank	$ 35m
Cr	Investment property	$ 30m
Cr	Gain on disposal	$ 5m

Reclassification:

Dr	Revaluation reserve	$ 2m
Cr	Retained earnings	$ 2m

2.3.12 Presentation

Statement of financial position:

Non-current assets
• Property, plant and equipment
• Investment property (present here)

Statement of profit or loss:

Gross profit
Other income (present here) • Rent received from investment property • Fair value gain from investment property revaluation
Other expenses (present here) • Fair value loss from investment property revaluation • Direct operating expenses-investment property generating rental income • Direct operating expenses-investment property not generating rental income

Other income and expenses will be accumulated to the retained earnings rather than other comprehensive income.

Statement of cash flows:

1. Cash flows from operations:

Non cash items adjustments:

• Depreciation (if cost model is used)
• Profit or loss from disposal
• Fair value changes (either in other income or expenses)

2. Cash flows from investing activities:

• Payment made to acquired investment properties
• Proceeds from sale of investment properties

2.3.13 Disclosures

1. Investment properties under fair value model:

	Land and buildings
Opening balance	x
Additions:	x
1. Acquisitions 2. Subsequent expenditure capitalised	
Net gain/loss from fair value revaluations	x
Closing balance	x

2. Investment properties under cost value model:

	Land	Buildings
Opening balance		
Cost	x	x
Accumulated depreciation and impairment losses	-	(x)
Depreciation this year	-	(x)
Impairment loss this year	(x)	(x)
Disposals	(x)	(x)
Additions:	**x**	**x**
1. Acquisitions		
2. Subsequent expenditure capitalised		
Closing balance		
Cost	x	x
Accumulated depreciation	-	(x)

* Please note, under the cost model the fair value of the investment property should also be disclosed.

2.4 IAS 23 Borrowing Costs

Topic outline:

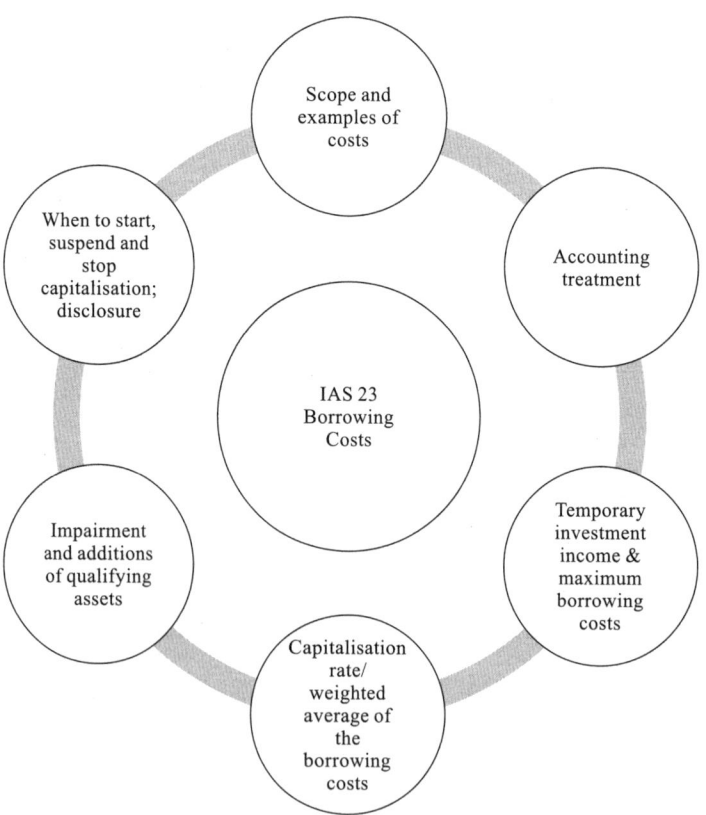

2.4.1 Borrowing for what?

No.	Easy Rules
1	**Core principle:** Borrowing costs that are directly attributable to the acquisition, construction or production of a qualifying asset form part of the cost of that asset. Other borrowing costs are recognised as an expense. (IAS 23:para.1)
2	**Examples of qualifying assets (substantial time to get ready for its intended use or sale):** • Inventories. For large quantities of inventories which are produced in large quantities on a repetitive basis such as cheese, wine and aircrafts (substantial time to produce). The standard allows an option (accounting policy) for the entity to either to capitalise the borrowing cost or not capitalising it. But inventories produced/manufactured over a short period of time are not qualifying assets. (IAS 23:para.4) • Manufacturing plants • Power generation facilities • Intangible assets such as development costs • Investment properties • Bearer plants • For biological asset (if it is a qualifying asset) acquired at fair value, the entity is not required to apply this standard to borrowing cost. (IAS 23:para.4)
3	Financial assets are not qualifying assets.
4	Assets that are ready for their intended use or sale when purchased are not qualifying assets. This means that management should assess the intention of the use and sale of the asset when it is acquired. Management should combine assets together to determine whether it is ready for their intended use or sale. (IAS 23:para.5)

Example 1: The intention of management 1

A telecom company acquired a 5G licence. The licence could be sold or licensed to a third party. However, management intends to use it to operate a wireless network. Development of the network starts when the licence is acquired.

Required: Should borrowing costs on the acquisition of the 5G licence be capitalised until the network is ready for its intended use?

Answer:

The answer is yes. This is because the licence has been exclusively acquired to operate the wireless network.

The acquisition of the licence is the first step in a wider investment project (developing the network). It is part of the network investment, which meets the definition of a qualifying asset.

The fact that the licence can be used or licensed to a third party when purchased is irrelevant.

Example 2: The intention of management 2

A company incurred borrowing costs regarding the government permit to build a building and an equipment which can be used to build lots of buildings in the future.

Required: Whether the borrowing costs for the government permit and equipment can be capitalised per IAS 23?

Answer: Yes for the building because this is the necessary step for the building to be built and the building is a qualifying asset. Therefore, we should consider the permit and building together, and the borrowing costs on the permit can be capitalised.

No for the equipment. Because the equipment will be used to build future buildings, hence at the time that the equipment was acquired, it is ready for its intended use.

2.4.2 What are included in borrowing costs?

No.	Easy Rules
1	**Interest expense**
2	**Finance charges for leases.** For example, a crane or a dockyard is leased for the purpose of constructing a ship. The ship is a qualifying asset. The interest on the finance lease of the crane or dockyard is capitalised as borrowing costs.
3	**Exchange differences from foreign currency loan** * (**accounting policy**)

(IAS 23: para. 6)

*** Example for exchange differences from foreign currency loan:**

A business based in the USA took a foreign currency loan in Japanese Yen of 100 million at the year start for the construction of its own factory and the loan is for one year.

The interest expense in Yen translated back to the US dollar is $ 0.45 million during the year.

The Japanese Yen of 100m translated back to the USD at the time that the loan was taken out and as at the Financial Statements year end are $ 0.9 million and $ 0.8 million.

Required: Accounting treatment.

Answer: The borrowing costs include:

1. Interest expense: (in our functional currency: USD)	$ 0.45m
2. Foreign exchange differences adjustment: gain ($ 0.9m– $ 0.8m)	$ (0.1)m *
Hence the net borrowing costs = $ 0.45m– $ 0.1m =	$ 0.35 m

* This is an exchange gain because instead of owing $ 0.9m to the bank but now it only owes $ 0.8m to the bank because of exchange rate differences. Hence the gain from foreign exchange rate differences should offset the interest expense. If there are foreign exchange losses, the interest expense should increase by the loss on re-translation.

2.4.3 Borrowing Costs Accounting Treatment

No.	Easy Rules
1	An entity shall capitalise borrowing costs that are directly attributable to the acquisition (such as the interest expense on the loan in order to get the government permit or license before producing outputs), construction or production of a qualifying asset as part of the cost of that asset.
2	This means that entities must capitalise all eligible borrowing costs except in some situations such as the optional treatment for large and repetitive quantities of inventories to be produced.
3	Capitalised borrowing costs should be added to the cost of the asset. Other borrowing costs which are not eligible should be recognised as expenses.

(IAS 23: para. 8)

Example:

As at the year start, a business began to construct a building with an estimated useful life of 40 years. The building costs are $ 35 million. The construction was completed in 9 months and brought into use in 12 months.

To complete the project, the business borrowed $ 20 million at the year start with the loan interest rate being 10%. The loan will be repaid in 12 months.

Required: Accounting treatment.

Answer: First 9 months: capitalise the borrowing costs: $ 20m×10% ×9/12 = $ 1.5m

	Dr	PP&E	$ 1.5m
	Cr	Accrued expense/Interest Payable/Cash	$ 1.5m

Last 3 months: expense the borrowing costs: $ 20m×10% ×3/12 = $ 0.5m

Dr	Interest expense/Finance costs	$ 0.5m
Cr	Accrued expense/Interest Payable/Cash	$ 0.5m

2.4.4 Temporary investment income

No.	Easy Rules
1	Borrowing costs available for capitalisation = Actual borrowing costs LESS investment income

(IAS 23:para. 12)

Example:

On 1 January, the business borrowed $ 1.5 million to finance the production of its two ships and each is expected to be completed in one year. Work has started during this year and the loan facility was drawn down and incurred on 1 January. The remaining funds are invested temporarily.

$ 000	Ship X	Ship Y
1 January	250	500
1 July	250	500
Total	500	1,000

The loan rate was 10% and the business can invest surplus funds at 8%.

Required: Calculate the capitalised borrowing costs for each asset. Ignore compound interest in the calculation.

Answer:

$ 000		Ship X		Ship Y
Borrowing costs From 1 January to 31 December $ 500×10%		50	Borrowing costs $ 1,000×10%	100
Minus: Temporary investment income From 1 January to 30 June $ 250×8%×6/12		(10)	Minus: Temporary investment income From 1 January to 30 June $ 500×8%×6/12	(20)
Capitalised borrowing costs		40	Capitalised borrowing costs	80

2.4.5 Capitalisation rate/Weighted average of the borrowing costs

No.	Easy Rules
1	Borrowings are obtained generally and applied in part to obtain a qualifying asset, we should use the "capitalisation rate".
2	Exclude borrowings for specific qualifying assets.

(IAS 23:para. 14)

Example:

The business has three types of loans during the year:

$ million	1 January	31 December
9% Bank loan repayable in 2 years' time	130	130
8.5% Bank loan repayable in 3 years' time	90	90
7.5% Loan notes repayable in 1 year's time	0	120

The 7.5% loan notes was issued to fund the construction of a building and the construction has begun this year.

At the start of this year, the business began construct a piece of equipment which is a qualifying asset using the existing borrowings. Expenditure drawn down for the construction was: $ 40 million at the start of this year and $ 30 million in October.

Required: Calculate the capitalised borrowing costs.

Answer: Capitalisation rate = 9%×(130/220*) + 8.5%×(90/220) = 8.8%

* This is calculated using the average bank loan during the year: $ 130 million and $ 90 million together to be a total $ 220 million.

Capitalised borrowing costs = ($ 40m×8.8%×12/12) + ($ 30m×8.8%×3/12) = $ 4.18m

2.4.6 Maximum borrowing costs

No.	Easy Rules
1	The maximum borrowing costs to be capitalised should not exceed actual borrowing costs incurred. This happens when the expenditure on qualifying asset is greater than its borrowings.

(IAS 23:para. 14)

Example:

Expenditure spent on the building is $ 100m but it only took $ 80m debt with the interest rate being 10%. The loan is for one year.

Required: Determine the amount to be capitalised.

Answer: Only $ 8m to be capitalised.

The maximum borrowing costs ($ 100m × 10% = $ 10m) should not exceed actual borrowing costs incurred ($ 80m×10% = $ 8m).

2.4.7 Impairment

No.	Easy Rules
1	Sometimes, the qualifying assets may be impaired (PP&E impairment or inventories where costs are lower than the net realisable value), the calculation of the capitalised borrowing costs should be based on the impaired qualifying asset. (IAS 23: para. 16)

2.4.8 When to capitalise?

No.	Easy Rules
1	All three events/transactions happen: 1. Incur expenditure 2. Incur borrowing costs 3. Activities to prepare the asset for its intended use or sale such as obtaining permits but do not include holding an asset when no production or development that changes the asset's condition is taking place such as the land is held without any associated development activity—does not meet with the third criteria. (IAS 23: para. 17)

2.4.9 Additions (increase qualifying assets) during the year

No.	Easy Rules
1	IAS 23 allows the average carrying amount of the asset during a period to be used as an approximation to the expenditure to which the capitalisation rate is applied in the period. (IAS 23: para. 14)

Example:

Date	Additions	Cumulative carrying amount	Weighted average carrying amount

	From 1 Jan–1 April:3/12	$ 300	$ 300	3/12× $ 300 = $ 75
	From 1 April–1 Sept:5/12	$ 500	$ 800($ 300+ $ 500)	5/12× $ 800 = $ 333
	From 1 Sept–31 Dec:4/12	$ 600	$ 1,400($ 800+ $ 600)	4/12× $ 1,400 = $ 467
			Total =	$ 875

The capitalisation rate may be applied to the weighted average carrying amount above of $ 875 instead of the simple average carrying amount of $ 850 [($ 300+ $ 1,400)/2].

2.4.10 Suspension of capitalisation

No.	Easy Rules
1	If the reason is normal, we should continue to capitalise the borrowing costs: • Factory closed down during holiday season • Production process is slow • High water levels delay construction of a bridge (if such high water levels are common during the construction period in the geographical region involved) then capitalisation of borrowing costs should not be suspended • Periods when engineers improve the technical specifications of the asset
2	If the reason is **abnormal**, we should suspend to capitalise the borrowing costs: • Workers go on strike • Fire damage • Flood <div style="text-align:right">(IAS 23:para.20–21)</div>

2.4.11 Cessation of capitalisation

No.	Easy Rules
1	Substantially all the activities to prepare the qualifying asset for its intended use or sale are completed.
2	Normally when physical construction of the asset is completed, although minor modifications may still be outstanding.

No.	Easy Rules
3	Assets completed in parts or stages (capitalisation should cease for each part as it is completed such as business part consisting of many buildings). (IAS 23:para.22-25)

Example:

1. Investment property for sale:

Investment property has been completed but the business needs time to find new tenants. Hence when the investment property is completed, the borrowing costs should cease to be capitalised.

2. Building complete-fire safety approval is outstanding:

An entity has completed the physical construction of a building but is not permitted to use it until fire approval is obtained. Often it is a formality to obtain the necessary approval for fire safety. In such cases it is appropriate to cease capitalisation on physical completion. If the building fails the inspection, and substantial additional work is then required, it may be necessary to resume capitalisation of borrowing costs.

3. Shopping centre:

Major construction work on the shopping centre is completed first but the fit-out work (which is essential for the intended use) continues. At this stage the building is not ready for use and the entity continues to capitalise borrowing costs. When the fit-out is substantially complete the entity ceases to capitalise borrowing costs on the shopping centre.

4. Late completion of the car park:

The multi-storey car park is capable of being used independently. If construction of the car park continues after work on the shopping centre is complete, borrowing costs continue to be capitalised on the car park. The treatment of the shopping centre is not affected by the later completion of the car park.

2.4.12 Disclosure

No.	Easy Rules
1	Amount of borrowing costs capitalised during the period
2	Capitalisation rate

(IAS 23:para.26)

Chapter 3

Intangible Assets

Topic outline:

- Recognition and amortisation
- Initial measurement using cost model: 3 situations
- Initial measurement using revaluation model
- Exchange of assets; useful life; amortisation period and methods; residual value
- Indefinite useful life; R&D; Other internally generated intangible assets
- Goodwill

IAS 38 Intangible Assets

3.1 *Recognition and Amortisation*

3.1.1　Initial recognition / Definition of intangible asset

No.	Easy Rules
1	An intangible asset (meet the control * definition) is an identifiable * * (acquired/rented/sold separately) non-monetary asset (not shares/debts) without physical substance * * *
2	* Control: **Condition 1: The entity can enjoy future economic benefits * * from the asset;** Economic benefits can be one of the followings: ● Use the intangible asset to increase sales ● Use the intangible assets to reduce costs ● Use the intangible assets to reduce market competition **External evidence should be considered in determining the future economic benefits.** For instance: ● a business is well known for its intangible assets such as secret formulae or brand to reduce competition or increase sales revenue; ● the business may have received several quotes from others who want to acquire the intangible assets; ● the business has been using its brand to charge a premium when products are sold. **Condition 2: The entity can restrict others from benefiting it.** ● An evidence of control is the legally enforceable right such as when the entity bought the license or signed the contract. This evidence is not always a necessary condition. ● Another evidence of control is where an entity develops a software and use it to control its sales revenue. ● The following items are not deemed to be controlled by the entity: 1. Staff technical knowledge-failed the condition 2 since staff may leave the business. However, if the technical knowledge is protected by a legal right, it meets with the above conditions. 2. Market share and customer loyalty-failed the condition 2 since customers may buy things from competitors. 3. Long term staff training benefits-failed the condition 2 since staff may leave the business. (IAS 38: para. 13–17)

No.	Easy Rules
3	An asset is identifiable if it either: a) is separable, i. e. is capable of being separated or divided from the entity and sold, transferred, licensed, rented or exchanged, either individually or together with a related contract, identifiable asset or liability, regardless of whether the entity intends to do so; or b) arises from contractual or other legal rights, regardless of whether those rights are transferable or separable from the entity or from other rights and obligations. (IAS 38: para. 12)
4	*** Physical substance: An intangible asset may have physical form such as a certificate (to a patent), or compact disc storing videos. But these physical forms are less important than the knowledge itself included in the asset, hence the substance of the asset is primarily intangible rather than intangible. (IAS 38: para. 8)

Example:

A company has a special recipe to produce a special drink which is very popular around the world. The recipe is protected by a patent. Some competitors have approached the company to buy the recipe but were rejected.

Required: Can this recipe be capitalised as an intangible asset?

Answer: Yes. Referring back to the definition of an intangible asset:

1. Control:

- Condition 1: future economic benefits: Met. Since sales may be improved if the special recipe is used.
- Condition 2: Restrict others from using it. The recipe is protected by a patent.

2. Identifiable:

The recipe is not acquired separately but it can be sold separately to others. Therefore, these criteria is met.

3. Non-monetary asset: this is neither currency held nor asset received in a fixed amount of money, i. e., not debt or equity. Hence this criterion is met.

4. Without physical substance: it may have physical form such as documents detailing the recipe, but the substance of the recipe is about the knowledge and therefore, it is intangible.

* **Note:** However, if the recipe is not protected by the patent but only controlled by the three key managers in the business, then this is the staff technical knowledge and it should not be capitalised as an intangible asset.

3.1.2 Examples of intangible assets into different classes

No.	Easy Rules
1	a) brand names; b) mastheads and publishing titles; c) computer software; d) licences and franchises; e) copyrights, patents and other industrial property rights, service and operating rights; f) recipes, formulae, models, designs and prototypes; and g) intangible assets under development. (IAS 38: para. 119)

3.1.3 Initial measurement

No.	Easy Rules
1	**Step 1**: Choose accounting policy: • Cost model (Initially carried at cost-accumulated amortisation and impairment); or • Revaluation model [Initially carried at cost (subsequently update to fair value)-accumulated amortisation and impairment]
2	**Step 2**: Subsequent measurement: For intangible assets which are carried at either cost or revaluation model, the subsequent measurement depends on whether the life of the intangible asset is finite (amortise) or indefinite (impairment reviewed each year). (IAS 38: para. 72)

3.1.4 Cost model

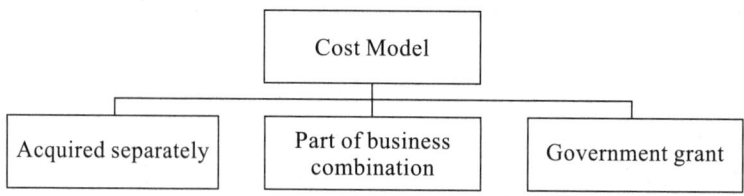

3.1.4.1 Situation 1: if the intangible asset is acquired separately

No.	Easy Rules
1	Initial/historical costs which **can** be included in the intangible asset value include: • Purchase price, including any import duties paid, but excluding any trade discount and reclaimable sales tax paid; • Legal fees in drafting the intangible asset contract; • Employee benefits costs bringing the asset to its working condition (employ extra staff specifically for obtaining the intangible asset); • Costs of testing whether the asset is functioning properly (such as testing the software).
2	Initial/historical costs **can not** be included in the intangible asset value include: • Start up costs; • Costs of introducing a new product or service (including costs of advertising and promotional activities); • Costs of conducting business in a new location or with a new class of customer (including costs of staff training); • Administration and other general overhead costs.

3.1.4.2 Situation 2: if the intangible asset is acquired as part of a business combination

No.	Easy Rules
1	We should use the fair value at the date of the acquisition as the initial cost of the intangible asset. (IAS 38: para. 10)

Example:

Company A acquired 100% shares in company B. At the date of purchase, the independent valuer provides a value of the company B's brand at $ 10 million. The brand is not recognised as an intangible asset in the individual company B's account.

Company A paid $ 18 million to acquire company B's net assets, the fair value of company B's equity at the date of acquisition was $ 6 million without its brand value.

Required:
1. Accounting treatment of company B's brand at the date of acquisition in the group account.
2. Goodwill amount shown in the group account.

Answer:
1. Accounting treatment:

Dr	Intangible asset	$ 10 million
Cr	Fair value of company B's equity	$ 10 million

- This is also known as "fair value adjustment" in the consolidated account. The intangible asset can subsequently be measured at cost or revaluation model (in very rate situations), and the subsequent measurement can either be to amortise the intangible asset or to test whether the asset is impaired at each reporting date.
- The intangible asset value of $ 10 million should be recognised separately from goodwill.

(IFRS 3: para. B31)

2. Goodwill:

Consideration paid	$ 18 million
−Fair value of company B's equity ($ 6 million + $ 10 million)	$ (16) million
Goodwill at the date of acquisition	$ 2 million

3.1.4.3 Situation 3: if the intangible asset is acquired by way of government grant

No.	Easy Rules
1	**Examples include:** • Government grants the entity to operate a TV or Radio station; • Government grants the entity the taxi license; • Government grants the entity the fishing license; • Government grants the entity the license to operate a toll road; • Construction permits granted by the government; • Mineral rights such as the right of drilling and mining; • The right granted by government to operate service contracts such as mortgage service contracts; • Import licences granted by government; • Production quota granted by government.

No.	Easy Rules
2	**Measurement:** • At cost (money that business paid to get the asset from the government, normally the amount is not significant which is known as "nominal amount", plus directly attributable costs to acquire the asset); or • At fair value (fair value provided by the independent valuer) • The above cost or fair value update and increase the debit side of the journal entry, i.e. **Dr** Intangible assets <div align="right">(IAS 38: para. 44)</div>
3	According to IAS 20 Accounting for Government Grants and Disclosure of Government Assistance: The credit side of the above entry depends on: **Dr** Intangible assets **Cr** ? 1. If there are no future performance conditions required: **Cr** income. 2. If there are future performance conditions needed to be fulfilled: **Cr** Deferred income liability, only when the future performance conditions are met, the income can then be recognised.

Example 1:

The business received a free of charge transferable license to operate a radio station for the next six years. The fair value of the license is $3 million.

The license will not be revoked during the next six years, however, if the business violates the local law by expressing incorrect political views, a severe fine will be charged.

Required: Accounting treatment.

Answer:

Dr	Intangible asset *	$3m
Cr	Income * *	$3m

* Either at cost or fair value, but free of charge in this case. Fair value is therefore used.

* * There are no conditions attached to the grant.

Only if the business violates the local law, the business should provide a provision liability or disclose a contingent liability per IAS 37 Provisions, Contingent Liabilities and Contingent Assets.

Example:

The business received a free of charge transferable license to operate a radio station on 1 January for the next six years. The fair value of the license is $3 million. The business can start operating the radio station by upgrading all of its facilities according to the contract.

On 1 March, the business finished upgrading all of its facilities and start operating the radio station.

The license will not be revoked during the next six years, however, if the business violates the local law by expressing incorrect political view, a severe fine will be charged.

Required: Accounting treatment.

Answer:

On 1 January:

Dr	Intangible asset *	$3m
Cr	Deferred income liability **	$3m

* Fair value is preferable.

** Since there are future performance conditions needed to be fulfilled.

On 1 March:

Dr	Deferred income liability	$3m
Cr	Income ***	$3m

*** Since on 1 March, all conditions are met.

3.1.5 Revaluation model

No.	Easy Rules
1	The revaluation model is applied after an asset has been initially recognised at cost. (IAS 38 : para. 77)
2	**Conditions**: 1. There must be an active market to determine the fair value of the intangible asset. Three conditions for an active market: • Items are homogeneous • Willing buyers and sellers in the market • Price available to the public. 2. The entire class of intangible assets must be revalued at the same time. 3. Revaluation surplus should be included in the revaluation surplus/reserve account and other comprehensive income section; Revaluation decrease should first reverse the original revaluation reserve, with the balancing figure going into the impairment loss expense. 4. When the intangible asset is disposed of, the accumulated revaluation reserve should be transferred to the retained earnings. (IAS 38 : para. 85 and 87)
3	In some jurisdictions, an active market may exist for freely transferable taxi licences, fishing licences or production quotas. However, an active market cannot exist for brands, newspaper mastheads, music and film publishing rights, patents or trademarks, because each such asset is unique. Also, although intangible assets are bought and sold, contracts are negotiated between individual buyers and sellers, and transactions are relatively infrequent. (IAS 38 : para. 78)

Example:

A taxi license with a value of $ 1 million has been revalued to $ 1.2 million as at the year end. However, it is subsequently revalued downwards to $ 0.7 million in the second year.

Before the end of the third year, the license is revalued up again to $ 1.3 million and then the license is disposed of at $ 5 million.

Required: Accounting treatments for the above transactions. For simplicity reasons, we assume that the above $ 1 million and $ 0.7 million are carrying value of intangible assets (netting off the cost and accumulated amortisation).

Answer:
1. Revaluation upwards:

Dr	Intangible asset ($1.2m-$1m)	$0.2m
Cr	Revaluation reserve	$0.2m

2. Revaluation downwards:

Dr	Revaluation reserve	$0.2m
Dr	Impairment loss	$0.3m
Cr	Intangible asset ($1.2m-$0.7m)	$0.5m

3. Revalue upwards again:

Dr	Intangible asset ($1.3m-$0.7m)	$0.6m
Cr	Revaluation reserve	$0.6m

4. Transfer from revaluation reserve to retained earnings since the asset is disposed of:

Dr	Revaluation reserve	$0.6m
Cr	Retained earnings	$0.6m

3.1.6　Exchange of assets

No.	Easy Rules
1	Principles for assets exchange in IAS 16 PP&E also apply in IAS 38.　　　　　　　　　　　　　　　　　　　　　　(IAS 38:para.45)

3.1.7 Useful life

No.	Easy Rules
1	1. Finite (limited); or 2. Indefinite (no foreseeable limit to the period over which the asset can generate future cash inflows) (IAS 38: para. 88)
2	**Factors to consider to determine the useful life of the intangible asset:** • Expected usage • Typical product life cycles • Technological, commercial or other types of obsolescence (economics of an industry; new legislations and loss of resources such as materials or labour) • Stability of the industry • Competitors' actions • Level of maintenance expenditure required • Legal or similar limits on the asset use such as expiry dates of related leases (IAS 38: para. 90)
3	A change in the useful life estimation is a change in an accounting estimate. (IAS 38: para. 109)

3.1.8 Amortisation period and method

No.	Easy Rules
1	Intangible assets are amortised if the life is finite. (IAS 38: para. 89)
2	Amortisation should start when the asset is available for use. For instance, the date that business receives regulatory and marketing approval of the intangible asset. (IAS 38: para. 97)
3	Amortisation should cease when the asset is classified as held for sale (IFRS 5) or de-recognised (sold) (earlier of the two). (IAS 38: para. 97)

No.	Easy Rules
4	**Amortisation methods:** **Method 1: Straight-line method:** This is used where the consumption of economic benefits is based on the passage of time such as patents and licenses granted for a finite period of time. This is a default method and it should be used when the economic benefits consumption pattern cannot be predicted reliably. **Method 2: Unit of production method:** This is used for intangible assets related to resource depletion such as rights to extract oil and gas resources. The intangible asset value is reduced by the number of units (tonnes of oil) being depleted. **Method 3: Revenue based method:** This method can ONLY be used when: 1. If the intangible asset is expressed as a measure of revenue; and 2. The revenue and the consumption of economic benefits of the intangible asset are highly correlated; **Examples of these include the right to operate a toll road or dig the gold mine:** 1. Such rights are expresses as a measure of revenue; 2. Revenue and consumption of economic benefits are highly correlated, i. e. until the cumulative amount of revenue earned, such rights would expire. (IAS 38: para. 98A) **Method 4: Reducing balance method:** This is normally used in taxable profits calculation. (IAS 38: para. 98)
5	**Journal entry for amortisation charge:** 	**Dr** Amortisation expense (P/L)	X	 	**Cr** Accumulated amortisation (SOFP)	X	
6	The calculation is to use the cost or revalued amount and to subtract its residual value and spread it over the economic useful life or units. Amortisation charge may not be taken to the statement of profit or loss as an expense. For instance, patents (intangible asset) acquired for the machine to produce certain inventories. The amortisation charge may be included in fixed production overhead expenses in inventories. The journal entry is as follows: 	**Dr** Inventories (Work-in-progress)	X	 	**Cr** Accumulated amortisation (SOFP)	X	

3.1.9 Residual value

No.	Easy Rules
1	The residual value of an intangible asset with a finite useful life shall be assumed to be zero unless: (1) A third party is committed to buy the intangible asset at the end of the useful life (a buyer signed a contract or paid the deposit); or (2) There is an active market for the asset and: (a) residual value can be determined by reference to that market; and (b) it is probable that such a market will exist at the end of the asset's useful life. <div align="right">(IAS 38: para. 100)</div>The residual value is the expected selling price and subtract any expected costs of disposal.
2	The residual value should be reviewed each year, and a change in residual value (consider any changes in price and other variables) would be a change in an accounting estimate and should be adjusted prospectively. <div align="right">(IAS 38: para. 102)</div>

3.1.10 Intangible assets with indefinite useful lives

No.	Easy Rules
1	An intangible asset with an indefinite useful life shall not be amortised. <div align="right">(IAS 38: para. 107)</div>
2	Review the assumption that the useful life of the intangible asset is indefinite each year. <div align="right">(IAS 38: para. 109)</div>
3	Examples of such intangible assets typically include: • goodwill • trademarks • perpetual franchises
4	We should conduct impairment review test for such intangible assets by considering the carrying value and the recoverable amount. If the carrying value is greater than the recoverable amount, an impairment loss expense should be recognised per IAS 36 Impairment of assets by: **Dr** Impairment loss expense **Cr** Intangible assets

No.	Easy Rules
5	If impairment indicators or management assumptions changed, i. e. management believes that the life of the intangible asset is no longer indefinite, management shall change the accounting estimate to amortise the intangible assets. (IAS 38:para. 109)

Examples when intangible assets lives are indefinite:

Example 1:

A pharmaceutical company acquired a well established branded drug. Management decides to assume that the life of this type of drug is indefinite. However, the assumption needs to be reviewed each year, for instance, by considering the technological and medical advances, since these factors may suggest that the life of this drug is finite rather than indefinite.

Example 2:

An indicator for intangible asset with indefinite useful lives may be that the intangible asset (such as broadcasting right) can be renewed at little cost each year.

Example 3:

The acquired airline route, if the acquiring company also provides supporting services such as airport gates, slots, and terminal facility leases and it can be seen that the acquiring company could generate future cashflows indefinitely. However, impairment review test should be done each year to confirm this useful life assumption.

Example 4:

The trademark has a remaining legal life of five years but is renewable every 10 years at little cost. The acquiring entity intends to renew the trademark continuously and evidence supports its ability to do so. An analysis of (1) product life cycle studies, (2) market, competitive and environmental trends, and (3) brand extension opportunities provides evidence that the trademarked product will generate net cash inflows for the acquiring entity for an indefinite period.

The trademark would be treated as having an indefinite useful life because it is expected to contribute to net cash inflows indefinitely. Therefore, the trademark would not be amortised until its useful life is determined to be finite. It would be tested for impairment in accordance with IAS 36 Impairment of Assets.

3.1.11 Research and Development (R&D) costs

No.	Easy Rules
1	**Research** is original and planned investigation undertaken with the prospect of gaining new scientific or technical knowledge and understanding. Examples include: • Activities aimed at obtaining new knowledge • The search for applications of research findings or other knowledge • The search for product or process alternatives • The formulation and design of possible new or improved product or process alternatives **Accounting treatment:** **Dr** Research expense (P/L) **Cr** Cash/Accrued expense/Payables
2	**Development** is the application of research findings or other knowledge to a plan or design for the production of new or substantially improved materials, devices, products, processes, systems or services prior to the commencement of commercial production or use. Examples include: • The design, construction and testing of pre-production prototypes and models • The design of tools, jigs, moulds and dies involving new technology • The design, construction and operation of a pilot plant that is not of a scale economically feasible for commercial production • The design, construction and testing of a chosen alternative for new/improved materials (IAS 38: para. 8, 56 and 57)

Practical examples of R&D in different industries:

Industry examples	Research	Development
Self driving cars	• Activities to obtain new knowledge on self-driving technology. • Search activities for alternatives for replacing metal components used in a company's current manufacturing process. • Search activities for a new operating system to be used in the car.	• Design and construction activities related to the development of a new self-driving prototype. • Design and construction of a new tool required for the manufacturing of a new product. • Testing activities on a new operating system that will replace the current one.

Industry examples	Research	Development
Gaming (also eligible for other software activities)	• Activities in analysing the requirements (including market research) of the game. • Activities in researching different coding system to be used in developing the game. • Costs spent for alternative "themes" to be used in the gaming industry.	• Design and construction activities related to development of a new video gaming prototype (for alpha or beta testing). • Time spent architecting, developing, testing and project managing the technology used in the game.
Oil and gas	• Activities in developing new knowledge regarding geological interpretations and reservoir models through seismic processing. • Activities in searching for different alternative places or technologies used in extracting oils. • Technical work to support bids.	• The development of drilling technologies to operate in more extreme wells with higher temperature and pressure requirements. • The appreciable improvement of the performance of equipment. • The development of new subsea infrastructure.
Pharmaceutical industry	• Activities in gaining new knowledge about the effect and side effect of the new medicine. • Activities in searching for alternative ingredients used in the medicine. • Time and costs spent in arguing the feasibility of the medicine introduced in the market such as gaining knowledge on the legal requirements and its overall cost and benefits analysis.	• Development of the prototype medicine. • Design a pilot plant to develop this particular type of medicine. • Testing the alternative ingredients used in the specified medicine to confirm the best option.

No.	Easy Rules
3	R&D costs will include all costs that are directly attributable to R&D activities, or that can be allocated on a reasonable basis. The standard lists the costs which may be included in R&D, where applicable (note that selling costs are excluded). • Salaries, wages and other employment-related costs of personnel engaged in R&D activities • Costs of materials and services consumed in R&D activities • Depreciation of property, plant and equipment to the extent that these assets are used for R&D activities • Overhead costs, other than general administrative costs, related to R&D activities; these costs are allocated on bases similar to those used in allocating overhead costs to inventories • Other costs, such as the amortisation of patents and licences, to the extent that these assets are used for R&D activities (IAS 38: para. 66)

Example: in pharmaceutical industry:

A laboratory is developing a drug to cure a special disease.

Required: List the potential development costs for this drug.

Answer:

- Medical materials used in the development of the drug and the clinical trials;
- Employee benefits for personnel involved in the investigation and trials, including employee benefits for dedicated internal employees;
- Compensation paid to patients or their relatives;
- Directly attributable costs such as fees to transfer a legal right and the amortisation of patents and licences that are used to generate the asset;
- Overheads that are directly attributable to develop the asset and can be allocated on a reasonable and consistent basis, such as allocation of depreciation of property, plant and equipment (PP&E) or rent;
- Legal costs incurred in presentations to authorities;
- Insurance costs for the risks of unexpected side-effects in patients participating in trials;
- Design, construction and testing of pre-production prototypes and models; and
- Design, construction and operation of a pilot plant that is not of an economically feasible scale for commercial production, including directly attributable wages and salaries.

Accounting treatment:

Before capitalisation conditions are met:

Dr Development expense (P/L)
Cr Cash/Accrued expense/Payables

After capitalisation conditions are met:
Dr Intangible asset—development costs (SOFP)
Cr Cash/Accrued expense/Payables

Please note, the earlier development expenditure should not be retrospectively recognised at a later date as part of the cost of an intangible asset.

Example:

The business incurred $6 million development costs which did not qualify for capitalisation criteria before August 20×9. From August 20×9 onwards, the development cost is qualified to be capitalised and the business incurred another $8 million.

Required: Accounting treatment.

Answer: The $6m development costs should be expensed to P/L since it did not meet with capitalisation criteria before August 20×9. The $8m development costs should be capitalised as intangible assets since they meet with capitalisation criteria after August 20×9. The previous $6m should not be retrospectively recognised at a later date as part of the cost of an intangible asset.

The subsequent measurement for capitalised development cost uses the same principle as we have seen before.

3.1.12 Other internally generated intangible assets

No.	Easy Rules
1	Internally generated brands, mastheads, publishing titles, customer lists and items similar in substance shall not be recognised as intangible assets.
2	Expenditure on internally generated brands, mastheads, publishing titles, customer lists and items similar in substance cannot be distinguished from the cost of developing the business as a whole. Therefore, such items are not recognised as intangible assets. (IAS 38: para. 63-64)

3.2 *Goodwill: IFRS 3 Business Combinations*

No.	Easy Rules
1	Goodwill is a good relationship between a business and its customers (reputation, prompt response to customers; staff personality in the business).

No.	Easy Rules
2	**Purchased goodwill:** • This takes place if the fair value of consideration plus non-controlling interest are more than the fair value of net assets acquired. • It should be subject to impairment review test at each reporting period but it should not be amortised.
3	**Negative goodwill:** • This takes place if the fair value of consideration plus non-controlling interest are less than the fair value of net assets acquired. • It should be taken to the consolidated statement of profit or loss and consolidated retained earnings. • This is also known as a gain on bargain purchase.

Chapter 4

Impairment of Assets

IAS 36   Impairment of Assets

Topic outline:

- Different standards about impairment
- Definitions
- Impairment indications
- Accounting entries
- Cash generating units
- Impairment reversal

4.1 Different Standards Dealing with Impairment

No.	Easy Rules
1	• Inventories (IAS 2); • Contract assets and assets arising from costs to obtain or fulfill a contract that are recognised (IFRS 15); • Deferred tax assets (IAS 12); • Assets arising from employee benefits (IAS 19); • Financial assets within the scope of IFRS 9; • Investment property measured at fair value (IAS 40); • Biological assets related to agricultural activity measured at fair value less costs to sell (IAS 41); • Other tangible and intangible assets (IAS 36 Impairment of assets).

4.2 *Definitions*

No.	Easy Rules
1	**Impairment loss:** • An impairment loss is the amount by which the carrying amount of an asset or a cash-generating unit exceeds its recoverable amount.
2	**Recoverable amount:** • The recoverable amount of an asset or a cash-generating unit is the higher of its fair value less costs of disposal and its value in use. (IAS 36: para. 6)

Example: Calculate an impairment loss expense:

A business has a piece of equipment and the management believes that this is impaired. The cost of the equipment is $30,000 and the carrying value at the date when the impairment review test has been performed was $17,000.

The fair value of the equipment is $25,000 and the commission costs to be paid to sell this equipment are expected to be $13,000. The value in use of this equipment is estimated to be $11,000.

Required: Calculate the impairment loss expense of this equipment.

Answer: Carrying value $17,000.

Recoverable amount is the higher of value in use ($11,000) and the fair value less costs of disposal ($25,000 - $13,000 = $12,000). Therefore, the recoverable amount is $12,000.

Since the carrying value of the equipment is higher than its recoverable amount, the $5,000 impairment loss expense should therefore be recognised ($17,000 - $12,000).

No.	Easy Rules
3	**Value in use:** • Value in use is the present value of the future cash flows expected to be derived from an asset or cash-generating unit. The net cash flows to be received or paid for the disposal of assets at the end of its useful life should also be included. (IAS 36: para. 6)
4	**Fair value less costs of disposal:** • The value is calculated by assuming the business disposes of the asset now rather than it continues to use the asset in the foreseeable future.

No.	Easy Rules
5	**Fair value**: • Fair value is the price that would be received to sell an asset or paid to transfer a liability in an orderly transaction between market participants at the measurement date. • If active market exists for the asset: fair value should be based on market price or recent transaction price in similar assets. • If active market does not exist for the asset: estimate the fair value using best estimate of what market participants might pay in an orderly transaction. (IFRS 13)
6	**Costs of disposal**: • Costs of disposal are incremental costs directly attributable to the disposal of an asset or cash-generating unit, excluding finance costs and income tax expense. (IAS 36: para. 6)
7	**Note**: • Future cash flows shall be estimated for the asset in its current condition. Estimates of future cash flows shall not include estimated future cash inflows or outflows that are expected to arise from: (a) a future restructuring to which an entity is not yet committed; or (b) improving or enhancing the asset's performance. • Costs of disposal, other than those that have been recognised as liabilities, are deducted in measuring fair value less costs of disposal. (IAS 36: para. 44 and 28)

Example: Costs of disposal liability

A company operates a mine with the cost of $ 100 million. The estimated costs of removal the mine at the end of its useful life are $ 10 million.

The company receives a quote from one of the buyers to be $ 80 million if the mine is sold.

The value in use of the mine after considering the removal costs is $ 50 million.

Required: Calculate the impairment loss expense of the mine if:

1. The $ 10 million removal costs can be capitalised in the mine costs and the provision liability;

2. The $ 10 million removal costs can not be capitalised in the mine costs and the provision liability.

Answer:
1. If the $10 million removal costs have been capitalised:

Dr	PP&E	$10m
Cr	Provision	$10m

The carrying value is therefore $110 million ($100m+$10m).

The fair value less costs of disposal = $80 million (in this case, we can not include $10 million removal costs in the calculation because $10 million liability has been recognised). Therefore, the recoverable amount is the fair value less costs of disposal being $80 million as this is higher than its value in use.

Therefore, the impairment expense = $110 million−$80 million = $30 million.

2. If the $10 million removal costs have not been capitalised:

The carrying value of the mine is $100 million.

The fair value less costs of disposal = $80 million−$10 million = $70 million (the removal costs should be included in the fair value less costs of disposal calculation).

Therefore, the impairment expense = $100 million−$70 million = $30 million.

Conclusion: In whatever cases, the impairment expense is $30 million.

4.3 *Identifying a Potentially Impaired Asset*

No.	Easy Rules
1	If there are impairment indicators of the asset, formal estimate of the assets' recoverable amount is required: The mandatory annual impairment test can be at any time during an annual period, provided the test is performed at the same time of the year. There is no requirement for an entity to test all these assets at the same time (including individual CGU's). If the asset is tested for impairment before the end of the reporting period, an additional test is required if there are indicators of impairment at the reporting date. (IAS 36: para. 8)

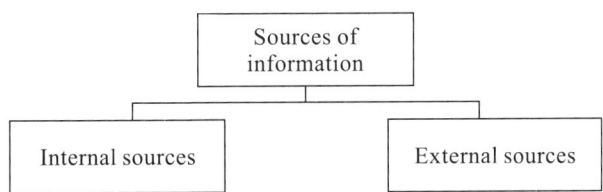

4.3.1　Internal sources of information

No.	Easy Rules
1	**Evidence of obsolescence or physical damage.**
2	**Asset becomes idle, plans to discontinue or restructure the operation to which an asset belongs, or plans to dispose of an asset before the previously expected date.** For instance, the machine is now idle due to a change in consumer needs.
3	**Reassessing the useful life of an asset as finite rather than indefinite.** For instance, government now changes the law regarding the broadcasting right (intangible asset) to be renewed at a large rather than a small cost. The business should therefore reassess its useful life as finite rather than indefinite.
4	**Evidence is available from internal reporting that indicates that the economic performance of an asset is, or will be, worse than expected.** For instance: • Cash flows needed for acquiring, operating or maintaining the assets are significantly higher than originally budgeted. • Actual net cash flows or operating profit resulting from the asset are significantly worse than budgeted. (IAS 36：para. 12)

4.3.2　External sources of information

No.	Easy Rules
1	**There are observable indications that the asset's value has declined during the period significantly more than would be expected as a result of the passage of time or normal use.** For instance, the company acquired a machine and expected to produce products in house rather than to use the outsourcing option in order to gain costs efficiency. However, due to changes in market factors, the supplier decides to change its pricing policy and charge a low price, the company's original estimate for cost efficiency isnot realised.

No.	Easy Rules
2	**Changes (took place or will take place) with an adverse effect on the technological, market, economic or legal environment in which the entity operates.** For instance: • Changes in import duty or sales tax affecting the use of machines to produce products; • The entry of a major competitor into the market; • Nationalisation of the firm by the local government; • A change in consumer demand due to improvement in technology that the business cannot handle; • Economic downturn such as: 　-Fall in index (such as FTSE, Dow Jones, Hang Seng index) 　-Tightening credit (an increase in interest rate) and less disposable income to citizens 　-Government increases rescue spending in saving companies in financial crisis 　-Impacts on commodity (materials/fuel) prices • Changes in foreign exchange rates (affecting business's imports or exports).
3	**The carrying amount of the net assets of the entity is more than its market capitalisation.** For instance, the market capitalisation of different companies can be found in real time in different websites such as https://ycharts.com/. The carrying amount of net assets include those tangible and intangible assets subtracting liabilities. Market may believe those assets are overvalued, or companies may find it very difficult to pay those liabilities back to creditors, and therefore the market capitalisation of the company is less than its net assets carrying value. We can often refer to the market to book (price to book) ratio for different companies, i.e. if the ratio is less than one, this could suggest impairment indicator exists. <div style="text-align:right">(IAS 36: para. 12)</div>

4.4 *Common Impairment Indicators in Different Industries*

No.	Easy Rules
1	**Car industry**: • Vehicles recall; • Idle plant due to excess capacity; • Changes in law requiring plant to shut down. **Bank**: • Sharp increase in bad debts; • Financial crisis; • Credit tightening; • Increase in interest rate. **Retail industries**: • Actual operating cash flows from individual stores less than budgets; • Economic downturn affecting customer disposal income. **Hotel industries**: • Substitutes or competitors entering in the market such as Airbnb; • Interest rate increases; • Issues such as food poisoning.

4.5 *Accounting Entries*

An asset or a cash generating unit (CGU) is impaired:

Normal accounting treatment: **Dr** Impairment expense **Cr** Asset at cost **Dr** Accumulated depreciation	**Or in FR** exam: **Dr** Impairment expense **Cr** Asset at carrying value

4.6 *Cash-Generating Units (CGUs)*

No.	Easy Rules
1	**Definition**: A cash-generating unit is the smallest identifiable group of assets that generates cash inflows that are largely independent of the cash inflows from other assets or groups of assets. (IAS 36: para. 6)

4.7 Examples of CGUs

No.	Easy Rules
1	An entire entity (parent or subsidiary entities within a group).
2	Departments or business units within an entity: for instance, each store in a retail business.
3	Production lines within a department, or within an entity: for instance, each magazine titles of a publisher.
4	Groups of items of property, plant and equipment within a production line, within a department, or within an entity: for instance, a plant or aircraft.

4.8 Considerations to Determine a CGU

No.	Easy Rules
1	If the business is run on a unit by unit basis (such as store by store basis) and the internal management report is organised to measure performance on a unit by unit (such as store by store basis), each unit is identified as a CGU.
2	If an active market exists for the output produced by the asset or a group of assets (such as assets combined in each factory), this asset or group should be identified as a CGU, even if some or all of the output is used internally. In simple words, if an active market exists, each unit does not need to completely/ partly depend on the other unit's demand and therefore, each unit is independent.
3	CGUs should be identified consistently from period to period for the same type of asset unless a change is justified. For instance, if there is a change in economic factors and there is no active market for the produced product, the original assessment of CGU should change. (IAS 36: para. 72)
4	If the asset is used to serve the business, the asset itself can not be identified as a CGU.

4.9 Practical Examples to Determine a CGU

Practical example 1: Retail store chain:
Store ABC belongs to retail store chain M. ABC makes all its retail purchases through M's

purchasing centre. Pricing, marketing, advertising and human resources policies (except for hiring ABC's cashiers and sales staff) are decided by M. M also owns five other stores in the same city as ABC (although in different neighbourhoods) and 20 other stores in other cities. All stores are managed in the same way as ABC. ABC and four other stores were purchased five years ago and goodwill was recognised.

Required: What is the cash-generating unit for ABC (ABC's cash-generating unit)?

Answer: In identifying ABC's cash-generating unit, an entity considers whether, for example:

- Internal management reporting is organised to measure performance on a store-by-store basis; and
- The business is run on a store-by-store basis on a region/city basis.

All M's stores are in different neighbourhoods and probably have different customer bases. So, although ABC is managed at a corporate level, ABC generates cash inflows that are largely independent of those of M's other stores. Therefore, it is likely that ABC is a cash generating unit.

Practical example 2: Factory for an intermediate step in a production process:

A significant raw material used for plant Y's final production is an intermediate product bought from plant X of the same entity. X's products are sold to X at a transfer price that passes all the margins to X.

Eighty percent of Y's final production is sold to customers outside of the entity. Sixty percent of X's final production is sold to Y and the remaining forty percent is sold to customers outside of the entity.

Required: For each of the following cases, what are the cash-generating units for X and Y?

Scenario 1: X could sell the product it sells to Y in an active market. Internal transfer prices are higher than market prices.

Scenario 2: There is no active market for the products that X sells to Y.

Answer:

Case 1:

X could sell its products in an active market and, so, generate cash inflows that would be largely independent of the cash flows from Y. Therefore, it is likely that X is a separate cash-generating unit, although part of its production is used by Y. It is likely that Y is also a separate cash-generating-unit. Y sells eighty percent of its products to customers outside of the entity. Therefore, its cash inflows can be regarded as largely independent.

Internal transfer prices do not reflect market prices for X's output. Therefore, in determining value in use of both X and Y, the entity adjusts financial budget/forecasts to reflect management's best estimate of future prices that could be achieved in arm's length transactions for those of X's products that are used internally.

Case 2:

It is likely that the recoverable amount of each plant cannot be assessed independently of the recoverable amount of the other plant because:

a) The majority of X's production is used internally and could not be sold in an active market. So, cash inflows of X depend on demand for Y's products. Therefore, X cannot be considered to generate cash inflows that are largely independent of those of Y.

b) The two plants are managed together.

As a consequence, it is likely that X and Y together are the smallest group of assets that generates cash inflows that are largely independent.

Practical example 3: Building half-rented to others and half-occupied for own use:

M is a manufacturing company. It owns a headquarters building that used to be fully occupied for internal use. After downsizing, half of the building is now used internally and half rented to third parties. The lease agreement with the tenant is for five years.

Required: What is the cash-generating unit for the building?

Answer: The primary purpose of the building is to serve as a corporate asset, supporting M's manufacturing activities. Therefore, the building as a whole cannot be considered to generate cash inflows that are largely independent of the cash inflows from the entity as a whole. So, it is likely that the cash-generating unit for the building is M as a whole.

Practical example 4: Mining company and railway:

A mining company owns a private railway that it uses to transport output from one of its mines. The railway now has no market value other than as scrap, and it is impossible to identify any separate cash inflows with the use of the railway itself.

Required: How to determine the CGU for the mining company?

Answer: The railway itself should not be treated as a CGU because:

1. The mining company is not managed using a unit by unit basis such as revenue streams from mining and from railway.

2. The railway is used to serve the mining company, i. e., to transport output from one of its mines.

And therefore, the mine as a whole should be treated as a cash generating unit.

Practical example 5: Bus routes:

A bus company has an arrangement with a town's authorities to run a bus service on five routes in the town. Separately identifiable assets are allocated to each of the bus routes, and cash inflows and outflows can be attributed to each individual route. Four routes are running at a profit and one is running at a loss.

Required: How to determine the CGU for bus mining company.

Answer: Four profitable routes cash inflows depend on the loss-making route because without the loss making route, the bus company cannot proceed with the project. Hence all five bus routes together should be treated as a CGU.

4.10 *Impairment Test for CGU*

No.	Easy Rules
1	**Allocation order**: 1. Specific asset which has been impaired 2. Reduce goodwill down to zero 3. Remaining balance on a pro-rata basis to the remaining unimpaired assets carrying amount (exclude current assets) (IAS 36: para. 60,104)

Example: A plant has been defined as a cash generating unit with the following information:

	$ 000
Allocated goodwill	2,400
Land	6,000
Plant and equipment	6,000
Intangible assets	2,000
Current assets (cash, inventories and receivables)	1,400
Carrying value	17,800

Due to changes in laws, the intangible asset has been subject to impairment review test and the recoverable amount of the intangible asset is now $ 1.5 million. The recoverable amount of the CGU is now $ 9.8 million.

Required: Accounting entries for the impairment expense on this CGU.

Answer: Total impairment expense = Carrying value − CGU Recoverable amount = $ 17.8m − $ 9.8m = $ 8m

The $ 8 m should be allocated using the following order:

$ 000	Order	Carrying value	Recoverable amount	Impairment expense
Allocated goodwill	2	2,400		2,400
Land	3	6,000		50% ×5,100 = 2,550

Plant and equipment	3	6,000		50% ×5,100 = 2,550
Intangible assets	1	2,000	1,500	500
Carrying value		17,800	9,800	8,000

Dr	Impairment expense	$ 8,000
Cr	Intangible assets	$ 500
Cr	Goodwill	$ 2,400
Cr	Land *	$ 2,550
Cr	Plant and equipment * *	$ 2,550

* Land:6,000/(6,000+6,000) × $ 5,100 remaining impairment expense.

* * Plant and equipment: $ 2,550 (6,000/(6,000+6,000)× $ 5,100 remaining impairment expense.

4.11 *Allocated Goodwill*

No.	Easy Rules
1	Goodwill arising from a business combination must be allocated to each of the acquirer's CGUs which are expected to benefit from synergies after business combination, this is because the goodwill itself does not generate cash flows independently of other assets. (IAS 36:para. 80)
2	For example, a business operating in financial services industry acquired a company with three product lines including automobile, aircraft and retail businesses. The goodwill arising from business acquisition was $ 30 million and this must be allocated into the four product lines including financial services, automobile, aircraft and retail businesses based on their weightings of projected cash flows, changes in net assets values or carrying amounts of the CGUs.

4.12 "Consistency" Rule

No.	Easy Rules
1	The carrying amount of a cash-generating unit shall be determined on a basis consistent with the way the recoverable amount of the cash-generating unit is determined.
2	If the disposal of a cash-generating unit would require the buyer to assume the liability. In this case, the fair value less costs of disposal of the cash-generating unit is the price to sell the assets of the cash-generating unit and the liability together (this means that the price the buyer pays include both the asset and liabilities purchased), less the costs of disposal.
3	To perform a meaningful comparison between the carrying amount of the cash-generating unit and its recoverable amount, the carrying amount of the liability is deducted in determining both the cash-generating unit's value in use and its carrying amount. (IAS 36: para 75 and 78).

Example: (adjusted from IFRS illustrative example)

A company operates a mine and it determines the whole mine to be a CGU. The carrying value of the CGU is $ 1,000 million.

The fair value less costs of disposal is estimated to be $ 800 million.

The value in use of the mine is estimated to be $ 1,200 million excluding restoration costs of $ 500 million.

The restoration costs have been recognised as a provision liability when the mine was first operated.

Required: Whether the above CGU is impaired?
Answer: No.

Carrying amount = $ 1,000 million − $ 500 million (restoration costs should be deducted here for comparison purposes) = $ 500 million

(IAS 36: para. 78)

Recoverable amount is the higher of value in use and fair value less costs of disposal:
Value in use = $ 1,200 million − $ 500 million (necessary restoration costs) = $ 700 million
Fair value less costs of disposal = $ 800 million (The $ 800m to be paid by the buyer is for both the asset and the liabilities that the buyer will bear)

Hence the recoverable amount is $ 800 million which is more than its carrying amount of $ 500 million and therefore, the CGU is not impaired.

4.13 *Impairment Reversal for an Individual Asset*

No.	Easy Rules
1	**Situations causing impairment reversal to take place:** **External sources of information:** ⅰ. there are observable indications that the asset's value has increased significantly during the period. ⅱ. significant changes with a favourable effect on the entity have taken place during the period, or will take place in the near future, in the technological, market, economic or legal environment in which the entity operates or in the market to which the asset is dedicated. ⅲ. market interest rates or other market rates of return on investments have decreased during the period, and those decreases are likely to affect the discount rate used in calculating the asset's value in use and increase the asset's recoverable amount materially. **Internal sources of information:** ⅳ. significant changes with a favourable effect on the entity have taken place during the period, or are expected to take place in the near future, in the extent to which, or manner in which, the asset is used or is expected to be used. These changes include costs incurred during the period to improve or enhance the asset's performance or restructure the operation to which the asset belongs. ⅴ. evidence is available from internal reporting that indicates that the economic performance of the asset is, or will be, better than expected.
2	**Rules:** • The increased carrying amount of an asset other than goodwill attributable to a reversal of an impairment loss shall not exceed the carrying amount that would have been determined (net of amortisation or depreciation) had no impairment loss been recognised for the asset in prior years. • For depreciated asset using cost model, the reversal of impairment loss should go to "gain" in the P/L. • For revalued asset, the reversal of impairment loss should go to "Revaluation reserve" in equity and OCI. • Impaired goodwill is never reversed. <div style="text-align:right">(IAS 36: para 111–121)</div>

Example:

A company acquired a building on 1 January 2011 at a cost of $ 300,000 with the estimated useful life of 10 years. The cost model is used for subsequent measurement. On 31 December 2012, the recoverable amount of the building is $ 160,000 after the impairment review test has been carried out.

On 31 December 2015, the market interest rate decreased, the resulting recoverable amount is now $400,000.

Required: Accounting entries.

Answer:

	$
Cost on 1 January 2011	300,000
−Accumulated depreciation (1 January 2011–31 December 2012) $300,000/10 years×2 years	(60,000)
Carrying amount on 31 December 2012	240,000
Impairment loss	(80,000)
Recoverable amount on 31 December 2012 (become the new cost)	160,000
−Accumulated depreciation (31 December 2012–31 December 2015) $160,000/remaining 8 years×3 years	(60,000)
Carrying value on 31 December 2015	100,000

On 31 December 2015, the recoverable amount is $400,000 which is higher than its carrying amount of $100,000, and therefore, the impairment loss can be reversed.

The amount of impairment loss can be reversed shall not exceed the carrying amount that would have been determined had no impairment loss been recognised for the asset in prior years.

If there are no impairment loss expenses of $8,000 recognised, we depreciate the asset using the original cost of $300,000 up to 31 December 2015 as follows:

If there were no impairment losses:

	$
Cost on 1 January 2011	300,000
−Accumulated depreciation (1 January 2011–31 December 2015) $300,000/10 years×5 years	(150,000)
Carrying value on 31 December 2015	150,000

Hence we can:

Dr	PP&E (carrying value) ($150,000 − $100,000)	$50,000
Cr	Gain	$50,000

Please note, if the asset has been subject to revaluation before, we should credit "Revaluation reserve" account in equity with the corresponding figure going to the "OCI—Other comprehensive income".

The above way is what we could use in the FR exam. However, the whole disclosure in real business is as follows (this is not required from the FR exam's perspective):

After the impairment has taken place:

	Year 3	Year 4	Year 5
Cost	$160,000	$160,000	$160,000
−Accumulated depreciation $160,000/8 years	$(20,000)	$(40,000)	$(60,000)
Carrying value	$140,000	$120,000	$100,000

If the impairment has not taken place:

	Year 3	Year 4	Year 5
Cost	$300,000	$300,000	$300,000
−Accumulated depreciation $300,000/10 years and for year 3–5	$(90,000)	$(120,000)	$(150,000)
Carrying value	$210,000	$180,000	$150,000

Hence we should:

Dr	Accumulated depreciation	$ 60,000
Cr	PP&E at cost *	$ 10,000
Cr	Gain	$ 50,000

* ($150,000 – $160,000) -the depreciation should be based on the adjusted amount of $150,000 over its remaining useful life.

Chapter 5

Revenue

IFRS 15 Revenue from Contracts with Customers

Topic outline:

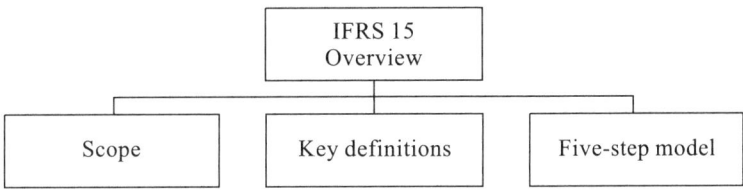

5.1 Scope

No.	Easy Rules
1	**IFRS 15 allies to all contracts with customers except:** An entity shall apply this standard to all contracts with customers, except the following: a) lease contracts within the scope of IFRS 16 Leases; b) insurance contracts within the scope of IFRS 4 Insurance Contracts; c) financial instruments and other contractual rights or obligations within the scope of IFRS 9 Financial Instruments, IFRS 10 Consolidated Financial Statements, IFRS 11 Joint Arrangements, IAS 27 Separate Financial Statements and IAS 28 Investments in Associates and Joint Ventures; and d) non-monetary exchanges between entities in the same line of business to facilitate sales to customers or potential customers. For example, this Standard would not apply to a contract between two oil companies that agree to an exchange of oil to fulfil demand from their customers in different specified locations on a timely basis. (IFRS 15: para. 5)

5.2 *Key Definitions*

```
┌──────────┐  ┌────────────────┐  ┌──────────────────────┐  ┌────────────────────┐
│  Income  │  │ Contract asset │  │ Incremental costs of │  │ Contract liability │
│          │  │                │  │ obtaining a contract │  │                    │
│          │  │                │  │   (contract cost)    │  │                    │
└──────────┘  └────────────────┘  └──────────────────────┘  └────────────────────┘

      ┌──────────────┐   ┌───────────────────┐   ┌──────────────┐
      │  Stand-alone │   │ Transaction price │   │ Performance  │
      │ selling price│   │                   │   │ obligation   │
      └──────────────┘   └───────────────────┘   └──────────────┘
```

(IFRS 15: Appendix A)

No.	Easy Rules
1	**Income** includes revenue and gains.
2	**Contract asset:** A contract asset can be: • mount due from customer/accrued income • Prepaid expense • Incremental costs to obtain the contract An entity's right to consideration in exchange for goods or services that the entity has transferred to a customer when that right is conditioned on something other than the passage of time (for example, the entity's future performance). This is different from accounts receivables because account receivables mean that a business has a right to collect payment from customers and the right is conditioned on the passage of time, i.e. after the invoice is sent to customer, the customer can decide when to pay the business. Contract asset can also be "prepaid expense". For instance, in order to allow the third party to work with the business, the business may prepay certain costs to support the third party (for instance, company A pays $1 million to company B in order to redecorate company B's store to sell company A's products. The $1 million is a prepaid expense or a contract asset). Incremental costs to obtain the contract should be capitalised as contract assets. Definition of incremental cost is provided below.

No.	Easy Rules
3	**Incremental costs of obtaining a contract (contract cost):** The incremental costs of obtaining a contract are those costs that an entity incurs to obtain a contract with a customer that it would not have incurred if the contract had not been obtained (for example, a sales commission). **To capitalise the incremental costs as contract asset:** ✓ Condition 1: These costs are clearly identified to the contract ✓ Condition 2: These costs can enhance the entity's resources to satisfy the performance obligations ✓ Condition 3: These costs can be recovered from the contract (contract revenue is more than the costs) Costs that relate directly to a contract (or a specific anticipated contract) include any of the following: a) direct labour (for example, salaries and wages of employees who provide the promised services directly to the customer); b) direct materials (for example, supplies used in providing the promised services to a customer); c) allocations of costs that relate directly to the contract or to contract activities (for example, costs of contract management and supervision, insurance and depreciation of tools, equipment and right-of-use assets used in fulfilling the contract); d) costs that are explicitly chargeable to the customer under the contract; and e) other costs that are incurred only because an entity entered into the contract (for example, payments to subcontractors). An entity shall recognise the following costs **as expenses** when incurred: a) general and administrative costs (unless those costs are explicitly chargeable to the customer under the contract, in which case an entity shall evaluate those costs as contract assets); b) costs of wasted materials, labour or other resources to fulfill the contract that were not reflected in the price of the contract; c) costs that relate to satisfied performance obligations (or partially satisfied performance obligations) in the contract (i.e. costs that relate to past performance); and d) costs for which an entity cannot distinguish whether the costs relate to unsatisfied performance obligations or to satisfied performance obligations (or partially satisfied performance obligations). (IFRS 15: para. 91–95)

No.	Easy Rules
4	**Contract liability**: An entity's obligation to transfer goods or services to a customer for which the entity has received consideration (or the amount is due) from the customer. In summary, contract liability can be: • The business has not provided services to customers yet, but customers settled money in advance, i.e. deferred income liability. • The invoiced amount to customer (account receivable) is greater than the work performed by the entity (contract asset), the remaining balance is recorded as a contract liability.
5	**Stand-alone selling price**: The price at which an entity would sell a promised good or service separately to a customer.
6	**Transaction price**: The amount of consideration to which an entity expects to be entitled in exchange for transferring promised goods or services to a customer, excluding amounts collected on behalf of third parties.
7	**Performance obligation**: A promise in a contract with a customer to transfer to the customer either: a) a good or service (or a bundle of goods or services) that is distinct; or b) a series of distinct goods or services that are substantially the same and that have the same pattern of transfer to the customer. (IFRS 15: Appendix A)

5.3 Five-Step Model [COPAR]

No.	Easy Rules
1	1. Contract Identification 2. Obligation identified 3. Price for transaction 4. Allocation of transaction price to obligation 5. Recognise revenue

Example:

Scenario 1: Contract asset:

Aaron enters into a 12-month telecom plan with the local mobile operator Tele plc. The

terms of plan are as follows:
- Aaron's monthly fixed fee is $ 100.
- Aaron receives a free mobile phone at the inception of the plan and Arron does not pay anything at the time when the contract is signed.

Tele plc sells the same mobile phones for $ 300 and the same monthly prepayment plans without mobile phone for $ 80/month.

Required: Accounting entries.

Answer:

1. Contract: Tele plc and Aaron enters into the contract where Aaron is required to pay a monthly network service fee and receive a free mobile phone.
2. Performance obligation: There is a promise by Tele plc to develop a free mobile phone and network service to Aaron each month.
3. The price for the contract is $ 1,200 for one year ($ 100 per month×12 months)
4. Allocation: based on stand-alone selling price

	Stand-alone price $	Proportion (%)	Actual revenue $
Mobile phone	$ 300	23.8%	1,200×23.8% = $ 286
Service	$ 960 (12× $ 80)	76.2%	1,200×76.2% = $ 914
	$ 1,260	100%	$ 1,200

5. Recognise revenue:

First, recognise revenue now if mobile phone is delivered and received by the customer.

Dr	Contract asset	$ 286
Cr	Revenue	$ 286

Second, recognise $ 76 each month ($ 914/12 months)

Dr	Receivable	$ 100
Cr	Contract asset ($ 286/12 months)	$ 24
Cr	Revenue	$ 76

Scenario 2: Contract liability

Aaron enters into a 12-month telecom plan with the local mobile operator Tele plc. The terms of plan are as follows:
- Aaron's monthly fixed fee is $ 80.

- Aaron receives a free mobile phone at the inception of the plan.

If Aaron pays $ 320 when the contract is signed with monthly fixed fee of $ 80 being settled at the end of each remaining 11 months.

Tele plc sells the same mobile phones for $ 300 and the same monthly prepayment plans without mobile phone for $ 80/month.

Required: Accounting entries.

Answer: First, recognise revenue now if mobile phone is delivered and received by the customer.

Dr	Cash	$ 319
Cr	Revenue	$ 286
Cr	Contract liability	$ 33

Second, recognise $ 83 revenue each month ($ 914/11 months)

Dr	Cash	$ 80
Dr	Contract liability ($ 33/11 months)	$ 3
Cr	Revenue	$ 83

5.4 IFRS 15 Five Steps in Detail

5.4.1 Step 1: Identifying the contract

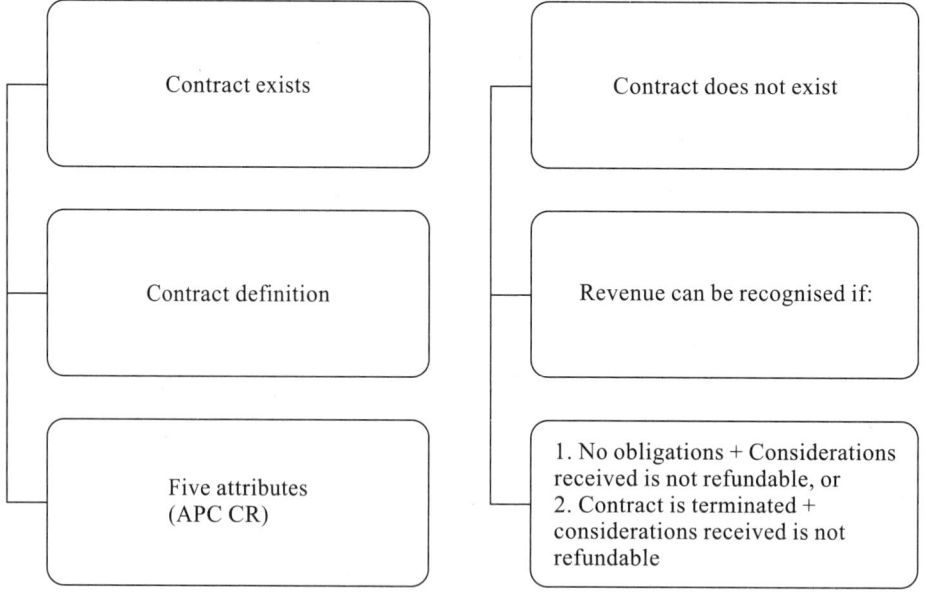

5.4.2 Situation 1: The contract exists

No.	Easy Rules
1	A contract is an agreement between two or more parties that creates enforceable rights and obligations. A contract can be written, oral or implied. • A written contract is normally enforceable in most countries, but a business needs to consult with its lawyer in advance, for instance, in most countries where a written contract is not for a lawful purpose, the contract is not enforceable. An example is a written contract to buy illegal drugs. • An oral contract may not be enforceable in some countries or for some items, for instance, in some countries, the contract regarding the sale of land must be written. In most countries, there should be other physical evidence such as emails, testimony from any witnesses or texts along with the verbal contract. • An implied contract is a contract that is not written nor verbal confirmation is needed. A common example is an implied warranty where a customer purchases a product on the assumption that the product will perform its intended function. For instance, a customer buying a TV assumes that the TV can be turned on.

A contract has five attributes: (**mnemonics: APC CR**)

An entity shall account for a contract with a customer that is within the scope of this standard only when all of the following criteria are met:

Key words	Explanations from IFRS 15: para. 9	Further explanations
Approved	The parties to the contract have approved the contract (in writing, orally or in accordance with other customary business practices) and are committed to perform their respective obligations;	Contract is approved by both parties. Contracts can be in different forms but business needs to identify whether the contract is enforceable in its own jurisdiction.
Payment terms	The entity can identify the payment terms for the goods or services to be transferred;	For instance, payment in advance or credit period is defined, including the discount offered to customers.

Key words	Explanations from IFRS 15: para. 9	Further explanations
Commercial substance	The contract has commercial substance (i.e. the risk, timing or amount of the entity's future cash flows is expected to change as a result of the contract); **An example given by IASB where the transaction lacks commercial substance:** For example, this Standard would not apply to a contract between two oil companies that agree to an exchange of oil to fulfill demand from their customers in different specified locations on a timely basis. Any related party transaction should be carefully reviewed to determine whether the transaction has commercial substance.	**1. Risk of future cash flows:** For instance, the exchange of the government bond to a piece of land. The risks for the government bond and the land would be different. **2. Timing of future cash flows:** The exchange of inventories to a piece of equipment by the business may have commercial substance because the timing to generate cash flows from the sale of inventories is generally quicker than the sale of the equipment. However, if the business exchanges an obsolete piece of equipment with its high value inventories, the transaction may lack commercial substance. **3. Amount of future cash flows:** The business may exchange its trademark with a new technology and the amount of revenue that the trademark can help the business generate is different from the amount of revenue generated by the new technology, i.e. there might be more cash flows generated from the new technology at the start than the trademark.

Key words	Explanations from IFRS 15:para. 9	Further explanations
<u>C</u>ollectability	It is probable that the entity will collect the consideration to which it will be entitled in exchange for the goods or services that will be transferred to the customer. In evaluating whether collectability of an amount of consideration is probable, an entity shall consider only the customer's ability and intention to pay that amount of consideration when it is due. The amount of consideration to which the entity will be entitled may be less than the price stated in the contract if the consideration is variable because the entity may offer the customer a price concession;	The collectability should be assessed continuously by the business. If the business deems the collectability of an amount of consideration is not probable (for instance, a business may have a low credit rating and hence the business can not apply the loan to pay the fees), the subsequent revenue should not be recognised until this criterion is met. Any accounts receivables should also be impaired or derecognised per IFRS 9 Financial Instruments.
<u>R</u>ights	The entity can identify each party's rights regarding the goods or services to be transferred.	Seller's right is to collect payments and the buyer's right is to get the promised goods or/ and services from the seller.

Example: Contract definition

The business sells and delivers a special product to the customer without a signed agreement based on the request by the customer to fill the urgent need. The seller's normal practice is to obtain written and customer signed sales agreements.

Required: Can an enforceable contract exist in this case?

Answer: It depends.

First, the business needs to confirm whether the contract not signed is enforceable in the country.

Second, the business needs to confirm whether five attributes of a contract are met.

Example: Contract attributes

A real estate developer entered into a contract with a customer for the sale of a building for $1 million and the customer takes procession of the building when the contract was signed.

However, the real estate developer concludes that the collectability of considerations from the customer is not probable due to economic factors. The customer paid $50,000 non-refundable deposits.

Required: How to treat the $50,000 non-refundable deposits?

Answer: Since the collectability of consideration criteria is not met, and the contract has not been terminated (sees situation 2 later).

The real estate developer should not recognise revenue regarding the $50,000.

However, the deposit of $50,000 should remain in the contract liability until the collectability of consideration from the customer is probable.

5.4.3 Situation 2: The contract does not exist

No.	Easy Rules
1	If there is no contract with the customer, i.e. the customer pays the business before the business provides goods or services: The business can recognise consideration received as sales revenue only when: (a) the entity has no remaining obligations to transfer goods or services to the customer and all, or substantially all, of the consideration promised by the customer has been received by the entity and is non-refundable; or (b) the contract has been terminated and the consideration received from the customer is non-refundable.
2	Otherwise, the business should recognise the consideration received as a contract liability until performance obligations are met. (IFRS 15: para. 15)

Example: IFRS 15: para. 15 application

A traveller bought a ticket from the cruise company and paid the full amount already. However, the traveller failed to check in before the deadline timing.

Required: Can the cruise company recognise the revenue of the ticket paid when the traveller failed to check in before the deadline timing?

Answer: It depends.

Case 1: If the cruise company has no further obligations to provide cruise ship services to the customer and the consideration received is not refundable, the cruise company can recognise the consideration received as revenue.

For instance, the cruise company received $ 5,000 ticket price from the traveler. The journal entry when the consideration was received:

Dr	Cash	$ 5,000
Cr	Contract liability	$ 5,000

If the cruise company can refund $ 500 to the customer:

Dr	Contract liability	$ 500
Cr	Cash	$ 500

The remaining $ 4,500 can be recognised in the sales revenue:

Dr	Contract liability	$ 4,500
Cr	Sales revenue	$ 4,500

Case 2: If the cruise company allows the traveler to change the schedule, the cruise company needs to re-arrange another cruise ship for the traveler and the service has not been performed. In this case, the consideration received should not be recognised as revenue and it should remain in the contract liability.

5.4.4 Step 2: Identifying performance obligations

```
Assess promised goods or services and whether they are distinct?
        ↓
If the good or service is distinct, each would be a performance obligation.
        ↓
Distinct (two conditions):
1. Customer can benefit;
2. Separately identifiable not integration service or not customized or not interelated with other products/services.
```

No.	Easy Rules
1	**At contract inception, an entity shall:** 1. Assess the goods or services promised [can be explicit (written promise in the contract) or implicit (through marketing materials that the business promises to provide services to others)] in a contract with a customer; and 2. Identify whether goods or services promised are distinct. A distinct good or service is a separate performance obligation.

No.	Easy Rules
2	**A good or service that is promised to a customer is distinct if both of the following criteria are met:** **1. The customer can benefit from the good or service either on its own or together with other resources that are readily available to the customer;** For instance, When building a school, a customer may not benefit from getting the permit itself from the government, but the customer can benefit from getting the permit from the government along with other steps such as school design and renovation (together with other resources readily available to the customer); and **2. The entity's promise to transfer the good or service to the customer is separately identifiable from other promises in the contract.** For instance, the good or service is not separately identifiable if one of the situations occurs: a) Integration services: Are products or services are used as inputs to produce a combined output? For instance, the customer can not benefit from each stage of the construction process of a building but rather, only when the whole building is completed, the customer can benefit from it. b) Customisation: Do products or services need to customise or modify other products or services in the contract? For instance, the seller may need to customise the installation work to the client given the complexity of the machine or software and this means that only the seller can provide this service. c) Interrelated: Are products or services highly interrelated? For instance, the customer can still use the product even without services provided by the seller and in this case, the product and service are not highly interrelated. (IFRS 15: para. 29)

Example 1:

A software business sells a software program to a customer with the following bundled features:

1. Software license
2. Installation service
3. Online and face to face training course
4. Software upgrade in next five years.

The software needs to be tailored to the client's operating system and it has to be installed by the software business, i.e. the client's existing operating system needs to change by adding additional features in order for the software to be used.

Required: How many performance obligations are in this software program?

Answer: There are **three or four** performance obligations in this case.

Promised good/service is distinct if two conditions are met:
1. Customers can benefit from it: this is met because the customer can use the software;
2. The promise from the seller to transfer the good or service is separately identifiable from other promises: this is not met because the installation service is tailored to the customer's operating system. Hence we could argue that only after the software is installed, the software can be used by the client. Therefore, the software license and the installation service should be combined as a performance obligation.

For the remaining promised services including training and upgrade services, they are not customised to the customer. They do not need to modify other promised services in the contract as well, for instance, the software can be used by the business after it has been installed and the business does not need to wait the training and upgrade services provided by the seller before the software can be used.

They are not highly interrelated to each other because clients may not attend the training service and it can still use the software. This is not an integration service as well because the client can use the software separately without training and upgrade.

Please note, if the installation service is not complex and can be provided by any third parties or the client can install it on its own without having to customise other promised services in the contract, in this case, there should be four performance obligations.

In some cases, the contract may contain restrictions such as the buyer must have the software installed only by the seller. The restriction itself does not affect the judgement about the number of performance obligations in this case, i.e. if the installation service needs to customise other promised goods or services in the contract, it is still not separately identifiable. But if not, the software license and the installation service are separately identifiable.

(IFRS 15: IE58F)

Example 2:
A blockchain training school provides lectures and study materials to students who enroll in the course. The lectures are provided to students by face to face. Upon enrollment, students can get the study materials from the school before attending the lectures.

Required: How many performance obligations?
Answer: Two performance obligations.

Performance obligations are distinct if both conditions are met:
1. Customers can benefit from it: this condition is met because the customer can gain new knowledge from lectures and study materials;
2. The promise from the seller to transfer the good/service is separately identifiable from other promises: this condition is met because the study materials do not customise the lectures, i.e. the students can attend the lectures without the study materials or vice versa. It also means that the study materials and the lectures are not highly interrelated nor integrated.

Example 3:
A construction company signed a contract with the customer to build a school building in-

volving the following stages:
- Stage 1: getting permits from local government
- Stage 2: building and interior design
- Stage 3: foundation
- Stage 4: construction of the structure
- Stage 5: piping and wiring
- Stage 6: installation of equipment and finishing

Required: How many performance obligations?

Answer: One performance obligation.

Performance obligations are distinct if both conditions are met:

1. Customers can benefit from it: this condition is met because the customer can take control of the school building after it is finished.

2. The promise from the seller to transfer the good or service is separately identifiable from other promises: this condition is not met. Because this is an example of integration service provided by the construction company, i. e. the construction company uses those six stages as inputs to provide the combined output which is the school. This means that the customer can only benefit from taking control of the school when all six stages are completed.

Example 4: (illustrative example from IFRS 15 Case 12)

An entity, a manufacturer, sells a product to a distributor who will then resell it to an end customer. In the contract with the distributor, the entity promises to provide maintenance services for no additional consideration (i. e. "free") to any party (i. e. the end customer) that purchases the product from the distributor. The entity outsources the performance of the maintenance services to the distributor and pays the distributor an agreed-upon amount for providing those services on the entity's behalf. If the end customer does not use the maintenance services, the entity is not obliged to pay the distributor.

Required: How many performance obligations.

Answer: The contract with the customer includes two promised goods or services:
(a) the product and
(b) the maintenance services.

Performance obligations are distinct if both conditions are met:

1. Customers can benefit from it: this condition is met because the customer can benefit from the product and services.

2. The promise from the seller to transfer the good or service is separately identifiable from other promises: this condition is met.

The entity is not providing a significant integration service because the presence of the product and the services together in this contract do not result in any additional or combined functionality.

In addition, neither the product nor the services modify or customise the other.

Lastly, the product and the maintenance services are not highly intergrated nor highly interrelated because the entity would be able to fulfill each of the promises in the contract independently of its efforts to fulfill the other (i.e. the entity would be able to transfer the product even if the customer declined maintenance services and would be able to provide maintenance services in relation to products sold previously through other distributors).

Example 5:

A business has a contract to license a right to produce a special drug to a customer and agreed jointly promote the drug in a specified region.

Required: How many performance obligations?

Answer: Two performance obligations.

Performance obligations are distinct if both conditions are met:

1. Customers can benefit from it: this condition is met because the customer can benefit from the drug production and marketing activities.

2. The promise from the seller to transfer the good or service is separately identifiable from other promises: this condition is met. Because the license is not highly interrelated with the co-promotion activity and this is because the customer could provide the co-promotion activity and license can be used without promotional activities.

5.4.5 Step 3: Determining the transaction price

Transaction price includes:
1. Fixed consideration
2. Variable consideration

⇨

Maximum variable consideration:
1. Highly probable
2. Significant reversal will not occur
Approaches:
1. Weighted probability approach
2. Most likely outcome.

⇨

Reassessment:
At the end of each reporting period.

No.	Easy Rules
1	**Definition of transaction price:** Transaction price is the amount of consideration to which an entity expects to be entitled in exchange for transferring promised goods or services to a customer, excluding sales tax. (IFRS 15: para. 47)
2	**Transaction price includes:** • Fixed consideration • Variable consideration

No.	Easy Rules
3	**Forms of variable considerations:** ● **Discounts**: cash discounts. If there is a credit sale and the seller expects the credit customer will take advantage of the cash discount offered, the cash discount should be initially subtracted from the total sales revenue when the transaction takes place. And if subsequently the customer does not take advantage of the cash discount, i.e. the customer settles the payment very late, the discount revenue should be recognised again in the P/L. If at the contract inception that the seller does not expect the credit customer to take advantage of the cash discount, the discount revenue should not be removed from the contract price. When the customer subsequently settles the payment and take advantage of the cash discount, i.e. paying early, the seller should reduce the sales revenue by the discount offered. ● **Rebates**: such as volume based rebates. For instance, if a customer purchases more than 1,000 items per year, instead of charging the customer $200 per unit, the customer is charged $170 per unit, i.e. $30 rebates per unit returned to the customer. ● **Refunds**: this is the direct refunds provided from the seller to the buyer given a certain performance condition is met. For instance, the above example $30 rebate is a refund provided back to the buyer. ● **Price concessions**: for instance, given the first time that the seller works with the buyer, the seller may be willing to reduce the price charged for longer business relationships. ● **Credits such as coupon offered**: for instance, a coffee shop may offer a credit to customers "buy 10 coffee and get 1 free". Another example is in the airline industries where the passengers can accumulate the mileage to reduce the future flight ticket price. ● **Penalties**: for instance, a construction company contracts with the customer to build a building and if the contract delays, the construction company may need to pay additional penalty fees. <div align="right">(IFRS 15: para. 51)</div>

No.	Easy Rules
4	**Two approaches to deal with variable considerations:** An entity shall estimate an amount of variable consideration by using either of the following methods, depending on which method the entity expects to better predict the amount of consideration to which it will be entitled: (a) **The expected value**—the expected value is the sum of probability-weighted amounts in a range of possible consideration amounts. An expected value may be an appropriate estimate of the amount of variable consideration if an entity has a large number of contracts with similar characteristics. (b) **The most likely amount**—the most likely amount is the single most likely amount in a range of possible consideration amounts (i. e. the single most likely outcome of the contract). The most likely amount may be an appropriate estimate of the amount of variable consideration if the contract has only two possible outcomes (for example, an entity either achieves a performance bonus or does not). <div align="right">(IFRS 15:para. 53)</div>
5	**Significant financing component:** However, the effects of the customer's credit risk and the material time value of money effect (more than one year) should be considered if a significant financing component exists. For instance, a seller sells the goods or services to the customer and allows the customer to settle the payment in 2 years. The discount rate used to discount the future cash received from the customer should reflect the customer's credit risk. However, customer's credit risk is not considered in other circumstances in the revenue recognition because this is covered in IFRS 9 Financial Instruments. <div align="right">(IFRS 15:para. 60)</div>
6	**The maximum amount of consideration to be recognised:** Variable contingent amounts are only included to the extent that it is highly probable that a significant reversal in the amount of cumulative revenue recognised will not occur when the uncertainty associated with the variable consideration is subsequently resolved. In simple words, revenue reversal means to reduce the total revenue by the amount of variable consideration. <div align="right">(IFRS 15:para. 56–57)</div>

No.	Easy Rules
7	**Factors that could increase the likelihood or the magnitude of a revenue reversal include, but are not limited to, any of the following:** a) the amount of consideration is highly susceptible to factors outside the entity's influence. Those factors may include volatility in a market, the judgement or actions of third parties, weather conditions and a high risk of obsolescence of the promised good or service. b) the uncertainty about the amount of consideration is not expected to be resolved for a long period of time. This means that during this period, the total gross revenue should be reduced by the amount of variable considerations. c) the entity's experience (or other evidence) with similar types of contracts is limited, or that experience (or other evidence) has limited predictive value. d) the entity has a practice of either offering a broad range of price concessions or changing the payment terms and conditions of similar contracts in similar circumstances. e) the contract has a large number and broad range of possible consideration amounts. For instance, the seller provides a management service to the buyer and receives the service fee at 5% based on the buyer company's asset value. (IFRS 15. para. 56–57)
8	**Reassessment:** At the end of each reporting period, an entity shall update the estimated transaction price (including updating its assessment of whether an estimate of variable consideration is constrained) to represent faithfully the circumstances present at the end of the reporting period and the changes in circumstances during the reporting period. (IFRS 15. para. 59)

Example 1: Discounts

Alpha company contracted with the customer to build a hospital with a total contract price of $ 50 million and the payment is settled in three progress payments. The final payment will be made upon completion of the project.

According to the past experience, customers would refuse to pay the final instalment arguing minor defects and the Alpha company would provide the discount for this.

Management expects to get only 80% of the consideration at the inception of the contract.

Required: What is the transaction price.

Answer: The transaction price should include the fixed payment and the variable consideration. In this case, the fixed payment is $ 50 million (gross revenue) and the variable consideration is $ 10 million ($ 50m×20%). We can also conclude it is highly probable that the significant reversal of the $ 10 million cumulative revenue will not occur given this is the past experience of Alpha company.

	Transaction price
Transaction price/gross revenue	$ 50 million
Discount	$ (10) million
Net revenue	$ 40 million

If the project is then 40% completed, the revenue to be recognised should be $ 40 million ×40% = $ 16 million.

If at the end of the project, the Alpha company does not offer discounts to the customer, the maximum revenue that Alpha company can recognise is $ 50 million.

Example 2: Rebates

On 1 January, Beta company signed a contract with the retailer to sell mobile phones. According to the contract, if the retailer could purchase up to 500 mobile phones in this year, a rebate of $ 60 per mobile phone can be returned back to the retailer. This means that the price before the rebate is $ 300 per mobile phone.

Case 1: as at 30th June, the retailer has only purchased 30 mobile phones from the Beta company.

Case 2: as at 30th September, the retailer has purchased 270 mobile phones from the Beta company.

Required: What is the transaction price for Beta company for the above two cases?

Answer:

Case 1: Since there are only 30 mobile phones are sold to the retailer in the first half of the year, and it may not be probable that additional 470 phones could be sold in the second half of the year. Beta company could conclude that it is not highly probable that the significant reversal of the cumulative revenue of $ 60 rebate could occur, hence the $ 60 rebate should NOT be considered in calculating the net revenue.

Therefore, the transaction price is $ 300 per mobile phone.

The revenue to be recognised is therefore $ 300/mobile phone×30 mobile phones = $ 9,000.

Case 2: Since at this date, 470 mobile phones have been sold. Hence it is highly probable that a significant reversal of the cumulative revenue of $ 60 rebate per mobile phone could occur. Therefore, the revenue to be recognised is $ 300-$ 60=$ 240/mobile phones×470 mobile phones = $ 112,800. Given the $ 9,000 revenue has been recognised in the first half of the year, the revenue to be recognised in the second half of the year should be $ 103,800 ($ 112,800-$ 9,000).

Example 3: Probability weighted approach

C company is contracted to provide consultancy advice to the client and here are the contingent performance targets:

If the client's sales revenue after implementing the C company's plan increases to:
- More than $ 50 million, additional bonus of $ 2 million can be paid to the C company. C company estimates there is 50% chance that this target can be met.
- More than $ 100 million, additional bonus of $ 3 million can be paid to the C company. C company estimates there is 30% chance that this target can be met.
- More than $ 150 million, additional bonus of $ 6 million can be paid to the C company. C company estimates there is 20% chance that this target can be met.
- The consultancy fee is fixed at $ 2.5 million.

Required: What is the transaction price?

Answer: The transaction price should include the fixed and variable consideration and the amount of variable consideration to be recognised should be to the extent that it is highly probable the significant reversal of cumulative revenue will not occur.

In this case, the fixed contract price is $ 2.5 million.

Since there are multiple options of the performance targets, a weighted probability approach should be used:

	Likely outcomes	Probability	Expected value
	Target 1: + $ 2million	50%	$ 1 million
	Target 2: + $ 3 million	30%	$ 0.9million
	Target 3: + $ 6 million	20%	$ 1.2 million
			$ 3.1 million

Hence the total contract price at the start is $ 5.6 million ($ 2.5 million + $ 3.1 million).

If for instance, at the end of the third quarter, C company revises its original estimate as follows:

	Likely outcomes	Probability	Expected value
	Target 1: + $ 2million	90%	$ 1.8 million
	Target 2: + $ 3 million	10%	$ 0.3million
	Target 3: + $ 6 million	0%	$ 0 million
			$ 2.1 million

The transaction price will then be revised to $ 2.5 + $ 2.1 million = $ 4.6 million.

Alternative approach there are only two outcomes:

Per IFRS 15, C company could decide to use the most likely amount to estimate the variable consideration associated with the incentive bonus. This is because there are only two possible outcomes (+ $ 2 million or + $ 3 million) and it is the method that the entity expects to better predict the amount of consideration to which it will be entitled. In this case, the transaction price may be revised to $ 2 million as the most likely outcome to occur if this approach is used.

(IFRS 15: para IE107)

5.4.6 Step 4: Allocating the transaction price to performance obligations

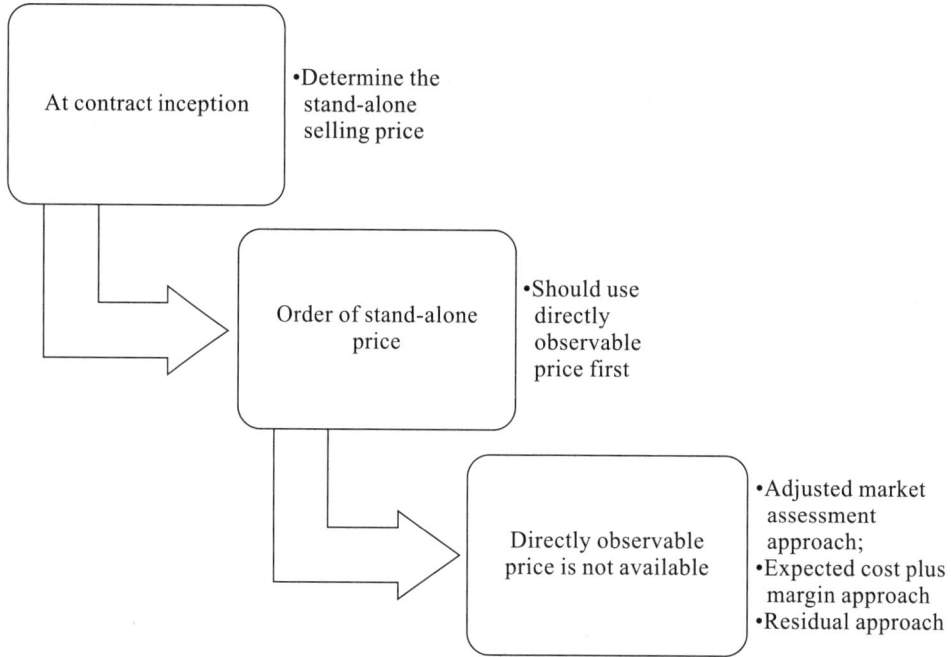

No.	Easy Rules
1	**Stand-alone selling price for each performance obligation is needed:** To allocate the transaction price to each performance obligation on a relative stand-alone selling price basis, an entity shall determine the stand-alone selling price at contract inception of the distinct good or service underlying each performance obligation in the contract and allocate the transaction price in proportion to those stand-alone selling prices. (IFRS 15: para. 76)

No.	Easy Rules
2	The stand-alone selling price is the price at which an entity would sell a promised good or service separately to a customer. (IFRS 15:para. 77)
3	**The order of stand-alone price:** • Observable price of a good or service that the entity sells separately in similar circumstances and to similar customers. • If the price is not directly observable, the entity can use the following methods: 1. **Adjusted market assessment approach:** the entity could refer to competitor's prices for similar goods or services. 2. **Expected cost plus a margin approach:** the entity could forecast its expected costs of satisfying a performance obligation and then add an appropriate margin for that good or service. 3. **Residual approach:** the entity can use the total transaction price less the sum of the observable stand-alone prices of other goods or services promised. This approach is only suitable if one of the following situations occurs: -The entity sells this good or service to different customers at different prices (a broad range of amounts). -The entity has not sold this good/service to any customers in the past. (IFRS 15. para. 75-79)

Example 1: Directly observable price

The entity regularly sells the following products A, B, C to similar customers in the country at $ 40, $ 50 and $ 10 and the price is directly observable in the market.

The entity sells a bundle of product A, B and C to a customer at $ 30.

Required: How to allocate the $ 70 transaction price to products A, B and C.

Answer:

Products	Stand-alone price	%	Allocation of revenue
A	$ 40	40%	$ 30×40% = $ 12
B	$ 50	50%	$ 30×50% = $ 15
C	$ 10	10%	$ 30×10% = $ 3
	$ 100	100%	Transaction price = $ 30

Example 2: Not directly observable price

The entity regularly sells the product A to similar customers in the country at $ 40.

Products B and C are not regularly sold separately to customers in the country and the observable price for those products are not directly observable. However, the entity refers to the competitor's pricing information for product B and determines that the adjusted market price for product B is $ 55.

For product C, since there is no competitors offering similar products, the entity estimates that the cost of producing the product C is $ 6 and the business policy of setting up the mark up is 10%, i.e. the expected selling price for product C using the cost plus margin approach is $ 6.6 ($ 6×1.1).

Since this is the first time that the entity signed a contract with the customer and the entity decides to give a special free of charge warranty service to the customer. The warranty service has not been provided by the entity before and the entity decides to use the residual approach to determine its stand-alone price.

The transaction price with the customer is $ 130.

Required: How to allocate the $ 130 transaction price to products A, B, C and the special warranty service.

Answer:

Product or service	Stand-alone price	
A	$ 40	The price is directly observable
B	$ 55	The price is set using the adjusted market approach
C	$ 6.6	The price is set using the expected cost plus margin approach
Warranty service	$ 28.4 *	The price is set using the residual approach
	$ 130	

* Warranty service: $ 28.4 = $ 130 − $ 40 − $ 55 − $ 6.6

In this example, we assume that the business has not sold the warranty service to any customers before, therefore, the $ 28.4 revenue can be recognised for the warranty service.

However, if we assume that the warranty service is regularly sold to customers at different prices, i.e. broad range from $ 5 to $ 10, and in this case, the $ 28.4 is outside the price range. The business should therefore review the observable data including sales and margin reports to establish the price for the warranty service using another suitable approach.

(IFRS 15: para. IE177)

5.4.7 Step 5: Recognise revenue when (or as) a performance obligation is satisfied

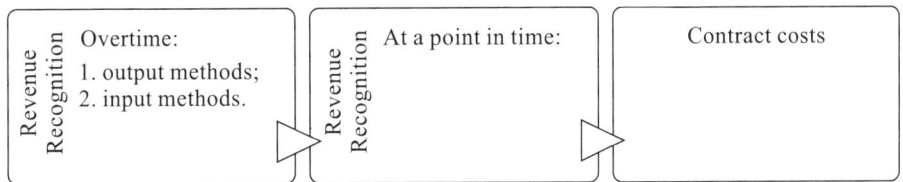

If a control of a promised good or service is transferred to the customer, the performance obligation is satisfied. The performance obligation can be satisfied at a point in time or over time.

5.4.7.1 Performance obligations satisfied over time when one of the following criteria is met

No.	Easy Rules
1	**Criteria one:** **The customer simultaneously receives and consumes the benefits as the performance takes place.** Examples include service provision such as cleaning service, monthly magazine subscription service, electricity or natural gas provision by the utility company, or tuition services.
2	**Criteria two:** **The entity's performance creates or enhances an asset that the customer controls as the asset is created or enhanced.** Examples include a construction company renovate the customer's shopping mall or adding additional features inside the shopping mall. However, if the construction company owns the shopping mall and the customer can finally obtain this after it is completed, this criteria is not met.

No.	Easy Rules
3	**Criteria three:** **The entity's performance does not create an asset with an alternative use to the entity and the entity has an enforceable right to payment for performance completed to date.** Examples include a construction company builds a shopping mall for the customer and the construction company will transfer the shopping mall to the customer when the shopping mall is finished, i.e. the asset is with no alternative use because of its practical limitations as customer contracts to build it. Another example is where a consultancy company provides management service to the business and the service is highly specialised to the customer. The right to payment does not have to be a fixed amount (payments can be made at intervals or on completion of the contract), at all times through put the contract duration, the entity must be entitled to an amount that at least compensates the seller for performance completed to date if the contract is terminated, i.e. cost plus reasonable margin. Please note, if the payment from the buyer can only cover the cost, this criteria is not met. (IFRS 15: para. 35)
4	**Two methods can be used to measure the progress.**
5	**Method one: output methods:** The progress under this method is determined by: • Surveys of performance completed to date (additional costs may be incurred in getting those reports); • Time elapsed (such as two year contract with payment being made at each year end); • Units produced or delivered (for design work, it would be hard to determine the progress using the output method). The method one may provide faithful representation, however, additional costs may need to be incurred in terms of the survey results. Alternatively, the progress is not easily determined in some situations such as for planning and design work.

No.	Easy Rules
6	**Method two: input methods:** The progress under this method is determined by: • Resources consumed; • Labour hours or machine hours used; • Costs incurred. This method is available if the entity decides the output methods can not faithfully represent the progress of the work provided (such as design work) or the costs can not be justified. However, the limitation of input methods is that additional adjustments need to be made. For instance, if a construction company contracts with a customer to build a building and the construction company buys an elevator for the customer. The cost of the elevator should not be included in the costs to date to measure the progress because this is not the cost to be involved in designing and manufacturing the asset. <div align="right">(IFRS:15 para. 41)</div>

5.4.7.2 Performance obligations satisfied at a point in time if none of the above criteria are met

No.	Easy Rules
1	If a performance obligation is not satisfied over time then it will be satisfied at a point in time. An entity shall consider the indicators of the transfer of control, which include, but are not limited to, the following:
2	**Indicator one: The entity has a present right to payment for the asset.** This means that the buyer is obligated to pay for an asset immediately, and this may imply that the control of the asset has been transferred to the buyer. However, this might not be the case when the contract states that at the contract inception, the customer is obliged to pay when the contract is signed but the seller has not provided the service yet. This commonly exists in education industries for the tuition services provided to students.

No.	Easy Rules
3	**Indicator two: The customer has legal title to the asset.** Usually if the customer owns the asset, the customer can sell it or exchange the asset for another asset or service and it deems that the control of the asset has been transferred to the buyer when the legal title remains in customer. However, an exception to this could be the party such as a bank holds the legal title of the asset for protective reasons, i. e. to secure the loan provided to the buyer. In this case, even though the legal title of the asset is transferred to the bank, the control of the asset is not deemed to be transferred to the bank and therefore, no sales revenue should be recognised at this point.
4	**Indicator three: The entity has transferred physical possession of the asset.** Normally, when a sale took place, the customer accepted it and possessed it physically and restricted any third parties to use the asset. In this case, control of an asset is transferred. However, exceptions to this may include: • **Consignment sale.** This normally takes place in car industry where the car manufacturer allows the car dealer to possess several cars in its showroom and if those cars can not be sold to the end customer, those cars can be returned back to the seller. • **Bill and hold arrangement.** This means that a customer paid money to the seller to buy a specified product but due to some reasons from the customer's side, the product is still physically processed in the seller's company. In this case, even though the seller processes the product, the control of an asset has been transferred to the buyer.
5	**Indicator four: The customer has the significant risks and rewards of ownership of the asset.** This means that the seller has completed its own obligation to transfer the asset or perhaps providing the necessary service for the asset to be used by the buyer. If there are problems with the asset in the future, it is not the risk that the seller needs to be responsible for. At the same time, the buyer could get the rewards from using the asset, selling the asset or exchanging the asset with any third parties for another asset or service. This would usually be seen that the control of asset has taken place. However, if separate services need to be provided in addition to the asset but has not been provided, part of that revenue should not be recognised at the point in time.

No.	Easy Rules
6	**Indicator five: The customer has accepted the asset.**
	This usually indicates that the customer has control of the asset when the customer signed and accepted the asset. However, there might be a contractual customer acceptance clause on when control of an asset is transferred such as allowing the customer to cancel the contract at any time if the customer is not happy with the asset, and in this case, the sales revenue should not be recognised at the point in time.
	(IFRS 15: para. 38)

5.5 *Incremental Costs of Obtaining a Contract (Contract Costs)*

Here is a useful recap on contract costs:

The incremental costs of obtaining a contract are those costs that an entity incurs to obtain a contract with a customer that it would not have incurred if the contract had not been obtained (for example, a sales commission).

To capitalise the incremental costs as contract asset:

✓ Condition 1: These costs are clearly identified to the contract

✓ Condition 2: These costs can enhance the entity's resources to satisfy the performance obligations

✓ Condition 3: These costs can be recovered from the contract (contract revenue is more than the costs)

Costs that relate directly to a contract (or a specific anticipated contract) include any of the following:

a) direct labour (for example, salaries and wages of employees who provide the promised services directly to the customer);

b) direct materials (for example, supplies used in providing the promised services to a customer);

c) allocations of costs that relate directly to the contract or to contract activities (for example, costs of contract management and supervision, insurance and depreciation of tools, equipment and right-of-use assets used in fulfilling the contract);

d) costs that are explicitly chargeable to the customer under the contract; and

e) other costs that are incurred only because an entity entered into the contract (for example, payments to subcontractors).

An entity shall recognise the following costs **as expenses** when incurred:

a) general and administrative costs (unless those costs are explicitly chargeable to the customer under the contract, in which case an entity shall evaluate those costs as contract assets);

b) costs of wasted materials, labour or other resources to fulfill the contract that were not reflected in the price of the contract;

c) costs that relate to satisfied performance obligations (or partially satisfied performance obligations) in the contract (i. e. costs that relate to past performance); and

d) costs for which an entity cannot distinguish whether the costs relate to unsatisfied performance obligations or to satisfied performance obligations (or partially satisfied performance obligations).

(IFRS 15:para. 91–95)

Example:

An accounting software company signed a five-year contract with a customer to manage the IFRS reporting requirements. It charges a yearly fee of $ 200,000. The accounting software company incurred the following costs:

Items	Costs
Hardware	$ 50,000
IFRS software	$ 30,000
Integration and installation costs	$ 10,000
Data conversion costs	$ 5,000

Required: How to deal with the above costs?

Answer:

Items	Costs	Treatment
Hardware	$ 50,000	PP&E
IFRS software	$ 30,000	Intangible assets
Integration and installation costs	$ 10,000	Contract assets
Data conversion costs	$ 5,000	

The integration and installation costs should be recognised as contract assets because:

1. These costs are clearly identified to the contract, i. e. costs arose as a result from the contract.

2. These costs enhance the hardware and IFRS software resources to satisfy the performance obligation, i. e. without these costs, hardware and IFRS software may well function.

3. These costs can be recovered from the contract, i. e. a five-year contract with total revenue of $ 1 million ($ 200,000×5 years) well covers the $ 15,000 contract costs.

5.6 *Common Types of Transactions*

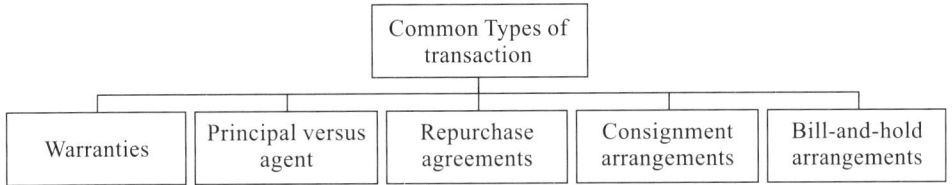

5.6.1 Type one: Warranties

No.	Easy Rules
1	If there is an option for the customer to purchase the warranty separately, it is deemed that the warranty can be separated from other promised goods or services in the contract, hence it should be accounted for under IFRS 15 as a separate performance obligation.
2	If the warranty is required by law and can not be purchased by the customer separately, it should be accounted for under IAS 37 Provisions, Contingent Liabilities and Contingent Assets.
3	The following situations are treated under IAS 37: A law that requires payment of compensation when products cause harm or damage. Promises to indemnify the customer for liabilities and damages arising from claims of patent, copyright, trademark or other infringement by the entity's products. (IFRS 15:B28-B33)

5.6.2 Type two: Principal versus agent

No.	Easy Rules
1	**Principal**: It controls the promised good/service before it is transferred to the customer. <u>Accounting treatment</u>: Recognise the revenue excluding the commission paid to the agent.
2	**Agent**: Its performance obligation is to arrange for the provision of goods or services by another party. <u>Accounting treatment</u>: Recognise the commission paid by the principal as revenue.

No.	Easy Rules
3	**Indicators that an entity controls the specified good or service before it is transferred to the customer and is therefore a principal include, but are not limited to, the following:** 1. The principal is primarily responsible for fulfilling the contract. 2. Inventory risk both before and after the goods have been ordered by a customer, during shipping or on return is borne by the principal. 3. The principal has discretion to establish prices and receives benefit. 4. The consideration is not in the form of a commission. 5. The principal has exposure to credit risk for the amount receivable from a customer. (IFRS 15:para. B34–38)

Example: IFRS illustrative example 45

An entity operates a website enabling customers to purchase goods from a range of suppliers. The suppliers deliver directly to the customers, who have paid in advance, and the entity receives a commission of 10% of the sales price.

The entity's website also processes payments from the customer to the supplier at prices set by the supplier. The entity has no further obligations to the customer after arranging for the products to be supplied.

Required: Whether the entity is a principal or agent?

Answer:

1. It is the suppliers who are responsible for fulfilling the contract, i.e. supply directly to the customer.

2. Suppliers are responsible for the inventories risks since it is the suppliers who directly supply goods to customers.

3. Prices are set by suppliers rather than by our entity.

4. The entity only receives 10% of the sales price as a commission rather than buying those goods at low price first and resells them at a higher price.

5. Customers are required to pay the consideration in advance and the entity is not exposed to any credit risks from the customers' default in this case nor the suppliers'.

Hence the conclusion is that the entity acts as an agent and it should account for 10% of the sales price as commission revenue.

Note: In some cases, judgements need to be exercised. For instance, the entity may need to jointly set the sales price together with the supplier, or the agent may also need to provide some services such as after sales services to the customer dealing with complaints etc. In this case, although some criteria are not met for the entity to be an agent, we need to focus on the substance of the transaction, i.e. business model [whether the entity buys products at low price and sells them at a higher price later to earn the gain (principal) rather than just the commission income (agent)]; who is responsible for providing the main service (produce and deliver goods) as opposed to the after sales service to the customers (main service: principal).

5.6.3 Type three: Repurchase agreements

No.	Easy Rules
1	Repurchase agreements exist when the seller sells the asset and promises or has the option to repurchase it back from the buyer. (IFRS 15: B64)
2	There are three forms of repurchase agreements: The seller has an obligation to repurchase the asset—a forward contract; The seller has the right to repurchase the asset—a call option; The seller must repurchase the asset at the customer's request—a put option. (IFRS 15: B65)

Here is the diagram showing the accounting treatments for the above three forms of repurchase agreements:

> Repurchase price < Original selling price but the customer does not have a significant economic incentive to exercise that right

- Outright sale per IFRS15 (in other words, customers are not very likely to resell this back to the original seller)

> Repurchase price < Original selling price and the customer has a significant economic incentive to exercise that right

- Leasing per IFRS16 (in simple words, customers are very likely to resell this back to the original seller)

> Repurchase price > Original selling price

- Financing agreement (IFRS g Financial Instrument)

Example:
Situation 1: (Repurchase price is lower than original selling price but the customer does not have an incentive to exercise the option—outright sale)

Company A sold the goods to the company B at $ 1 million and the company B has an option to sell these goods back to the company A at $ 0.7 million. At the contract inception date, it was concluded that the company B has no significant economic incentive to resell these goods back to the company A.
Required: Accounting treatment.
Answer: In this case, it can be concluded that the outright sale accounting treatment should be

applied.

Dr	Bank	$ 1m
Cr	Revenue	$ 1m

Company A would also need to derecognise the inventory assets when they are sold:

Dr	Costs of sales	x
Cr	Inventories	x

Situation 2:(**Repurchase price is lower than original selling price-Leasing**)

Company A sold the product to customer B at $ 1 million and company A must repurchase this back in one year's time at $ 0.8 million. At the contract inception date, it was concluded that the company has a significant economic incentive to repurchase the product back.

Required: Accounting treatment.

Answer: Since the repurchase price is lower than its original selling price, and the company A must repurchase it back in one year's time, hence we should apply the lease accounting treatment to this transaction.

In this case, company A (lessor) should continue recognise the asset in its account, and when the asset is bought back at $ 0.8 million, the rental income of $ 0.2 million should be recognised.

Sold:

Dr	Bank	$ 1m
Cr	Contract liability	$ 1m

Repurchase:

Dr	Contract liability	$ 0.8m
Cr	Bank	$ 0.8m

Recognise the remaining $ 0.2m as the operating lease income:

Dr	Contract liability	$ 0.2m
Cr	Income	$ 0.2m

Situation 3:(Repurchase price is higher than original selling price – Financing agreement)

Company A sold the product to customer B at $1 million and company A must repurchase this back in one year's time at $1.2 million.

Required:Accounting treatment.

Answer:Since the repurchase price is higher than the original selling price, hence the additional $0.2 million should be recognised as a financing component, i. e. financing liability.

When $1 million cash is collected from the company A:

Dr	Bank	$1m
Cr	Financial liability-loan	$1m

Interest expense needs to be provided for this $1m loan:

Dr	Finance cost / Interest expense	$0.2m
Cr	Financial liability-loan	$0.2m

When $1.2 million is repaid:

Dr	Financial liability-loan	$1.2m
Cr	Bank	$1.2m

5.6.4   Type 4:Consignment arrangements

1	When an entity delivers a product to another party (such as a dealer or a distributor) for sale to end customers, the entity shall evaluate whether that other party has obtained control of the product at that point in time. A product that has been delivered to another party may be held in a consignment arrangement if that other party has not obtained control of the product.

| 2 | Indicators that an arrangement is a consignment arrangement include, but are not limited to, the following:
the product is controlled by the entity until a specified event occurs, such as the sale of the product to a customer of the dealer or until a specified period expires;
the entity is able to require the return of the product or transfer the product to a third party (such as another dealer); and
the dealer does not have an unconditional obligation to pay for the product (although it might be required to pay a deposit).
(IFRS 15:B77-78) |

Accounting treatments:

Risks and rewards transferred to the customer = Record the sale	Risks and rewards NOT transferred to the customer = No sale
Manufacturer/Consignor Derecognise transferred inventory and record sales revenue: **Dr** Account receivables **Cr** Sales revenue **Dr** Costs of sales **Cr** Inventories **Dealer/Consignee** Records purchases & liabilities (reduce deposits); and includes goods in inventory (record asses & liabilities): **Dr** Purchases **Cr** Payables **Dr** Payables (deposits paid) **Cr** Cash **Dr** Inventories **Cr** Costs of sales	**Manufacturer/Consignor** Keep transferred goods in inventories. **Dealer/Consignee** Makes no accounting entries in the books, i.e. no inventories recognition until the transfer of control takes place; Any deposit should be included under "other receivables": **Dr** Other receivables **Cr** Cash

Example:
    A car dealer obtains inventory from the manufacturer on a consignment basis.

    The purchase price is set at delivery.

    Usually, the dealer pays the manufacturer for the car the day after the dealer sells to a customer.

    However, if the car remains unsold after three months, then the dealer is obliged to purchase the car, i. e. there is no right of return.

    The dealer is responsible for maintenance and insurance from delivery.

Required: Accounting treatment for the manufacturer at the time of delivery.

Answer: At the time of delivery, the transfer of control of those cars have been passed to the dealer indicated by the following factors:

    • The dealer faces the inventory obsolescence risks because the dealer has no right to return those cars;

    • Prices are set at delivery and the dealer is obliged to pay that amount even if the car is subsequently reduced in price or damaged;

    • The dealer insures and maintains those cars, i. e. bearing the risks of damage of cars break down;

    • Cars can be sold to the public without any limits and hence the dealer controls those cars.

    Therefore, the manufacturer should record the revenue and de-recognise those cars from inventories from the date of delivery.

5.6.5　Type 5: Bill-and-hold arrangements

No.	Easy Rules
1	This arrangement means that goods are sold (seller billed the customer) but not dispatched to customers yet. From the seller's perspective, to recognise revenue, four criteria must be met: 1. The reason for the bill-and-hold must be substantive. Examples may include: • Customers request it because there is limited space to store the product; • Customers want to lock in the price today when paid; • Customers have sufficient cash now to pay; • There is a delay in customer's production schedule, hence the customer pays now but needs goods later. 2. The product must be separately identified as belonging to the customer. For instance, every car has its own serial number to separate one from the other. 3. The product must be ready for physical transfer to the customer. This means that if customer wants the seller to dispatch the asset, the asset can be immediately dispatched. 4. The entity cannot have the ability to use the product or to transfer it to another customer. This means that the seller specifically stores the asset for the customer and the asset only belongs to this customer.

No.	Easy Rules
2	If all four criteria are met, the seller should recognise revenue at a point in time when the customer pays the asset. However, if there are other services to be provided by the seller, services may be accounted for as a separate performance obligation and the revenue for the service should be recognised over time.
3	If any one of the above criteria is not met, the seller should not recognise the sales revenue, but instead, the contract liability.

(IFRS 15: B79–82)

Example:

Table plc sells tables and it accepts full payment from the customer to lock in today's price. Delivery can be on hold for up to two years. If delivery is needed, customer needs to give one week notice to Table plc to make the table. The customer has paid for $100,000 for the table.

Required: How should the seller record this transaction?

Answer: The above transaction does not meet with the criteria in the bill-and-hold arrangements:

1. The reason for the bill-and-hold must be substantive. In this case, the customer wants to lock in today's price and accepts that the seller holds this table up to two years. This criterion is met.

2. The product must be separately identified as belonging to the customer. However, we are not told in this case that table is unique. Hence this criterion is not met.

3. The product must be ready for physical transfer to the customer. In this case, the delivery is not immediate because one week notice needs to be given by the customer and therefore, this criterion is not met.

4. The entity cannot have the ability to use the product or to transfer it to another customer but in this case, it is very likely that the table can be sold to other customers. Hence this criterion is not met.

The accounting entry for the seller should:

Dr	Cash		$100,000
Cr	Contract liability		$100,000

5.7 Presentation

No.	Easy Rules
1	This Standard uses the terms "contract asset" and "contract liability" but does not prohibit an entity from using alternative descriptions in the statement of financial position for those items. If an entity uses an alternative description for a contract asset, the entity shall provide sufficient information for a user of the financial statements to distinguish between receivables and contract assets. (IFRS 15: para. 109)

5.8 Disclosure

No.	Easy Rules
1	The objective of the disclosure requirements is for an entity to disclose sufficient information to enable users of financial statements to understand the nature, amount, timing and uncertainty of revenue and cash flows arising from contracts with customers. To achieve that objective, an entity shall disclose qualitative and quantitative information about all of the following: a) its contracts with customers; b) the significant judgements, and changes in the judgements, made in applying this Standard to those contracts; and c) any assets recognised from the costs to obtain or fulfill a contract with a customer. (IFRS 15: para. 110)

5.9 Contract in Progress

No.	Easy Rules
1	In construction industries, construction company may need to take some time (normally more than one year) to build a property such as a shopping mall. The revenue should therefore be recognised over time either using output or input methods. These uncompleted contracts are called "contract in progress".

No.	Easy Rules
2	The objective is to confirm the value both in the statement of profit or loss and in the statement of financial position.
3	**The statement of profit or loss shows the profit or loss of the contract only in the current year:** <table><tr><td>Revenue (% completion×total revenue)</td><td>x</td></tr><tr><td>−Costs of sales(% completion×total costs including costs to date and estimated costs to complete)</td><td>x</td></tr><tr><td>=Profit/(Loss)</td><td>x/(x)</td></tr></table>
4	Please note, to calculate the figure for the current year, we need to use the cumulative revenue or costs of sales and to subtract the previous year's revenue or costs of sales.
5	**The statement of financial position shows the following items:** (1) Contract asset (unbilled revenue) or Contract liability (overbilled revenue); (2) Net receivables (if the business bills the customer $100,000 and receives cash of $40,000, the net receivables would be $60,000). In summary: Net receivables = Amounts invoiced−Cash received
6	To calculate the contract asset or contract liability, we could use the following proforma: (**CPI**) <table><tr><td>Costs incurred to date</td><td>x</td></tr><tr><td>+Profit/−Loss to date</td><td>x/(x)</td></tr><tr><td>−Invoiced (receivables)</td><td>(x)</td></tr><tr><td>If positive: contract asset</td><td></td></tr><tr><td>If negative: contract liability</td><td>x/(x)</td></tr></table>
7	If the contract is initially forecasted to be a loss making contract, the profit or loss in the statement is: <table><tr><td>Revenue (% completion × total revenue)</td><td>x</td></tr><tr><td>−Costs of sales (**Balancing figure**)</td><td>x</td></tr><tr><td>= (Loss)</td><td>(x)</td></tr></table> (IFRS 15: para. 41−45)

Steps in dealing with construction contract questions:

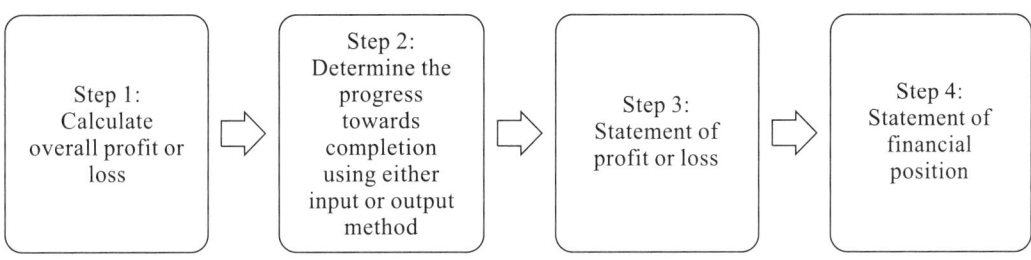

1. If the expected outcome is a profit

• Revenue and costs should be recognised per the progress of the contract.

2. If the expected outcome is a loss

• The whole loss should be recognised immediately.

3. If the expected outcome or progress is unknow (often due to it being in the very early stages of the contract)

• Revenue should be recognised only to the level of recoverable costs incurred and this results in no profits being recorded on a contract with unknown outcomes. (see example 10)

Example 1: Overall profit or loss

The information about the contract in progress is as follows:

	$ m
Total contract price	1,000
Costs incurred to date	300
Estimated costs to complete	200

Required: Calculate the profit or loss of this contract.

Answer: $ 500 million ($ 1,000m− $ 300m− $ 200m).

Example 2: Overall profit or loss

The information about the contract in progress is as follows:

	$ m
Total contract price	1,000

Costs incurred to date include: • Materials, labour and overheads • Specialist plant acquired	150 200
Estimated costs to complete	200

Required: Calculate the profit or loss of this contract.

Answer: $450m ($1,000m − $150m − $200m − $200m).

Example 3: **Percentage of completion**

	$ m
Total contract price	1,000
Costs incurred to date	300
Estimated costs to complete	200
The value of performance obligations satisfied to date (The work certified to date)	550

Required: Calculate the percentage of completion using:

1. Output method;
2. Input method.

Answer:

1. Output method $= \dfrac{\text{Work certified to date}}{\text{Total contract price}} = \dfrac{\$550m}{\$1,000m} = 55\%$

2. Input method $= \dfrac{\text{Costs incurred to date}}{\text{Total Costs}} = \dfrac{\$300m}{\$300m + \$200m} = 60\%$

Example 4: **Determine the revenue and costs recognised in the P/L**

The information about the contract in progress is as follows:

	$ m
Total contract price	1,000
Costs incurred to date	300
Estimated costs to complete	200

The company uses the input method to estimate the percentage of completion.

Required: Determine the profit or loss in the current period in the statement of profit or loss.

Answer: Percentage of completion = $300m/($300m+$200m) = 60\%$

	$ m
Revenue $1,000m × 60%	600
−Costs of sales $500m × 60%	(300)
Profits	300

Example 5: Loss making contract

The information about the contract in progress is as follows:

	$ m
Total contract price	450
Costs incurred to date	300
Estimated costs to complete	200

The company uses the input method to estimate the percentage of completion.

Required: Determine the profit or loss in the current period in the statement of profit or loss.

Answer:

Step 1: The overall profit or loss of the contract: loss = $(50)m ($450m−$300m−$200m)

Step 2: Percentage of completion: 60% (same as in example 4)

Step 3: P/L:

	$ m
Revenue $450m×60%	270
−Costs of sales (balancing figure)	(320)
Full loss	(50)

Example 6: Contract asset

The information about the contract in progress is as follows:

	$ m
Total contract price	1,000

Costs incurred to date	300
Estimated costs to complete	200
Progress billing	400

The company uses the input method to estimate the percentage of completion.

Required: Show the contract asset balance in the statement of financial position.

Answer:

Step 1: Determine the overall profit or loss of the contract: profit: $ 500m

Step 2: % of completion: 60%.

Step 3: Statement of profit or loss:

	$ m
Revenue $ 1,000m×60%	600
−Costs of sales $ 500m×60%	(300)
Profit	300

Step 4: Statement of financial position:

	$ m
Costs incurred to date	300
+Profit to date	300
−Invoiced (receivables)	(400)
Contract asset	200

Example 7: Contract liability

The information about the contract in progress is as follows:

	$ m
Total contract price	1,000
Costs incurred to date	300
Estimated costs to complete	200

Amount invoiced for work certified to date	800
Cash received from the customer	600

The company uses the input method to estimate the percentage of completion.

Required: Show the contract liability and net receivable balance in the statement of financial position.

Answer:

Step 1: Determine the overall profit or loss of the contract: profit: $ 500m

Step 2: % of completion: 60%.

Step 3: Statement of profit or loss:

	$ m
Revenue $ 1,000m×60%	600
−Costs of sales $ 500m×60%	(300)
Profit	300

Step 4: Statement of financial position:

	$ m
Costs incurred to date	300
+Profit to date	300
−Invoiced (receivables)	(800)
Contract liability	200

Net receivable = Amount invoiced−Cash received = $ 800m− $ 600m = $ 200m

Example 8: Contract loss and contract liability

The information about the contract in progress is as follows:

	$ m
Total contract price	450
Costs incurred to date	300
Estimated costs to complete	200
Amount invoiced for work certified to date	800

The company uses the input method to estimate the percentage of completion.

Required:Show the contract liability balance in the statement of financial position.

Answer:

Step 1:The overall profit or loss of the contract:loss = $(50)m ($450m-$300m-$200m)

Step 2:Percentage of completion:60% (same as in example 4)

Step 3:Statement of profit or loss:

	$ m
Revenue $ 450m×60%	270
-Costs of sales (balancing figure)	(320)
Full loss	(50)

Step 4:Statement of financial position:

	$ m
Costs incurred to date	300
-Loss to date	(50)
-Invoiced (receivables)	(800)
Contract liability	(550)

Example 9:Changes in sales revenue and costs

The information about the contract in progress is as follows:

$ m	Year 1	Year 2
Total contract price	1,000	1,000
Costs to date	300	400
Estimated costs to complete	350	390

Input method is used to estimate the percentage of completion each year.

Required:Determine the revenue and costs to be recognised in year 1 and year 2.

Answer:

Step 1:Overall profit or loss:both contracts are profitable.

Step 2:

Percentage of completion in year 1 = 300/650 = 46%

Percentage of completion in year 2 = 400/790 = 50%

Step 3: Statement of profit or loss:

$ m	Year 1	Year 2
Revenue	1,000×46% = 460	50%×1,000−460 = 40
Costs	(300+350)×46% = (300)	(400+390)×50%−300 = (95)
Profits/(Loss)	160	(55)

Example 10: Work can't be certified and revenue should be recognised to the costs to date

The information about the contract in progress is as follows:

	Contract D
Contract price	1,000
Work certified to date	—
Costs incurred to date	300
Estimated costs to complete	Unknown

Required: Prepare the P/L extract.

Answer:

Step 1: Overall profit or loss: profitable contract.

Step 2: Percentage of completion: 0

Step 3: P/L:

	Contract D $ 000
Revenue	300 (recoverable costs)
Costs of sales	300 (recoverable costs)
Gross profit/loss	—

In some circumstances (for example, in the early stages of a contract), an entity may not be able to reasonably measure the outcome of a performance obligation, but the entity expects to recover the costs incurred in satisfying the performance obligation. In those circumstances, the entity shall recognise revenue only to the extent of the costs incurred until such time that it can reasonably measure the outcome of the performance obligation.

(IFRS 15: para. 45)

Example 11: Integrated example

Four contracts in process information is as follows:

	Contract A $ 000	Contract B $ 000	Contract C $ 000	Contract D $ 000
Contract price	500	890	420	750
Work certified to date	375	534	280	—
Costs incurred to date	384	700	468	20
Estimated costs to complete	48	115	168	650
Amount invoiced for work certified to date	360	520	224	—

Required: Prepare profit or loss and statement of financial position extracts. Assuming the output method is used to estimate the percentage of completion.

Answer:

Step1: Overall profit or loss of each contract:

	Contract A $ 000	Contract B $ 000	Contract C $ 000	Contract D $ 000
Contract price	500	890	420	750
Costs incurred to date	(384)	(700)	(468)	(20)
Estimated costs to complete	(48)	(115)	(168)	Unknown
Total estimated profits/(loss)	68	75	(216)	Unknown

Step 2: Percentage of completion:

- Contract A: 375/500 = 75%
- Contract B: 534/890 = 60%
- Contract C: 280/420 = 66.7%
- Contract D: 0/750 = 0%

Step 3: Statement of profit or loss:

	Contract A $ 000	Contract B $ 000	Contract C $ 000	Contract D $ 000
Revenue (% × contract price or recoverable costs)	375	534	280	20 (recoverable costs)
Costs of sales (% × total cost or balancing figure if loss making)	(324)	(489)	bal: (496)	20 (recoverable costs)
Gross profit/loss	51	45	(216)	—
Total estimated profits/(loss)	68	75	(216)	80

Step 4: Statement of financial position extract:

	Contract A $ 000	Contract B $ 000	Contract C $ 000	Contract D $ 000
Costs incurred to date	384	700	468	20
Profits/losses recognised to date	51	45	(216)	—
Amount invoiced for work certified to date	(360)	(520)	(224)	—
Contract assets	75	225	28	20

Contract C:

The loss of $ 216,000 must be recognised immediately.

Contract D:

Although work has been performed on this contract but no work has yet been certified. We therefore could not recognise a profit in the P/L. For those costs incurred becoming the costs of sale, the revenue should be forced to become the same costs of sales to bring the profit to nil.

Chapter 6

Non-Current Assets Held for Sale and Discontinued Operations

Topic outline:

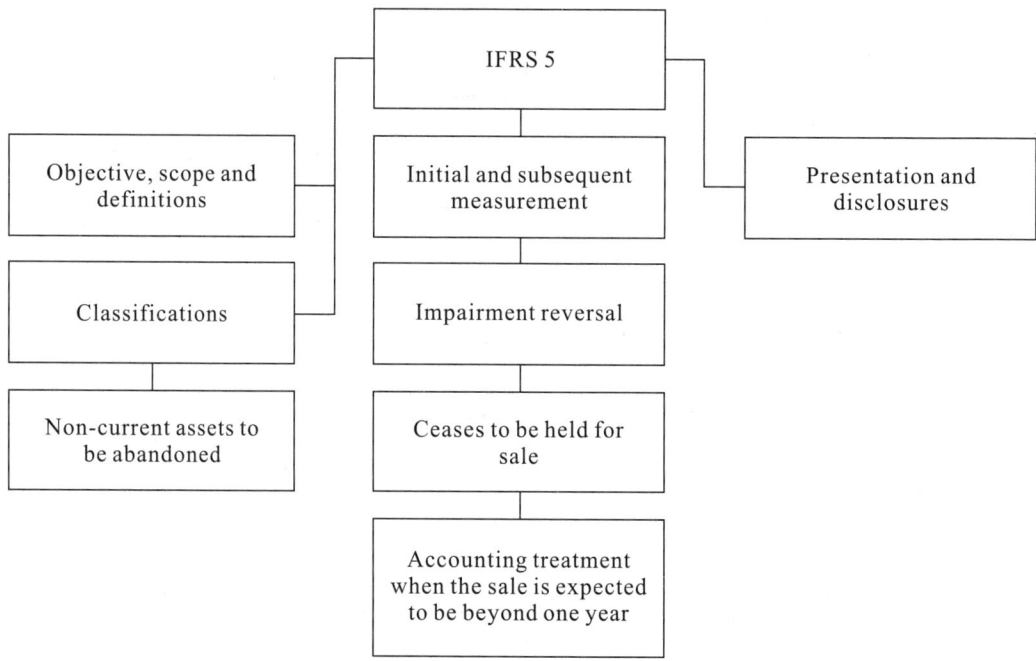

6.1 Objective

No.	Easy Rules
1	The objective of this IFRS is to specify the accounting for assets held for sale, and the presentation and disclosure of discontinued operations. In particular, the IFRS requires: a) assets that meet the criteria to be classified as held for sale to be measured at the lower of carrying amount and fair value less costs to sell, and depreciation on such assets to cease; and b) assets that meet the criteria to be classified as held for sale to be presented separately in the statement of financial position and the results of discontinued operations to be presented separately in the statement of comprehensive income. (IFRS 5:para.1)

6.2 Scope

No.	Easy Rules
1	The classification and presentation requirements of this IFRS apply to all recognised non-current assets and to all disposal groups of an entity. The measurement requirements of this IFRS apply to all recognised non-current assets and disposal groups. The measurement provisions of this IFRS do not apply to the following assets, which are covered by the IFRSs listed, either as individual assets or as part of a disposal group: a) deferred tax assets (IAS 12 Income Taxes). b) assets arising from employee benefits (IAS 19 Employee Benefits). c) financial assets within the scope of IFRS 9 Financial Instruments. d) non-current assets that are accounted for in accordance with the fair value model in IAS 40 Investment Property. e) non-current assets that are measured at fair value less costs to sell in accordance with IAS 41 Agriculture. f) contractual rights under insurance contracts as defined in IFRS 4 Insurance Contracts. (IFRS 5:para.2-5)

6.3 *Definitions*

No.	Easy Rules
1	**Disposal group:** A group of assets to be disposed of, by sale or otherwise (abandoned or closed), together as a group in a single transaction, and liabilities directly associated with those assets that will be transferred in the transaction Disposal group can be: • A subsidiary • A cash generating unit • A single operation in the entity (production line or geographical area)
2	**Discontinued operation:** A component of an entity that either has been disposed of or is classified as held for sale and: a) represents a separate major line of business or geographical area of operations, b) is part of a single co-ordinated plan to dispose of a separate major line of business or geographical area of operations or c) is a subsidiary acquired exclusively with a view to resale. (IFRS 5: Appendix A)

6.4 *Classification of Non-current Assets (or Disposal Groups) as Held for Sale*

No.	Easy Rules
1	An entity shall classify a non-current asset (or disposal group) as held for sale if its carrying amount will be recovered principally through a sale transaction rather than through continuing use. If not, the non-current asset still remains as in the non-current asset section and if it qualifies the definition of discontinued operations, additional disclosure should be made. (IFRS 5: para. 6)

No.	Easy Rules
2	The following criteria should be met so that a non-current asset or a disposal group can be classified as held for sale: **A. The sale is highly probable (significantly more likely than not):** **1. Locate a buyer:** • the appropriate level of management must be committed to a plan to sell the asset (or disposal group), and an active programme to locate a buyer and complete the plan must have been initiated. • the asset (or disposal group) must be actively marketed for sale at a price that is reasonable in relation to its current fair value. **2. Expected to complete the sale within one year from the date of classification:** • Actions required to complete the plan should indicate that it is unlikely that significant changes to the plan will be made or that the plan will be withdrawn. • Examples of this criterion arenot met: -an entity that is a commercial leasing and finance company is holding for sale or lease equipment that has recently ceased to be leased, and the ultimate form of a future transaction (sale or lease) has not yet been determined. -an entity is committed to a plan to "sell" a property that is in use as part of a sale and leaseback transaction, but the transfer does not qualify to be accounted for as a sale • **Exceptions** where the asset is sold "beyond one year" but qualifies "within one year" criterion: Events or circumstances may extend the period to complete the sale beyond one year. An extension of the period required to complete a sale does not preclude an asset (or disposal group) from being classified as held for sale if the delay is caused by events or circumstances beyond the entity's control, and there is sufficient evidence that the entity remains committed to its plan to sell the asset (or disposal group). Examples include: a) An entity is committed to a plan to sell a manufacturing facility in itspresent condition and classifies the facility as held for sale at that date. After a firm purchase commitment is obtained, the buyer's inspection of the property identifies environmental damage not previously known to exist. The entity is required by the buyer to make good the damage, which will extend the period required to complete the sale beyond one year. However, the entity has initiated actions to make good the damage, and satisfactory rectification of the damage is highly probable.

	b) A building is classified as held for sale by the business, and the business has active program to locate the buyer, and it is probable that the building can be sold. However, given the business has not sold the building within one year, the business reduces its sale price. Therefore, the building can still be held for sale. If the business then increases the price, but the building can not be sold within one year, the building should not be classified as held for sale any more. **3. The probability of shareholders' approval (if required in the jurisdiction) should be considered as part of the assessment of whether the sale is highly probable.**
3	**A. Available for immediate sale:** A non-current asset (or disposal group) is available for immediate sale if an entity currently has the **intention** and **ability** to transfer the asset (or disposal group) to a buyer in its present condition. Here are some examples: • If the building is to be transferred to the buyer, no additional time is needed to vacate the building, the building can, therefore, be reclassified as held for sale. However, if additional time is needed to vacate, renovate the building (particularly if the building is acquired through foreclosure) or meeting with environmental or fire safety regulations, the building would not be classified as held for sale until the building is vacated/renovated/meeting with conditions. • If a factory is to be transferred to the buyer, the uncompleted orders are to be transferred to customers as well, this would therefore not affect the timing of the transfer. However, if the seller intends to complete those uncompleted orders first, before transferring the factory to the buyer, then the factory should not be classified as a non-current asset held for sale until those uncompleted orders are completed. (IFRS 5: para. 7–12)

Example: Classification of non-current assets held for sale

On 31 October year one, the business decides to sell a piece of land as the price has increased recently.

On 31 December year one, the board agreed with the decision to sell the piece of land. The management approached various real estate agents and agreed the sales commission when the land would be sold. Theprice to sell the land is near its fair value. The management estimates it may take 5 months after the date of reclassification to sell the land.

However, according to the environmental law, the management needs to restore the land to its original condition, and the management estimates that it will be fully completed on 15 February year two.

The business has received a firm purchase commitment from the buyer as at 31 December year one, and the buyer can do the restoration work on behalf of the business per the contract.

Required: When should the above piece of land be classified as a non-current asset held for sale?

Answer: The piece of land can be reclassified as a non-current asset held for sale as at 31 December year one:

1. The sale is highly probable; this can be confirmed by:
   - the board resolution to sell the piece of land on 31 December year one;
   - active sale program was set up, i.e. agreeing on the sales commission with the agent;
   - a firm purchase commitment has been obtained from the buyer;
   - sale price is up to the fair value.

2. The management expects to complete the sale within one year after the date of reclassification.

3. Although the land needs to be restored according to the relevant law, the buyer can do this work on behalf of the business, and this means that the piece of land can be immediately sold by the business on 31 December year one.

6.5 *Non-Current Assets to Be Abandoned*

No.	Easy Rules
1	An entity shall not classify as held for sale a non-current asset (or disposal group) that is to be abandoned. This is because its carrying amount will be recovered principally through continuing use. However, if the disposal group to be abandoned meets the criteria in discontinued operations, the entity shall present the results and cash flows of the disposal group as discontinued operations at the date on which it ceases to be used. Non-current assets (or disposal groups) to be abandoned include non-current assets (or disposal groups) that are to be used to the end of their economic life and non-current assets (or disposal groups) that are to be closed rather than sold.
2	An entity shall not account for a non-current asset that has been temporarily taken out of use as if it had been abandoned. (IFRS 5; para. 13–14)

Example: Classification of non-current assets held for sale

An entity ceases to use a manufacturing plant because the demand for its product has declined. However, the plant is maintained in workable condition, and it is expected that it will be brought back into use if demand picks up.

Required: Whether the plant is regarded as abandoned?

Answer: The plant is not regarded as abandoned and it should be accounted for per IAS 16 PP&E.

6.6 Initial Measurement of Non-Current Assets Held for Sale

No.	Easy Rules
1	An entity shall measure a non-current asset (or disposal group) classified as held for sale at the lower of its carrying amount and fair value less costs to sell. (IFRS 5: para. 15)

Example:

On 31 December year one, a plant is qualified as "non-current asset held for sale" and its carrying value at the date of classification is $50 million. The fair value of the plant at the date of classification is $60 million and the fair value less costs to sell is estimated to be $3 million.

Required: Accounting treatment.

Answer:

Dr	Non-current assets held for sale (lower of carrying amount and fair value less costs to sell)	$50m
Cr	PP&E (at carrying value) *	$50m

* Alternatively, the derecognition of PP&E at carrying value should be:

Dr	Accumulated depreciation	x
Cr	PP&E at cost	x

No.	Easy Rules
2	An entity shall recognise an impairment loss for any initial or subsequent write-down of the asset (or disposal group) to fair value less costs to sell. (IFRS 5: para. 20)

Example:

On 31 December year one, a plant is qualified as "non-current assets held for sale" and its carrying value at the date of classification is $50 million. The fair value of the plant at the date of classification is $30 million and the fair value less costs to sell is estimated to be $3 million.

Required: Accounting treatment.

Answer:

Dr	Non-current assets held for sale ($30m-$3m)	$27m
Cr	PP&E at carrying value	$50m
Dr	Impairment loss	$23m

6.7 Subsequent Measurement

No.	Easy Rules
1	An entity shall not depreciate (or amortise) a non-current asset while it is classified as held for sale or while it is part of a disposal group classified as held for sale. (IFRS 5: para. 25)

Example:

An entity has reclassified a factory as a non-current asset held for sale as at 31 December year one for $60 million. The entity estimates that the value of the non-current assets held for sale has further decreased to $45 million due to the emergence of impairment indicators.

Required: Accounting treatment.

Answer:

Dr	Impairment loss	$15m
Cr	Non-current assets held for sale	$15m

Please note, the non-current assets held for sale should not be further depreciated.

6.8 Impairment Reversal

No.	Easy Rules
1	An entity shall recognise a gain for any subsequent increase in fair value less costs to sell of an asset, but not in excess of the cumulative impairment loss that has been recognisedeither in accordance with this IFRS 5 (impairment losses incurred after the asset has been classified as non-current assets held for sale) or previously in accordance with IAS 36 Impairment of Assets (i.e. if there are no impairment losses after the asset has been classified as non-current assets held for sale but there were losses before the asset was classified as non-current assets held for sale). (IFRS 5: para. 21)

Example:

As at the reporting date, $5 million worth intangible assets are classified as non-current assets held for sale per IFRS 5. Subsequently, $1.5 million impairment loss incurred regarding the non-current assets held for sale. Two months later, the fair value less costs to sell of the intangible asset increases up to $10 million.

Required: Accounting treatment for the impairment reversal.

Answer:

Impairment loss incurred:

Dr	Impairment loss	$ 1.5m
Cr	Non-current assets held for sale	$ 1.5m

Reversal of impairment loss:

Dr	Non-current assets held for sale	$ 1.5m
Cr	Impairment loss	$ 1.5m

Although the fair value less costs to sell increases to $10m, but it should not in excess of the cumulative impairment loss that has been recognised.

6.9 Ceases to Be Held for Sale

No.	Easy Rules
1	The entity shall measure a non-current asset (or disposal group) that ceases to be classified as held for sale or as held for distribution to owners (or ceases to be included in a disposal group classified as held for sale or as held for distribution to owners) at the lower of: a) its carrying amount before the asset (or disposal group) was classified as held for sale, adjusted for any depreciation, amortisation or revaluations that would have been recognised had the asset (or disposal group) not been classified as held for sale or as held for distribution to owners, and b) its recoverable amount at the date of the subsequent decision not to sell or distribute. (IFRS 5: para. 27)

Example:

A plant was reclassified as a non-current asset held for sale as at 31 December year one. The original cost of the plant was $10 million and the accumulated depreciation up to the date of reclassification was $3 million. Should the asset not be classified as non-current assets held for sale, the depreciation charge would be $100,000 per month. At the time the asset was classified as held for sale, its fair value less costs to sell was higher than its carrying amount. Six months later, the criteria for non-current assets held for sale ceases to exist. The recoverable amount at the date of the decision not to sell is $6 million.

Required: Accounting treatment.

Answer:

1. At the time of reclassification:

Dr	Non-current assets held for sale (lower of fair value less costs to sell and its carrying value)	$7m
Cr	PP&E	$7m

2. At the time that the asset was ceased to be classified as held for sale:

Should the reclassification not take place: initial carrying value $7m-additional 6 months depreciation ($0.1m×6months) = $6.4m

The recoverable amount at the date of the decision not to sell: $6m

Therefore, $6m is chosen in this case since this is lower than the carrying value should the reclassification not take place:

Dr	PP&E	$6m
	Non-current assets held for sale	$7m
Cr	Impairment loss	$1m

6.10 Accounting Treatment When the Sale Is Expected to Be Beyond One Year

No.	Easy Rules
1	When the sale is expected to occur beyond one year, the entity shall measure the costs to sell at their present value. Any increase in the present value of the costs to sell that arises from the passage of time shall be presented in profit or loss as a financing cost. (IFRS 5: para. 17)

Example: **Classification of non-current assets held for sale**

On 31 December year one, a piece of land is qualified as "non-current assets held for sale" and its carrying value at the date of classification is $50 million. The fair value of the land at the date of classification is $30 million and the fair value less costs to sell is estimated to be $3 million. The sale is not completed within one year, and the management expects the sale will complete beyond one year. However, the delay is caused by events beyond the entity's control, and there is sufficient evidence for this. The fair value of the land at this time is still $30 million, but the present value of estimated costs has been increased to $4 million due to passage of time.

Required: Accounting treatment.

Answer: When it is beyond one year:

Initial fair value less costs to sell: $30 million – $3 million = $27 million
Updated fair value less costs to sell: $30 million – $4 million = $26 million.

Dr	Finance costs	$ 1m
Cr	Non-current assets held for sale	$ 1m

6.11 *Presentation of a Non-Current Asset or Disposal Group Classified as Held for Sale*

No.	Easy Rules
1	An entity shall present a non-current asset classified as held for sale and the assets of a disposal group classified as held for sale separately from other assets in the statement of financial position.
2	The liabilities of a disposal group classified as held for sale shall be presented separately from other liabilities in the statement of financial position.
3	Those assets and liabilities shall not be offset and presented as a single amount.
4	The major classes of assets and liabilities classified as held for sale shall be separately disclosed either in the statement of financial position or in the notes.

(IFRS 5: para. 38)

Presentation example:

Assets	
Non-current assets	X
Current assets	Y
Non-current assets classified as held for sale	Z

Assets	
Total assets	X+Y+Z
Equity and liabilities	
Equity	A
Liabilities	
Non-current liabilities	B
Current liabilities	C
Liabilities directly associated with non-current assets classified as held for sale	D
Total equity and liabilities	A+B+C+D

6.12 *Additional Disclosures*

No.	Easy Rules
1	An entity shall disclose the following information in the notes in the period in which a non-current asset (or disposal group) has been either classified as held for sale or sold: a) a description of the non-current asset (or disposal group); b) a description of the facts and circumstances of the sale, or leading to the expected disposal, and the expected manner and timing of that disposal; c) the gain or loss recognised and, if not separately presented in the statement of comprehensive income, the caption in the statement of comprehensive income that includes that gain or loss; (IFRS 5: para. 41)

6.13 Presenting Discontinued Operations

Presentation:

XYZ GROUP - STATEMENT OF COMPREHENSIVE INCOME FOR THE YEAR ENDED 31 DECEMBER 20X2 (illustrating the classification of expenses by function)

(in thousands of currency units)	20×2	20×1
Continuing operations		
Revenue	×	×
Cost of sales	(×)	(×)
Gross profit	×	×
Other income	×	×
Distribution costs	(×)	(×)
Administrative expenses	(×)	(×)
Other expenses	(×)	(×)
Finance costs	(×)	(×)
Share of profit of associates	×	×
Profit before tax	×	×
Income tax expense	(×)	(×)
Profit for the period from continuing operations	×	×
Discontinued operations		
Profit for the period from discontinued operations[a]	×	×
Profit for the period	×	×
Attributable to:		
Owners of the parent		
Profit for the period from continuing operations	×	×
Profit for the period from discontinued operations	×	×
Profit for the period attributable to owners of the parent	×	×
Non-controlling interests		
Profit for the period from continuing operations	×	×
Profit for the period from discontinued operations	×	×
Profit for the period attributable to non-controlling interests	×	×
	×	×

(a) The required analysis would be given in the notes.

(IFRS 5: Implementation Guidance example 11)

No.	Easy Rules
1	**Disclosures in Statement of profit or loss:** There should be a single figure on the face of the statement for the total of: • Profit after tax • Gain or loss on disposal of assets • Gain or loss arising from the adjustment in value from carrying value to fair value
2	**Statement of profit or loss or note-the single figure should be analysed into:** • Revenues, expenses, profit/loss before tax and income tax expense of the discontinued operation • The related tax expense • Gain or loss arising from the adjustment in value from carrying value to fair value • Gain or loss on disposal of assets
3	**Statement of cash flows-there should be a disclosure of net cash flows for the discontinued operations for:** • Net cash flows from operating, investing and financing activities • A description of the discontinued operation • A description of the facts and circumstances of the sale • Expected manner and timing of the disposal (held for sale only)

Example: Classification of a discontinued operation

The business produces ice creams, and a net profit analysis by the product group is prepared.

The Exotic Fruit range has done particularly badly over the last quarter because the business was unable to source an ingredient due to flooding in the country where our sole supplier of the ingredient is based. Directors have pointed out that if we stopped producing the Exotic Fruit range, we would be able to sell the fruit feeder machine that we use specifically for this range. Subsequently, the Exotic Fruit range was classified as held for sale. However, the Exotic Fruit range only accounts for 0.01% of the group's revenue.

Required: Whether the closure of the exotic fruit range qualifies a discontinued operation.

Answer: A discontinued operation is a component of an entity that either has been disposed of or is classified as held for sale, and:

a) It represents either a separate major line of business or a geographical area of operations; or

b) It is part of a single co-ordinated plan to dispose of a separate major line of business or geographical area of operations; or

c) It is a subsidiary acquired exclusively with a view to resale, and the disposal involves loss of control.

Given those criteria we could not classify the discontinuation of the Exotic Fruit range as a "discontinued operation" because the range is a small percentage of our total business (0.01%) and would not, therefore, be deemed as a "major" line of business. We also do not have a plan to dispose of any other product rangesat this time, therefore, the closures are not part of a plan to dispose of a separate major line of business or geographical area of operations.

The above disposal group should be measured per IFRS 5 as Non-current assets held for sale following the lower of its carrying value and the fair value less costs to sell on the reclassification date.

Example: Presentation and disclosure

There are three divisions that the business operates: A, B and C.

The following trial balance is available for these three divisions:

	Dr	Cr
Sales revenue for division A&C		2,400
Sales revenue for division B		650
Operating expenses for division A&C	1,650	
Operating expenses for division B	525	
Finance costs for all continuing activities	70	
Income tax	180	

The income tax charge for the year includes $150,000 on continuing activities and $30,000 for discontinued activities.

During the year, the disposal loss of the asset for division B was $40,000. $80,000 was spent on restructuring divisions A&C when division B was terminated.

Required: Prepare the statement of profit or loss for the discontinued operations per IFRS 5.

Answer:

Continuing operations:	$ 000
Sales revenue	2,400
Operating expenses	(1,650)
Operating profits	750
Restructuring costs (note 1)	(80)
Finance costs	(70)

Profit before tax	600
Income tax expense	(150)
Profit for the year from continuing operations	450
Discontinued operations:	
Profit for the year from discontinued operations (note 2)	55
Profit for the year	505

Note 1: Restructuring cost:

This is a material item because of its unusual nature and should be presented as a separate item on the statement of profit or loss rather than included in operating expenses.

Note 2: Profit for the year from discontinued operations:

	$ 000
Sales revenue	650
Operating expenses	(525)
Operating profits	125
Loss on asset disposal	(40)
Tax expense	(30)
Profit for the period	55

Disclosure note:

- During the year, the business closed down division B, and the results are separately disclosed. A loss on the asset disposal was $ 40,000 because of the operation is discontinued.
- Additionally, restructuring costs incurred were $ 80,000 to rationalise the remaining division A and C.

Chapter 7

IFRS 16 Leases

Topic outline:

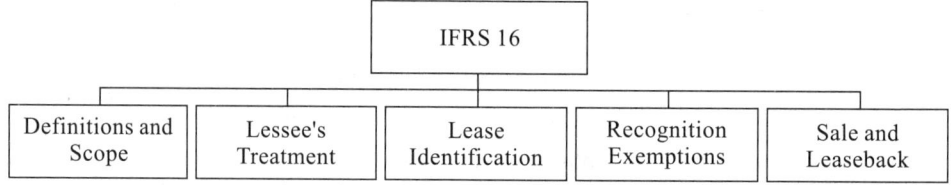

7.1 Definitions and Scope of a Lease

7.1.1 Definitions

No.	Easy Rules
1	**Lease:** A contract, or part of a contract, that conveys the right to use an asset (the underlying asset) for a period of time in exchange for consideration.
2	**Underlying asset:** An asset that is the subject of a lease, for which the right to use that asset has been provided by a lessor to a lessee.
3	**Right-of-use asset:** An asset that represents a lessee's right to use an underlying asset for the lease term.

No.	Easy Rules
4	**Lease term:** If the contract is a lease or contains a lease, the lease term starts from the date when the underlying asset(s) is (are) available for use by the lessee and: 1. Rent-free periods 2. The non-cancellable period of the lease 3. Periods covered by an option to extend the lease if the lessee is reasonably certain to exercise that option 4. Periods covered by an option to terminate the lease if the lessee is reasonably certain not to exercise that option
5	**Interest implicit in the lease:** This is the rate of interest that causes the present value of - the lease payments (variable lease payments not based on index or rate should not be included in the calculation; payments for non-lease components should also be excluded.) - the unguaranteed residual value (i.e., suppose the lessor expects the asset value at the end of the lease term to be $10,000 and the lessee guarantees $8,000 payable, this means the remaining $2,000 asset value is unguaranteed.) to equal the sum of - the fair value of the underlying asset and - any initial direct costs of the lessor (this includes lease commissions, legal fees, costs of negotiating the contract, costs of arranging collateral, payments made to the existing lessee to obtain the lease. However, payments such as general overheads and costs to obtain offers for potential leases are not considered to be initial direct costs.)
6	**Incremental borrowing rate:** This is the rate of interest that a lessee would have to **pay to borrow** over a **similar term**, and with a **similar security**, the funds necessary to obtain an asset of a **similar value** to the right-of-use asset in **a similar economic environment**. <div align="right">(IFRS 16: Appendix A)</div>

7.1.2 Scope of IFRS 16 Leases

No.	Easy Rules
1	Although this standard covers the majority lease transactions, the following transactions are not covered by this standard: • Leases to explore for or use minerals, oil, natural gas and similar non-regenerative resources; • Leases of biological assets within the scope of IAS 41 Agriculture held by a lessee; • Service concession arrangements within the scope of IFRIC ® 12 Service Concession Arrangements; • Licences of intellectual property granted by a lessor within the scope of IFRS 15; and • Rights held by a lessee under licensing agreements within the scope of IAS 38 Intangible Assets (IAS 38) for such items as motion picture films, video recordings, plays, manuscripts, patents and copyrights. (IFRS 16:para.3-4)

7.2 Lessee's Accounting

7.2.1 Initial measurement

No.	Easy Rules
1	At the commencement date when the lessor makes the underlying asset available for use by the lessee, the lessee recognises: A lease liability A right-of-use asset (IFRS 16:para.22)
2	If that rate can not be readily determined, the lessee's incremental borrowing rate should be used. (IFRS 16:para.41)

No.	Easy Rules
3	The lease payments include the following items: 1. Fixed rental payments. 2. In-substance fixed payment. 3. Variable payments depending on an index (such as CPI) or rate (such as interest rate). 4. Amounts expected to be payable under residual value guarantees [for instance, if The lessee guarantees the value of the leased asset at the end of the lease term to be $ 1 million and we expect the asset would be at least worth $ 0.2 million when the lease term expires, hence the we (lessee) expect to pay $ 0.8 million. In this example, $ 0.8 million is included in the lease liability calculation. Therefore, it is the amount payable to be included in the calculation rather than the full residual value guarantees]. 5. Options to purchase the asset that are reasonably certain to be exercised. 6. Termination penalties, if the lease term reflects the expectation that these will be incurred. 7. Subtract any lease incentives receivable. (IFRS 16: Appendix A)

Example: Lease liability calculation

The lease payment is $ 60,000 in the lease contract and the lease term is five years.

The lessee's incremental borrowing rate is 5%.

Required: Calculate the present value of the lease liability if:

1. The lease payment is made at the start of each year.
2. The lease payment is made at the end of each year.

Reference:

• The 5% incremental borrowing rate with the value of $ 1 having a cumulative present value in four year's time of $ 3.546.

• The 5% incremental borrowing rate with the value of $ 1 having a cumulative present value in five year's time of $ 4.329.

Answer:

1. The lease payment is made at the start of each year:

$ 60,000×(1+3.546) = $ 272,760

2. The lease payment is made at the end of each year.

$ 60,000×4.329 = $ 259,740

The accounting entry for the lease liability is as follows:

Dr	Right-of-use asset	$ 272,760 or $ 259,740
Cr	Lease liability	$ 272,760 or $ 259,740

7.2.2 Two approaches

No.	Easy Rules
1	**Approach 1**: Account for non-lease components separately from lease components: **Step 1**: Separate the total consideration or rental payment into lease and non-lease components. **Step 2**: Discount rental payments related to lease components at the lessee's incremental borrowing rate. **Step 3**: Recognise the right-of-use asset and lease liability. **Step 4**: Charge non-lease components directly to the statement of profit or loss.
2	**Approach 2**: Account for non-lease components together with lease components. This would result in a large amount of liability to be recognised. It is highly unlikely that businesses with large non-lease components would adopt this approach. (IFRS 16: para. 13 and 15)

7.2.3 Lease liability presentation

No.	Easy Rules
1	The lease liability at the end of each year should be split into the non-current and current liabilities as a best practice. However, IFRS 16 also allows the entity not to split those liabilities into the current and non-current portion, but to disclosed them in the notes. [IFRS 16: para. 47 (b)]

Example:

The lessee entered into a contract to lease a piece of specialised equipment for three years. The lessor agrees to maintain the equipment during the three-year period. The lessee must pay $ 90,000 at the end of each year.

If contracted separately, it has been determined that the stand-alone price for the lease of the equipment is $ 190,000 and the stand-alone price for the maintenance services is $ 50,000.

The lessee's incremental borrowing rate is 6% per year.

Required: Accounting treatment.

Answer:

Initial Measurement:

Approach 1: The lessee accounts for non-lease components separately from lease components:

Step 1: The lessee needs to separate the total consideration of $90,000 into lease and non-lease components based on their standard-alone selling price:

Components	Stand-alone selling price	Proportion	Allocated consideration
Specialised equipment	$190,000	79%	$71,250
Maintenance	$50,000	21%	$18,750
Sum	$240,000	100.00%	$90,000

Step 2: Discount the consideration allocated to lease components at the lessee's incremental borrowing rate to calculate the lease liability:

Years	Cash Flows	Discount Rate @ 6%	Present Value
Year 1	$71,250	0.943	$67,217
Year 2	$71,250	0.890	$63,412
Year 3	$71,250	0.840	$59,823
			$190,452

Step 3: Recognise the right-of-use asset and lease liability:

Dr	Right-of-use asset	$190,452
Cr	Lease liability	$190,452

Step 4: Charge the non-lease components directly to the statement of profit or loss:

Dr	Expense	$18,750
Cr	Cash	$18,750

Subsequent Measurement:
Right-of-use asset:
Year 1:

Dr	Depreciation expense	$ 63,484
Cr	Right-of-use asset	$ 63,484

Year 2:

Dr	Depreciation expense	$ 63,484
Cr	Right-of-use asset	$ 63,484

Year 3:

Dr	Depreciation expense	$ 63,484
Cr	Right-of-use asset	$ 63,484

Lease liability:

Years	Opening liability	Interest @ 6%	Outstanding liability	Instalment	Closing liability
Year 1	$ 190,452	$ 11,427	$ 201,879	$ (71,250)	$ 130,629
Year 2	$ 130,629	$ 7,838	$ 138,467	$ (71,250)	$ 67,217
Year 3	$ 67,217	$ 4,033	$ 71,250	$ (71,250)	0

- Interest is calculated by multiplying the opening liability by the interest rate of 6% (**actuarial method**: to apply the rate to the amount of capital outstanding to calculate the finance charge for that period.)
- Therefore, at the start of the lease, the finance charges will be larger because the outstanding lease liability is large in earlier years. Towards the end of the lease's life, the finance charge will be smaller because the outstanding lease liability is smaller.
- Outstanding liability is calculated by adding opening liability and the interest expense together.
- Instalment is also known as rental payment, in the above case, the fixed rental payment at the end of each year is $ 71,250.
- Closing liability is calculated by subtracting the instalment from the outstanding liability.

Interest expense or finance costs:
Year 1:

	Dr	Finance costs	$ 11,427
	Cr	Lease liability	$ 11,427

Year 2:

	Dr	Finance costs	$ 7,838
	Cr	Lease liability	$ 7,838

Year 3:

	Dr	Finance costs	$ 4,033
	Cr	Lease liability	$ 4,033

Instalment/rental payment:
Year 1, 2 and 3:

	Dr	Lease liability	$ 71,250
	Cr	Bank	$ 71,250

Lease liability presentation:
At the end of the 1st year:

Total lease liability	$ 130,629
Current liability	$ 63,412
Non-current liability	$ 67,217

At the end of 2nd year:

Total lease liability	$ 67,217
Current liability	$ 67,217
Non-current liability	0

At the end of the 3rd year:

Total lease liability	0
Current liability	0
Non-current liability	0

In the above case, the current liability is calculated by subtracting the finance costs from instalments. The reason is that the next rental payment due will contain interest, therefore, the interest is deducted from the rental payment to only become the capital repayment amount.

In this example, we assume that the rental payment is made at the end of each year. In some cases, the lessee may be required to make the lease payment at the beginning of each year. And if this is the case, the interest column is placed after the outstanding liability column whereas the instalment column is placed before the outstanding liability column.

Example: Lease payments made in advance:

Let's revised the case to be the lease payment is made in advance:

Years	Opening liability	Instalment	Outstanding liability	Interest @ 6%	Closing liability
Year 1	190,452	−71,250	119,202	11,427	130,629
Year 2	130,629	−71,250	59,379	7,838	67,217
Year 3	67,217	−71,250	−4,033	4,033	—

To determine what are the current and non-current liabilities in year one, the short cut rule applies:

- Non-current liability: next year's figure after instalment
- Current liability: total liability and to subtract the non-current liability amount
- Interest expense is based on opening liability.

Required: Accounting treatment.

Answer:

Non-current liability (next year's figure after instalment)	$ 59,379
Current liability (balancing figure)	$ 71,250
Total liability in year one	$ 130,629

Note:

The current liability of the business in year one is the amount $ 71,250 due in year two because the amount does not include the interest charge in year two and represents the principal amount. Therefore, from year one's perspective, the non-current liability is $ 59,379 (after $ 71,250) in year two.

Approach 2: The lessee accounts for non-lease components together with lease components:

Years	Cash Flows	Discount Rate @ 6%	Present Value
Year 1	$ 90,000	0.943	$ 84,906
Year 2	$ 90,000	0.890	$ 80,100
Year 3	$ 90,000	0.840	$ 75,566
			$ 240,572

Journal entry:

Dr	Right-of-use asset		$ 240,572
Cr	Lease liability		$ 240,572

7.3 *Lessee's Accounting in Detail: Right-of-Use Assets*

7.3.1 Initial measurement of right-of-use asset

No.	Easy Rules
1	The cost of the right-of-use asset shall comprise: a) the amount of the initial measurement of the lease liability b) any lease payments made at or before the commencement date, less any lease incentives received; c) any initial direct costs incurred by the lessee; and d) an estimate of costs to be incurred by the lessee in dismantling and removing the underlying asset, restoring the site on which it is located or restoring the underlying asset to the condition required by the terms and conditions of the lease, unless those costs are incurred to produce inventories in which case they would be accounted for inaccordance with IAS 2 Inventories. The lessee has the obligation for those costs either at the commencement date or as a consequence of having used the underlying asset during a particular period. The obligation of these costs is accounted for per IAS 37 Provisions, Contingent Liabilities and Contingent Assets (to discount the estimated costs to its present value and included in both right-of-use asset and provision liability). (IFRS 16, para. 24)

No.	Easy Rules
2	Examples of estimated removal costs: Lessee installed a significant amount of equipment and customised leasehold improvements in the property. Alternatively, it makes changes to the property internal configuration and these need to be removed at the end of the lease term.

Example:

A company signed a 10-year agreement with the lessor to lease a building with a remaining useful life of 5 years. The lease payments are $50,000 per year payable at the start of each year.

The lessee incurs initial direct costs of $20,000 and receives lease incentives (payments made by the lessor to the lessee, or the reimbursement or assumption by the lessor of costs of the lessee) of $5,000.

The present value of lease liability is $150,000 discounted at the interest rate implicit in the lease. At the end of the contract, the lessee is required by law to restore the building and the discounted costs to date are $60,000.

Required: Calculate the right-of-use asset.

Answer:

Items	Amount	Dr	Cr
Payment in advance	$50,000	Right-of-use asset	Cash
Initial direct costs	$20,000	Right-of-use asset	Cash
Lease incentives	$5,000	Cash	Right-of-use asset
Lease liability	$150,000	Right-of-use asset	Lease liability
Future costs	$60,000	Right-of-use asset	Provision liability

Hence the total right-of-use asset value is $275,000.

7.3.2 Subsequent measurement of right-of-use asset

No.	Easy Rules
1	**A: If it belongs to a class of property, plant and equipment:** 1. **Cost model:** initial cost-accumulated depreciation-impairment losses **Depreciation:** • If the asset ownership is transferred to the lessee at the end of the lease term, or if the cost reflects a purchase option which the lessee is expected to exercise, depreciation should be charged over the asset's remaining useful economic life. • If not, depreciation is charged over the shorter of the useful life and the lease term. (IFRS 16: paras. 31, 32). **Revaluation model:** revaluation surplus is taken to the reserve.

No.	Easy Rules
2	B: Meet the definition of investment property per IAS 40 (i.e. right-of-use assets which are sub-leased under operating leases to earn rental income), fair value model applies. (IFRS 16: para. 34)

Example:

From the previous example, explain the subsequent measurement of the right-of-use asset if:

Case 1: the building will be transferred to the lessee at the end of the contract;

Case 2: the building will not be transferred to the lessee at the end of the contract.

Required: Accounting treatment for the above two cases.

Answer:

Case 1: The right-of-use asset should be depreciated over the building's remaining useful economic life of five years:

	Dr	Depreciation expense ($ 275,000/5 years)	$ 55,000
	Cr	Right-of-use asset	$ 55,000

Case 2: The right-of-use asset should be depreciated over the shorter of the building's remaining useful economic life of 5 years and the lease term of 10 years, in this case, again, 5 years should be chosen:

	Dr	Depreciation expense ($ 275,000/5 years)	$ 55,000
	Cr	Right-of-use asset	$ 55,000

7.4 Lease Identification

7.4.1 Reasons for identifying a lease

No.	Easy Rules
1	Lease accounting treatments can only be applied to lease transactions. A contract is, or contains, a lease if the contract conveys the right to control the use of an identified asset for a period of time in exchange for considerations. This means the lessee: • could obtain substantially all of the economic benefits from the use of the identified asset • have the right to direct the use of the identified asset (IFRS 16 para. 9)

7.4.2 Lease identification diagram

To identify whether the contract is or contains a lease, IFRS 16 Appendix B (para. B31) provides the following useful diagram:

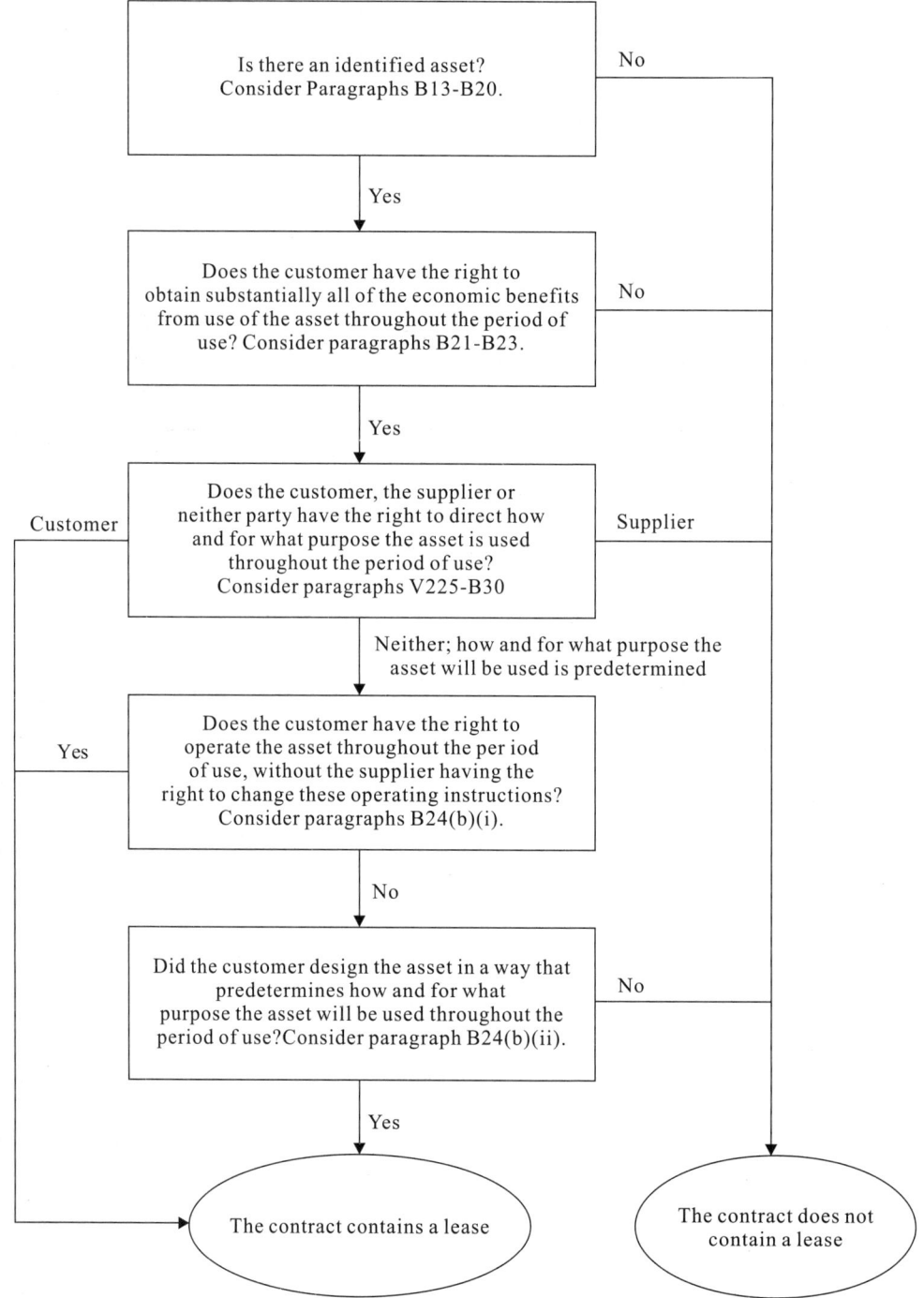

To summarise the above diagram, if:

1. This is not an identified asset, the contract does not contain a lease.
2. The customer does not benefit from the use of the identified asset, the contract does not contain a lease.
3. The customer benefits and directs the use of the asset, the contract contains a lease.
4. The customer benefits from the use of the identified asset, but the supplier directs its use, the contract does not contain a lease.
5. Neither party could direct the use of the asset, but the customer has the right to operate the asset without the supplier to change those operating instructions, or the customer designs the asset in a way predetermining how the asset is used, the contract contains a lease.

7.4.3 Identified asset

No.	Easy Rules
1	The asset is identified if either one of the following situations occurs: • The asset is explicitly specified in the contract (the asset specified can only be used in this contract) • The asset is implicitly specified at the time that it is made available for use by the customer (for instance, the asset is implicitly specified at the time that the asset is made available to the customer). (IFRS 16:B13)

7.4.4 Capacity portion

No.	Easy Rules
1	A capacity portion of an asset is an identified asset if it is physically distinct (i.e. a floor of a building) or
2	A capacity or other portion of an asset that is not physically distinct (i.e. a capacity portion of a fibre optic cable or a pipeline) is not an identified asset unless it represents substantially all of its capacity and thereby provides the customer with the right to obtain substantially all of the economic benefits from use of the asset.

7.4.5 Practical applications for an identified asset

Case 1: Specified asset but not an identified one

The lessee enters into a two-year lease agreement with the lessor to use one of its trucks to transport its gnome trapping equipment. The lessor can use any of its trucks when required.

Analysis:

The above contract does not contain a lease because it does not contain an identified asset.

The above lease agreement contains a specified asset as it is explicitly specified in the contract that the lessee can use one of its trucks.

(IFRS 16 para. 13)

However, the lessee does not have the right to use this truck if the supplier/lessor has the substantive right to substitute the truck throughout the period of use. The reason why the supplier's right is substantive is because both of the following conditions are met:

(IFRS 16 para. 14)

- **Condition 1**: The lessor/supplier has the practical ability to substitute alternative truck throughout the period of use. This means that The lessee cannot prevent the lessor from substituting the truck and;
- **Condition 2**: The lessor would benefit economically from the exercise of its right to substitute the truck (i.e. the economic benefits associated with substituting the truck are expected to exceed the costs associated with substituting it. This is evidenced by the lessor would substitute this when required).

However, the specified asset is identified if any one or both of the above two conditions is/are not met.

Case 2: The lessor's right to substitute the asset only on or after a specified event occurs

The lessee enters into a two-year lease agreement with the lessor to use one of its helicopters to find out when gnomes are coming. If there are problems with the helicopter, the supplier is obliged to substitute and repair it for the lessee.

Analysis:

The above contract contains an identified asset and therefore, it contains a lease.

In the above case, the lessor's right to substitute an asset is not substantive because the lessor has an obligation to substitute the asset only on or after the occurrence of a specified event, and this means that the lessor does not have the practical ability to substitute alternative trucks throughout the period of use.

(IFRS 16 para. 15 and para. 18)

Case 3: Protective right

The lessee enters into a two-year lease agreement with the lessor to use one of its trucks to transport its special soft drinks in Ciland. But the lease agreement also contains terms and conditions that trucks cannot be used outside Ciland.

Analysis:

The above contract contains a lease because the asset is identified.

In the above case, the contract contains a protective right because it includes terms and conditions designed to protect the lessor's interest in the asset(s) or its personnel, or to ensure the lessor's compliance with laws or regulations. These are examples of protective rights.

In the above case, the protective right is to limit where the lessee can use the truck.

Other examples of protective rights may include:
- specify the maximum amount of use of an asset
- limit where or when the customer can use the asset
- require a customer to follow particular operating practices
- require a customer to inform the supplier of changes in how an asset will be used

Protective rights typically define the scope of the customer's Right-of-Use but do not, in isolation, prevent the customer from having the right to direct the use of an asset.

(IFRS 16 para. 30)

Case 4: Asset capacity (asset is not physically distinct)

This following example is adjusted from IFRS 16 illustrative example 3.

The lessee enters into a 20-year contract with the lessor for the right to use a specified amount of capacity within a cable connecting Ciland to Biland. The specified amount is equivalent to us having the use of the full capacity of 2 fibre strands within the cable (the cable contains 21 fibres with similar capacities).

Lessor makes decisions about the transmission of data (i. e. lessor lights the fibres, makes decisions about which fibres are used to transmit. The lessee makes decisions about the electronic equipment that lessor owns and connects to the fibres).

Analysis:

1. The above contract does not contain a lease because:
2. The asset is not physically distinct and;

It does not represent substantially all of the capacity of the asset.

The reason why this is not distinct is because the lessee can only use a specified amount of capacity rather than using specific strands of cable.

The capacity is only 9.5% (2/21) of the total capacity of the cable and does not represent substantially all of the capacity of the asset.

However, if the capacity is more than 95% (say, 20 cables out of 21) can be used by the lessee, it represents substantially all of the capacity of the asset, and thereby provides The lessee with the right to obtain substantially all of the economic benefits from use of the asset, and in this case, although the capacity of an asset is not physically distinct, it still contains a lease.

(IFRS 16 para. 20)

Case 5: Asset capacity (asset is physically distinct)

The lessee enters into a 20-year contract with a lessor for the right to use 2 of 21 specific strands of fibre optic cable connecting Ciland and Biland. The lessee has the exclusive right to use these strands to transfer their data.

Analysis:

This contains a lease because two specific strands of fibre optic cable are specified and physically distinct from the other 19 cables because only 2 cables are for the lessee's use.

(IFRS 16 para. 20)

Besides, the lessor's right to substitute the cables throughout the period of use is not substantive.

Case 6: Supplier's substitution right considerations (exclude some future events)

This following example is adjusted from IFRS 16 illustrative example 4.

The lessee enters into a contract with a property owner (lessor/ supplier) to use Retail Unit A to sell its special soft drinks for a five-year period. Retail Unit A is part of a larger retail space with many retail units.

The lessee is granted the right to use Retail Unit A. Supplier can require the lessee to relocate to another retail unit. In that case, the supplier is required to provide the lessee with a retail unit of similar quality and specifications to Retail Unit A and to pay for The lessee's relocation costs. Supplier would benefit economically from relocating the lessee only if a major new tenant were to decide to occupy a large amount of retail space at a rate sufficiently favourable to cover the costs of relocating the lessee and other tenants in the retail space.

However, although it is possible that those circumstances will arise, at the inception of the contract, it is not likely that those circumstances will arise.

Analysis:

This contains a lease because:

1. The asset is specified in the agreement: Retail Unit A;
2. The asset is identified because the lessor's right to substitute the cables throughout the period of use is not substantive:

a. The lessor can have the practical ability to substitute alternative retail unit throughout the period of use and this means that the lessee could not prevent the lessor from relocating to another retail unit.

b. However, given the supplier/lessor needs to pay The lessee's relocation costs and provide similar quality and specifications to the original Retail Unit A when this is reallocated, and the supplier only benefits from this when the future new tenant/customer is found (future tenant is not the fact when the lease contract is entered into), the lessor would benefit economically from the exercise of its right to relocate The lessee's Retail Unit A.

The following considerations should also be excluded when the contract is entered into:

- The introduction of new technology that is not substantially developed at the inception of the contract;
- A substantial difference between the customer's use of the asset, or the performance of the asset, and the use or performance considered likely at the inception of the contract; and
- A substantial difference between the market price of the asset during the period of use, and the market price considered likely at the inception of the contract.

This is because an entity's evaluation of whether a supplier's substitution right is substantive is based on facts and circumstances at the inception of the contract and shall exclude consideration of future events that are not considered likely to occur at inception of the contract.

(IFRS 16 para. 16)

7.4.6 The right to control the use of an identified asset can be divided into

a. the right to obtain substantially all of the economic benefits from use of an identified asset and

b. the right to direct the use of an identified asset.

7.4.6.1 Economic benefits

No.	Easy Rules
1	**Right to obtain economic benefits from use:** The following hints are used to determine whether the lessee/customer has the right to obtain substantially all of the economic benefits from the use of the asset throughout the period of use: 1. The lessee could use the asset exclusively throughout that period; 2. The lessee could hold or sublease the asset.
2	**The economic benefits include:** 1. Its primary output and by-products (including potential cash flows derived from these items); 2. Other economic benefits from using the asset that could be realised from a commercial transaction with a third party; (IFRS 16 para. 21) 3. The economic benefits should be from the use of the asset within the defined scope of a customer's right to use the asset. For instance, if the territory or the usage for the use of the asset is limited, an entity shall consider only the economic benefits from the use of the asset within that territory or permitted usage and not beyond. (IFRS 16 para. 22)

7.4.6.2 Right to direct the use of the identified asset

No.	Easy Rules
1	**The lessee has the right to direct the use of an asset if either**: **1. The customer/lessee has the right to direct how and for what purpose the asset is used throughout the period of use.** A customer has the right to direct how and for what purpose the asset is used if, within the scope of its Right-of-Use defined in the contract, it can change how and for what purpose the asset is used throughout the period of use, the following decision making rights should be considered when making this assessment: (IFRS 16 para. 24) • rights to change the type of output that is produced by the asset • rights to change when the output is produced • rights to change where the output is produced • rights to change whether the output is produced, and the quantity of that output (IFRS 16 para. 26) Rights that are limited to operating or maintaining the asset do not grant the right to change how and for what purpose the asset is used. (IFRS 16 para. 27) **2. The relevant decisions about how and for what purpose the asset is used are predetermined and**: • The supplier/lessor does not have the right to change operating instructions to stop the customer's right to operate the asset on its own or to direct others to use the asset. • The customer designed the asset (or specific aspects of the asset) in a way that predetermines how and for what purpose the asset will be used throughout the period of use. (IFRS 16 para. 24)

Case 1: Supplier directs the use of the asset

This following example is adjusted from IFRS 16 illustrative example 1.

The lessee entered into a lease agreement requiring the lessor to transport a specified quantity of gnome trapping equipment by using a specified type of rail car for 5 years. Supplier provides the rail cars, driver and engine as part of the contract.

Supplier can choose to use any one of a number of engines to fulfill each of customer's requests, and one engine could be used to transport not only our equipment, but also the goods of other customers.

The cars and engines are stored at supplier's premises when not being used to transport our equipment.

Analysis:

The lessee does not direct the use, nor have the right to obtain substantially all of the economic benefits from use, of an identified car or an engine. The reasons are:

Right to direct the use:

1. The lessee does not have the right to direct how and for what purpose the asset is used throughout the period of use because it is up to the supplier to choose which retail car and engine to fulfill customer's request but it is not up to the customer to do so.

2. The lessee does not have the right to operate the cars and engines or to direct others to operate the cars and engines in a way that it determines throughout the period of use because as per the terms and conditions in the agreement, unused cars are stored at supplier's premises.

3. The lessee does not design the cars and engines and engines or part of them in a way that predetermines how and for what purpose the cars and engines will be used throughout the period of use.

Economic benefits:

1. The lessee could not use the car exclusively throughout that period because retail cars or engines could be provided by the supplier to other customers.

2. The lessee could not hold or sublease the asset throughout that period because if the retail car is not used, it would be stored at supplier's premises.

Therefore, The lessee does not have the right to obtain substantially all of the economic benefits from the use of an identified car or an engine.

Therefore, The lessee does not direct the use of an identified car or an engine.

Case 2: Payments based on % of the gross revenue

This following example is adjusted from IFRS 16 illustrative example 4.

The lessee entered into a contract for the lease of a store in a shopping centre to sell its special soft drinks for 10 years. The rental terms include payments equal to 12% of the gross sales revenue generated from the store.

The lessee has the right to determine which products are to be sold and the store design.

The contract requires The lessee to make fixed payments to the lessor, as well as variable payments that are a percentage of sales from the store.

The lessor provides cleaning and security services, as well as advertising services, as part of the contract.

Analysis:

The lessee has the right to obtain substantially all of the economic benefits from the use of the store. The reasons are as follows:

1. The lessee could use the store in the shopping centre exclusively throughout that period and get 100% of the revenue.

2. The lessee could hold or sublease the store to others throughout that period.

The lessee can direct the use of the store in the shopping centre. The reasons are:

1. The lessee has the right to direct how and for what purpose the store is used throughout the period of use. For instance, the lessee can decide how the store is designed and which products are to be sold.
2. The lessee can change how and for what purpose the store is used throughout the period of use:
   - rights to change the type of output that is produced by the asset. For instance, the lessee can change the product mix to be sold in the store.
   - rights to change when the output is produced. For instance, the lessee can decide when to sell those products.
   - rights to change where the output is produced. For instance, the lessee can also introduce an online store and sell those products online.
   - rights to change whether the output is produced, and the quantity of that output. For instance, the lessee can decide how many different types of products to be sold.

   -Rights that are limited to operating or maintaining the asset do not grant the right to change how and for what purpose the asset is used. In this case, although it is the lessor who is responsible for providing cleaning, security and advertising services, The lessee still directs the use of the store.

   Finally, although a portion of the cash flows derived from sales from the store will flow from The lessee to the lessor, this represents consideration that The lessee pays the lessor for the right to use the store. It does not prevent the lessee from having the right to obtain substantially all of the economic benefits from the use of the store, i. e., those cash flows paid as consideration shall be considered to be part of the economic benefits that the customer obtains from use of the asset.

(IFRS 16 para. 23)

Case 3: Lessee designs the leased asset

This following example is adjusted from *IFRS 16 illustrative example* 9.

The lessee enters into a 30-year contract with the supplier to install operate and maintain a wind plant for The lessee's energy supply. The lessee involves an external specialist to determine the location of the wind farm and the engineering equipment to be used.

The lessee has the exclusive right to receive and the obligation to take any energy produced.

Analysis:

The nature of the wind plant is such that all of the decisions about how and for what purpose the asset is used are predetermined because:
- the type of output (i. e. energy) and the production location are predetermined in the agreement; and
- when, whether and how much energy is produced is influenced by the sunlight and the wind farm location selection.

Besides, The lessee designed specific aspects of the wind plant because external experts are involved in determining the location as the location is key to the asset's performance. Therefore, The lessee has the right to direct the use of the asset.

7.5 *Recognition Exemptions*

According to IFRS 16 Leases, there are two situations that the lessee may not need to show the leased assets and liabilities.

Accounting treatment when the traditional lease accounting is exempted:

Dr	Operating expense	x
Cr	Cash	x

7.5.1 Situation 1: Short term leases where the lease term is generally less than 12 months

No.	Easy Rules
1	If the business elects this recognition exemption, it should be based on the class of underlying asset. For instance, the class of motor vehicles, the class of office equipment and the class of properties. If the business elects this exemption only for the class of office equipment but not for other classes of assets, this accounting policy needs to be adopted for similar motor vehicles in the future. (IFRS 16: para. B8)

Case 1: Lease term structured to be less than 12 months

The lessee needs to review the lease term to confirm whether it is a short-term lease. For instance, if the contract lease term is 11 months and 28 days, but with an extension option to another 3 months, and it's reasonably certain that the option will be exercised by the lessee, and in this case, it is not a short-term lease.

Case 2: Lease with a short remaining term

For instance, before we adopt the new standard, the lessee entered a lease agreement in 2016 with a 4-year non-cancellable period and an option to extend the contract to another 3 years. In 2019, we adopt the new standard and we find that the asset we leased would no longer fit our strategy, hence it is reasonably certain that the contract would not be renewed. In this case, we can conclude that the remaining lease term is less than one year, and we could treat this contract as a short term lease.

As the first-time adoption of IFRS 16, we could follow one of the two approaches in case 2:

- **Approach 1**: To recognise the leased asset and liability and to provide depreciation as well as finance costs based on the right-of-use asset and lease liability.
- **Approach 2**: To adopt the recognition exemption, i.e. to recognise the rental expense and cash paid for the rental expense. If the expense is not paid, the accrued expense liability should be recognised. (this is the same as the operating lease accounting treatment in the previous IAS 17 Leases).

7.5.2 Situation 2: Underlying asset in the lease has a low value

No.	Easy Rules
1	The Board does not specify how much the asset is worth would be seen as low value. However, it provides the following examples for low-value assets: • Tablets • Personal computers • Small items of office furniture (such as chairs, desks, office partitions, water dispensers, photocopier devices and printers) • Telephones
2	In practice, if the asset value is not greater than \$ 5,000, it may be seen as a low-value item. However, due to the changes in inflation, technological and supply chain factors, the \$ 5,000 may be used as a basepoint to determine whether the asset is a low-value item or not rather than use this as a hard threshold.
3	If the business adopts the recognition exemption accounting treatment on the basis of low-value assets, this treatment is made on a lease by lease basis. This means that similar accounting treatment is not applied to a similar class of assets. An underlying asset can be of low value only if: a) the lessee can benefit from the use of the underlying asset on its own or together with other resources that are readily available to the lessee; and b) the underlying asset is not highly dependent on, or highly interrelated with, other assets. (IFRS 16 para. 5)

Case 3: Leased assets are highly dependent on other assets

To improve our transaction processing system, the lessee leases several servers and some individual modules from two companies. Individual modules are leased to increase the storage of those servers each with a value of less than \$ 3,000.

Required: Can we apply the recognition exemption accounting treatment to the above modules?

Analysis:

In this case, the lease of both servers and modules are not considered as low-value items. First, servers are not in the above list of the low value of items provided by the Board. Second, those modules cannot be used separately, they are highly dependent on those servers, i. e. modules need to be used together with servers. Hence modules cannot be considered as low-value assets.

Case 4: Assets not material to the lessee

The lessee has a budget of $ 5,000 million and we leased a $ 1 million asset.

Required: Can we apply the recognition exemption accounting treatment to the above asset?

Analysis:

We cannot conclude that the value of this asset is low simply because it is not material to our business, i. e. only 0.02% of our total budget volume. According to IFRS 16 paragraph B4, the assessment is not affected by the size, nature or circumstances of the lessee. Therefore, we cannot apply the recognition exemption accounting treatment to this transaction.

Case 5: Leased assets in aggregate material to the lessee

The lessee has 30 computers and each of them cost $ 4,000. Hence the total value of those 30 computers is $ 120,000.

Required: Can we still apply the recognition exemption accounting in this case?

Analysis: The answer is yes.

According to IFRS 16 Leases paragraph B4, the assessment of whether an underlying asset is of low value is performed on an absolute basis. Leases of low-value assets qualify for recognition exemption regardless of whether those leases are material to the lessee. This means that individual asset value is focused on instead of its total value.

Case 6: Lease of second-hand car

The lessee leased a $ 3,500 second-hand car during the year. Can we apply the recognition exemption accounting treatment to this transaction?

Analysis:

We cannot apply the recognition exemption accounting treatment in this case. According to IFRS 16 paragraph B6, a lease of an underlying asset does not qualify as a lease of a low-value asset if the nature of the asset is such that, when new, the asset is typically not of low value.

In this case, the value of the new car should exceed $ 3,500 and it is not an example in the low-value asset list provided by the Board. This means that although the car is second hand by nature, this does not affect the assessment of whether it is of low value. However, the conclusion about whether the value is low should be based on when the car was new.

7.6 *Sale and Leaseback Transactions*

7.6.1 Introduction to sale and leaseback transaction

A sale and leaseback transaction means a business sells the asset and then it leases it back. This is a typical way to raise finance and to use the underlying asset at the same time.

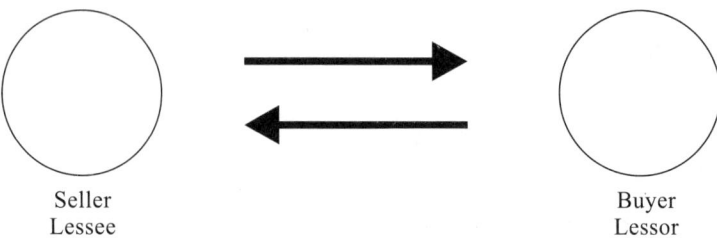

Seller
Lessee

Buyer
Lessor

7.6.2 Accounting treatment for sale and leaseback transaction

No.	Easy Rules
1	The accounting treatment depends on whether the transfer of an asset is a sale or not. (IFRS 16:para. 98)

7.6.3 Transfer of asset is a sale

No.	Easy Rules
1	If the transfer of an asset by the seller (lessee) satisfies the requirements of IFRS 15 Revenue from Contracts with Customers to be accounted for as a sale of the asset.
2	The seller (lessee) shall measure the right-of-use asset arising from the leaseback at the proportion of the previous carrying amount of the asset that relates to the right-of-use retained by the seller (lessee). Accordingly, the seller (lessee) shall recognise only the amount of any gain or loss that relates to the rights transferred to the buyer (lessor).
3	**Off market adjustments:** If the fair value of the consideration for the sale of an asset does not equal the fair value of the asset, or if the payments for the lease are not at market rates, an entity shall make the following adjustments to measure the sale proceeds at fair value: 1. any below-market terms shall be accounted for as a prepayment of lease payments; and 2. any above-market terms shall be accounted for as additional financing provided by the buyer-lessor to the seller (lessee). The entity shall measure any potential adjustments on the basis of the more readily determinable of: 1. the difference between the fair value of the consideration for the sale and the fair value of the asset; and 2. the difference between the present value of the contractual payments for the lease and the present value of payments for the lease at market rates. (IFRS 16 para. 100-102)

7.6.4 Transfer of asset is not a sale

No.	Easy Rules
1	If the transfer of an asset by the seller (lessee) does not satisfy the requirements of IFRS 15 to be accounted for as a sale of the asset:
2	The seller (lessee) shall continue to recognise the transferred asset and shall recognise a financial liability equal to the transfer proceeds. It shall account for the financial liability applying IFRS 9.

(IFRS 16: para. 103)

Case 1: Sale and leaseback with the proceeds from the sale being the fair value of the asset:

The lessee sells a warehouse to the buyer at the fair value of $ 5 million and the carrying value of the warehouse was $ 1.3 million at the time of sale. The sale meets with the sale definition per IFRS 15 Revenue from Contracts with Customers.

The lessee enters into a contract with the buyer for the right to use the warehouse for the next 6 years while the remaining economic useful life of the asset is 6 years. Annual rental payments of $ 600,000 are made at the end of each year. The interest rate implicit in the lease is 10%. The present value of the annual lease payments is $ 2.6 million. The remaining economic useful life of the asset is much greater than the lease term.

Required: Accounting treatment.

Answer: From the lessee/seller's perspective:

Dr	Bank	$ 5 million
Dr	Right-of-Use asset	$ 0.7 million
Cr	Asset at carrying value	$ 1.3 million
Cr	Lease liability	$ 2.6 million
Cr	Profit on sale (balancing figure) *	$ 1.8 million

* Alternatively, the profit on sale can be calculated as the proportion on the total profit on disposal of $ 3.7 million ($ 5 million – $ 1.3 million):

$$\frac{\$ 5 \text{ million} - \$ 2.6 \text{ million}}{\$ 5 \text{ million}} \times \$ 3.7 \text{ million} = \$ 1.8 \text{ million}$$

(IFRS 16 para. 100 (a))

Case 2: Sale and leaseback with the proceeds from sale different from the fair value of the asset

The lessee enters into a sale and leaseback transaction on the warehouse and leases it back for 3 years. The initial sale meets with the sale definition with IFRS 15 Revenue from contracts with customers.

At the date of sale, the following information is available:

Carrying value of the warehouse $ 800,000
Fair value of the warehouse $ 1,200,000

The present value of lease liability is $ 713,250. The company's incremental borrowing rate is 10%.

Required: Accounting treatment under:
- Scenario 1: If the proceeds are $ 1,400,000
- Scenario 2: If the proceeds are $ 900,000

Answer:

Scenario 1: If the proceeds are $ 1,400,000:

The sale proceeds are greater than its fair value at the sale date, and the sale meets with the sale definition, the excess value is considered as further financing.

Step 1: Derecognise the asset at its carrying value: Cr PP&E $ 800,000

Step 2: Calculate the excess in fair value as additional financing from the buyer: $ 200,000 ($ 1,400,000 − $ 1,200,000)

(IFRS 16 para 101 (b) and para 102 (a))

Step 3: Record the lease:

1. Recognise the lease liability: use the present value of the lease payments and subtract the additional financing: $ 713,250 − $ 200,000 = $ 513,250.

Hence to **Cr** Lease liability $ 513,250.

(IFRS 16 para 102 (b))

2. Recognise the right-of-use asset at the proportion of the carrying value recovered through the transaction: $ 800,000 × $ 513,250 / $ 1,200,000 = $ 342,167.

Hence to **Dr** Right-of-Use asset $ 342,167.

Step 4: Calculate the gain or loss from the sale and leaseback transaction:

1. Total disposal profits = $ 400,000 ($ 1,200,000 − $ 800,000)

2. The proportion of asset transferred to the lessor/buyer

$$= \frac{\text{Asset carrying value} - \text{Right-of-use asset}}{\text{Asset carrying value}}$$

$$= \frac{\$ 800,000 - \$ 342,167}{\$ 800,000}$$

$$= 57.229\%$$

3. Hence the profits to be recognised = 57.229% × $ 400,000 = $ 228,917

Dr	Bank	$ 1,400,000
Dr	Right-of-Use asset	$ 342,167
Cr	PP&E at carrying value	$ 800,000
Cr	Lease liability	$ 513,250
Cr	Financial liability	$ 200,000
Cr	Gain on disposal	$ 228,917

Scenario 2: If the proceeds are $ 900,000:

Step 1: Derecognise the asset at its carrying value: **Cr** PP&E $ 800,000.

Step 2: Calculate the reduction in fair value as a prepayment of lease payment to the buyer: $ 300,000 ($ 900,000 - $ 1,200,000).

(IFRS 16 para 101 (a) and para 102 (a))

Step 3: Record the lease:

Recognise the lease liability as the present value of the lease payments: $ 713,250.

Hence to **Cr** Lease liability $ 713,250.

Recognise the Right-of-Use asset at the proportion of the carrying value recovered through the transaction: $ 800,000 × $ 713,250 / $ 1,200,000 = $ 475,500.

Hence to **Dr** Right-of-Use asset $ 475,500.

Step 4: Calculate the gain or loss from the sale and leaseback:

1. Total disposal profits = $ 400,000 ($ 1,200,000 - $ 800,000)

2. The proportion of asset transferred to the lessor/buyer

$$= \frac{\text{Asset carrying value} - \text{Right-of-Use asset}}{\text{Asset varying value}}$$

$$= \frac{\$ 800,000 - \$ 475,500}{\$ 800,000}$$

$$= 40.56\%$$

Hence the profits to be recognised = 40.56% × $ 400,000 = $ 162,250.

Dr	Bank	$ 900,000
Dr	Right-of-Use asset	$ 475,500
Cr	PP&E at carrying value	$ 800,000
Cr	Lease liability	$ 713,250
Cr	Prepayment	$ 300,000
Cr	Gain on disposal	$ 162,250

Disclosures requirements for lessees

1	• Depreciation charge for the right-of-use assets • Finance costs of lease liabilities • Expenses relating to short term and low value assets • Details of sale and leaseback transactions • The carrying value of right-of-use assets at the end of the reporting period, by class of underlying asset • Additions to right-of-use assets (IFRS 16:para. 53)

Chapter 8

IAS 37 & IAS 10

IAS 37: Provisions, Contingent Liabilities and Contingent Assets
IAS 10　Events After the Reporting Period

8.1 *Provisions*

8.1.1　Definitions

No.	Easy Rules
1	A provision is a liability of uncertain timing or amount. If a business is invoiced, the liability should be "payables". If a business is not invoiced, the business should accrued the liability as "accrued expense". The uncertainty for accruals is much less than for provisions. (IAS 37: para. 10)

8.1.2　Recognition of provisions

Mnemonics (**POR**)	Explanations
Probable outflow	It is probable that an outflow of resources embodying economic benefits will be required to settle the obligation
Obligation	An entity has a present obligation (legal or constructive) as a result of a past event.

Mnemonics (POR)	Explanations
Reliably estimate	A reliable estimate can be made of the amount of the obligation. If the item is a one-off item, the best estimate will be the most likely outcome. If the item is made up of a number of items, for instance, a warranty provision for repairing goods, the expected value method should be used to calculate the probability of all events happening. (IAS 37:para. 14 and 39)

8.1.3 Meaning of "probable"

No.	Easy Rules
1	The word "probable" means that the event is more likely than not to occur. This indicates that the probability is more than 50%. (IAS 37:para. 15)

Example:Similar transactions

A company sells goods with warranty under which customers are covered for the repairs costs of any production defects which becomes apparent in the first three months of purchase. The company's past experience and future expectations indicate the following pattern of likely repairs:

% of goods sold	Defects	Costs of repairs
50%	Need minor repairs	$ 1m
40%	Need medium repairs	$ 2m
10%	Need major repairs	$ 3m

Required:What is the provision required?

Answer:The cost is calculated using "expected values":50% × $ 1m + 40% × $ 2m + 10% × $ 3m = $ 1.6m

Dr	Expense	$ 1.6m
Cr	Provision liability	$ 1.6m

Example:Single item

A company is sued by its competitor and the case is pending. The lawyer advised it is probable (70%) that A company needs to pay $ 5 million to compensate its competitor loss.

There is 30% chance that A company needs to pay only $ 1 million.

Required: Provision accounting.

Answer: This involves a single item which is a court case, i. e. provision is made in full for the most likely outcome. The most likely outcome is where 70% chance that A company needs to pay $ 5 million.

Dr	Expense	$ 5m
Cr	Provision liability	$ 5m

8.1.4　Time value of money

No.	Easy Rules
1	If the effect of the time value of money is material, the amount of a provision should be the present value of the expenditure required to settle the obligation. (IAS 37: para. 45)
2	The discount rate should be a pre-tax rate that reflects current market assessments of the time value of money. In other words, the current interest and inflation rate should be considered. Tax law may change in the future and therefore, the discount rate should be based on the "pre-tax" one.
3	The discount rate should not reflect risks for which future cash flow estimates.
4	However, future events which are reasonably expected to occur such as new legislation, changes in government, changes in technology may affect the amount required to settle the entity's obligation should be considered. For instance, when estimating the future costs of cleaning up the environmental pollution, the reduction in future costs by technology can be estimated, i. e. the provision liability can be reduced by that estimate. For example, instead of providing $ 1 million as the provision liability for future environmental pollution clean-up costs, we may reasonably estimate because of an improvement in technology, i. e. the technology is at the development stage, the future costs can be revised to $ 0.7 million. Therefore, a provision liability can be based on $ 0.7 million rather than $ 1 million in this case.
5	If both the discount rate and the future cash flows reflect future risks, this would result in double counting problems.
6	Expected disposal of assets should not be considered in measuring a provision. (ISA 37: para. 51)

No.	Easy Rules	
7	Accounting treatment:	
	When future costs are discounted:	
	Dr PP&E	x
	Cr Provision liability	x
	Unwind the provision liability by the discount rate:	
	Dr Finance cost	x
	Cr Provision liability	x

Example:

Company B operates in an oil industry.

It purchased an oilfield at $100 million and expects to pay the environmental clean-up costs of $10 million in three years' time.

The discount rate is 10% in this example, the discount factor (3 years) is 0.751.

Company B expects to sell the oilfield to the government in three years' time for $2 million.

Required: Accounting treatment.
Answer:
When an oilfield is bought:

Dr	PP&E	$100m
Cr	Cash	$100m

When future costs are discounted:

$10 million×0.751 = $7.51 million.

Dr	PP&E	$7.51m
Cr	Provision liability	$7.51m

Expected disposal of assets should not be considered in measuring a provision. Therefore, $2 million is ignored.

In year 1: unwind the provision liability at 10%:

Dr	Finance cost $ 7.51m×10%	$ 0.751m
Cr	Provision liability	$ 0.751m

Liability unwinding:

Years	Opening provision liability	Finance cost @10%	Closing provision liability
1	$ 7.51m	$ 0.751m	$ 8.261m
2	$ 8.261m	$ 0.826m	$ 9.087
3	$ 9.087	$ 0.909m	$ 10m

Therefore, the interest expense for the three-year period accounting treatments are as follows:

Dr	Finance costs	$ 0.751m; $ 0.826m; $ 0.909m
Cr	Provision liability	$ 0.751m; $ 0.826m; $ 0.909m

8.1.5 Meaning of obligations

No.	Easy Rules
1	**Legal obligation:** This is the "must do" for the business to comply with relevant laws such as labour law, environmental law, contract law or other relevant laws and regulations.
2	**Constructive obligation:** This is an obligation from an entity's action where: • By an established pattern of past practice, published policies or a sufficiently specific current statement the entity has indicated to other parties that it will accept certain responsibilities; and • As a result, the entity has created a valid expectation on the part of those other parties that it will discharge those responsibilities.

No.	Easy Rules
3	**Further illustration of constructive obligation:** A business may have a published refund policy that any customers can claim the refund within 7 days after buying any products. If a business has a past practice of having such policies, it creates a valid expectation that the business has an obligation of refunding customers. However, sometimes, such policies may not be so clear. For instance, refund policy should be easily found on the business website and this means after customers buy products or services from the business, customers have a valid expectation that if they are not happy with those products or services, they can claim the refund. But if a business has a past history of publishing such policies but they never refunded to customers (for instance, the business may have received numerous complaints from customers about the delay and red tape of the refund), the valid expectation criteria is not met. An example of the sufficiently specific current statement is that after a leakage of oil, a business may publicly announce a compensation package to those affected. (IAS 37: para. 15 and 17)

8.1.6 Reimbursements

No.	Easy Rules
1	Reimbursement represents the expenditure to be recovered from an insurance contract, indemnity clause or supplier's warranties.
2	Reimbursement should be recognised only when it is virtually certain that reimbursement will be received if the entity settles the obligation, i.e. to recognise the receivables asset: **Dr** Receivables **Cr** Income
3	The reimbursement should be treated as a separate asset and should not be offset against the provision liability in the statement of financial position. The asset amount recognised should not be greater than the provision liability itself.
4	The income from the reimbursement should not be offset against the expense related to provision in the statement of profit or loss. (IAS 37: 53-58)

8.1.7 Changes in provisions

No.	Easy Rules
1	Provisions should be reviewed at the end of each reporting period and adjusted to reflect the current best estimate. If it is no longer probable that a transfer of resources will be required to settle the obligation, the provision should be reversed by: **Dr** Provision liability **Cr** Expense
2	A provision should be used only for expenditures for which the provision was originally recognised. For instance, a provision may have been set for warranties. However, if there is a decrease in warranties provision, and an increase in environmental clean-up costs provision, we should separate those provisions in order not to conceal the impact of two different events. (IAS 37: para. 59 and 61)

8.1.8 Future operating losses

No.	Easy Rules
1	No provision should be recognised for future operating losses because they do not meet the liability definition. (IAS 37: para. 63) For instance, a business can not provide a provision liability simply based on the assumption that it would suffer from $ 10 million future operating losses in one year's time.

8.1.9 Onerous contracts

No.	Easy Rules
1	This standard defines an onerous contract as a contract in which the unavoidable costs of meeting the obligations under the contract exceed the economic benefits expected to be received under it. The unavoidable costs under a contract reflect the least net cost of exiting from the contract, which is the lower of the cost of fulfilling it and any compensation or penalties arising from failure to fulfill it. (IAS 37: para. 68)

Example:
    A business enters into a lease contract to lease a factory. However, at the end of the second year, the country is in economic recession and the business estimates that the costs of fulfilling the contract would exceed the benefits and determines that the contract is onerous.

The business estimates the costs of fulfilling the contract, i.e. rental expenses to be discounted to today's term are $ 600,000.

The costs of terminating the contract, i.e. penalty expenses are $ 450,000.

Required: Accounting treatment for the above onerous contract.

Answer: The unavoidable costs under a contract reflect the least net cost of exiting from the contract, which is the lower of the cost of fulfilling it and any compensation or penalties arising from failure to fulfill it. In this case, we should choose $ 450,000.

Dr	Expense	$ 450,000
Cr	Provision liability	$ 450,000

When the penalty is subsequently paid:

Dr	Provision liability	$ 450,000
Cr	Cash	$ 450,000

8.1.10 Provisions for restructuring

No.	Easy Rules
1	Restructuring is a programme that is planned and is controlled by management and materially changes either: • The scope of a business undertaken by an entity • The manner in which that business is conducted (IAS 37: para. 10)
2	**Examples of restructuring**: • The sale or termination of a line of business. However, in this case, abinding sale agreement should be available so that a provision liability can be recognised because if this is not the case, the entity may change the mind and withdraw from the sale even if its intentions have been announced publicly. • The closure of business locations in a country or region or the relocation of business activities from one country region to another. • Changes in management structure, for instance, the elimination of a layer of management. • Fundamental reorganisations that have a material effect on the nature and focus of the entity's operations. (IAS 37: para. 70 & 78)

No.	Easy Rules
3	Whether or not the provision liability should be recognised for the restructuring depends on whether the following criteria are met:

Mnemonics (POR)	Explanations
Probable outflow	It is probable that an outflow of resources embodying economic benefits will be required to settle the obligation.
Obligation	An entity has a present obligation (legal or constructive) as a result of a past event. To meet the "obligation" criterion: An entity must have a detailed formal plan for the restructuring: • About which business or part of the business would be restructured; • About principal locations affected; • About approximate number of staff affected; • About the approximate amount incurred; • About when the plan will be implemented. It must have raised a valid expectation in those affected that it will carry out the restructuring by starting to implement that plan or announcing its main features to those affected by it. (IAS 37: para. 72)
Reliably estimate	A reliable estimate can be made of the amount of the obligation.

No.	Easy Rules
4	**Restructuring provision costs:** Only direct expenditures should be included and these direct expenditures should be: 1. Necessarily entailed by the restructuring; and 2. Not associated with the ongoing activities of the entity. (This means the business stops the employment and staff are not going to work with us.) (IAS 37: para. 80)
5	The following costs should specifically not be included in a restructuring provision: • Retraining staff • Relocating continuing staff • Marketing • Investment in new systems and distribution networks (IAS 37: para. 81)

Example:Provision recognition
Whether the following situations would a provision be recognised?
1. The board determined a detailed closure plan of the northeast division by the year end, details have been communicated with the staff affected.
2. The business intends to spend huge expenditure in retraining the staff and improving marketing activities.
Answer:
1. A provision should be made.
2. No provision should be made because the business has no obligations of doing this.

Example:Provision costs
A business decided to sell a line of business and a binding agreement has been entered into.
The business decided to reallocate staff to the nearest factory and expect to incur $ 6 million costs. Some staff will be retained as a result of the restructuring and will be made redundant and the redundancy fee is expected to be $ 5 million.
The business will move the production facility to another factory at a cost of $ 10 million.
The business must pay the penalty regarding the lease termination of $ 1 million should the restructuring goes ahead.
The business will spend $ 19 million cost to retrain staff and invest in new systems.
Required: Explain the total provision costs to be recognised.
Answer:
1. Reallocation costs of $ 6m should not be included because this is the ongoing activity costs.
2. Redundant fee of $ 5m should be included because this is directly related to the restructuring and not ongoing activity costs.
3. $ 10m reorganisation costs can not be included because this is the ongoing cost, i. e. the business continues to use the facility.
4. $ 1m penalty cost should be included.
5. $ 19m should not be included.
The total restructuring costs are therefore $ 6m:

Dr	Expense	$ 6m
Cr	Provision	$ 6m

8.1.11 Summary

Items	Accounting treatment
Warranties/Refunds	Accrue a provision liability if such policy is published
Future operating losses	No provision liability
Environmental contamination	Accrue a provision liability if the company's policy is to clean up the contamination although there is no legal requirement to do so
Onerous contract	Accrue a provision liability
Firm offers staff training	No provision liability
Major overhaul or repairs	No provision liability
Restructuring by sale of an operation/line of business	Accrue a provision liability only after a binding sale agreement
Restructuring by closure of business locations or reorganisation	Accrue a provision liability only after a detailed formal plan is adopted and announced publicly.

8.1.12 Provision disclosure

No.	Easy Rules
1	Disclosure of details of the change in carrying value of a provision from the beginning to the end of the year.
2	Disclosure of the background to the making of the provision and the uncertainties affecting its outcome.

(IAS 37: paras. 84 and 85)

Example of disclosure by Tesco plc:

Restructuring provisions of the £ 195m net charge (£ 221m charge, £ 26m release) recognised in the year, £ 182m (2018: £ 102m) has been classified within exceptional items as "Net restructuring and redundancy costs" and related to store and head office restructuring in the UK & ROI £ 131m (2018: £ 102m), Central Europe £ 27m (2018: £ nil), Asia £ 26m (2018: £ nil) and Tesco Bank £ 2m release (2018: £ nil).

8.2 *Contingent Liabilities*

No.	Easy Rules
1	**A contingent liability is:** a) possible obligation that arises from past events and whose existence will be confirmed only by the occurrence or non-occurrence of one or more uncertain future events not wholly within the control of the entity; or
2	b) a present obligation that arises from past events but is not recognised because: (1) it is not probable that an outflow of resources embodying economic benefits will be required to settle the obligation; or (2) the amount of the obligation cannot be measured with sufficient reliability. (IAS 37: para. 10)

8.2.1 Disclosure of contingent liabilities

No.	Easy Rules
1	An estimate of its financial effect;
2	An indication of the uncertainties relating to the amount or timing of any outflow; and
3	The possibility of any reimbursement. (IAS 37: para. 86)

8.2.2 Disclosure exemption

No.	Easy Rules
1	In extremely rare cases, disclosure of some or all of the information required can be expected to prejudice seriously the position of the entity in a dispute with other parties on the subject matter of the provision, contingent liability or contingent asset. In such cases, an entity need not disclose the information, but shall disclose the general nature of the dispute, together with the fact that, and reason why, the information has not been disclosed. (IAS 37: para. 92)

No.	Easy Rules
2	For instance, this could be the case that the business is involved in criminal cases such as money laundering activities or terrorism activities. A full disclosure of these may seriously prejudice the entity's position. Details of the general nature of the provision or contingencies must still be provided, together with an explanation of why it has not been disclosed.

8.3 Contingent Assets

No.	Easy Rules
1	A contingent asset is a possible asset (this means it is not a certain asset) that arises from past events and whose existence will be confirmed only by the occurrence or non-occurrence of one or more uncertain future events not wholly within the control of the entity.
2	A contingent asset should be disclosed if it is probable, i.e. probability is more than 50%.
3	If the probability is virtually certain, i.e. more than 95%, then a receivable asset (certain asset rather than a possible asset) should be recognised by: **Dr** Receivable **Cr** Income (IAS 37:para. 10)

Disclosure of contingent assets

No.	Easy Rules
1	Where an inflow of economic benefits is probable, an entity shall disclose a brief description of the nature of the contingent assets at the end of the reporting period, and, where practicable, an estimate of their financial effect. (IAS 37:para. 89)

Example:
   Mic plc is in a legal dispute and the outcome is unknown at the moment. Please advice the accounting treatments.
1. It expects to pay approximately $ 5 million.
2. Possible damages are $ 200,000 but Mic plc does not expect to pay them.
3. Mic plc expects to have to pay damages but is unable to estimate the amount.

4. Mic plc expects to receive damages of $60,000 from the insurance company and this is virtually certain.

5. Mic plc expects to probably receive damages of $50,000.

6. Mic plc thinks it may receive damages, but it is not probable.

Answer:

1. Provision liability should be recognised.

2. A contingent liability should be disclosed.

3. A contingent liability should be disclosed.

4. A receivable asset should be recognised by:

Dr Receivable

Cr Income

5. A contingent asset should be disclosed.

6. No disclosure should be made.

Example:

In year one, A business provides a guarantee of B business's borrowings and at this time, the credit rating of B business is good.

In year two, the credit rating of business B deteriorates and business B is about to go bankrupt and the probability of paying the amount owed to the business B's creditors by the business A is now probable.

Required: Accounting treatment in year one and two from business A's perspective.

Answer: In year one, a contingent liability should be disclosed.

This is a possible obligation (will repay the money if business B defaults on payments) that arises from past events (providing guarantee) and whose existence will be confirmed only by the occurrence or non-occurrence of one or more uncertain future events (business B may default on its borrowings) not wholly within the control of the entity (business B is not the subsidiary of business A).

In year two, the probability of repaying the money to business B's creditor is probable because it is now probable that a transfer of resources will be required to settle the obligation, i. e. paying business B's creditors. A provision should be recognised in this case.

Example:

Bosco plc is being taken to court by a customer for injury due to one of the products Bosco plc sells. The customer is claiming damages of $75,000. Bosco plc's lawyers said that there is a 35% chance that the company would have to settle the claim as the court case is in its final stages.

Answer:

- Not probable because it's only 35% change
- With legal obligation because this is required by law
- The amount is reliably measured because it's $75,000

A contingent liability should be disclosed:

1. Nature of the event: court case;

2. Financial effect: $ 75,000 cash outflow from Bosco plc;

3. Uncertainty: the amount is only possible, and the timing would be in last stage of the court case.

Example:

MJY plc signed a contract with Bosco plc to do the refurbishment work for MJY plc. Bosco plc sub-contracted a company to provide part of refurbishment of the retail stores of MJY plc. But after the refurbishment service has been provided that MJY plc found there're certain areas the sub-contractor did not meet the standard. So MJY plc decides to sue Bosco plc for damages of $ 45,000. Then Bosco plc counter sue MJY Ltd for this issue. And from the lawyer of Bosco plc that there's an 80% of chance that the sub-contractor will have to pay $ 35,000 regarding this issue to Bosco plc. And the lawyer also estimates that there's a 60% of chance that Bosco plc will have to pay $ 45,000 to MJY plc as well.

Answer:

- It's probable because it's 80% chance of cash outflow
- There is legal obligation
- The cost can be reliably measured with $ 35,000

A contingent asset should be disclosed for Bosco plc.

But for the sub-contractor, there should be a provision to be recognised:

Dr Expense $ 35,000

Cr Provision $ 35,000

The following disclosure should also be made by Bosco plc:

1. Nature of event: court case

2. Financial effect: cash inflow of $ 35,000 will be received by Bosco plc.

IAS 10 Events After the Reporting Period

8.4 *Adjusting Event*

No.	Easy Rules
1	An event after the reporting period that provides further evidence of conditions that existed at the reporting period.

No.	Easy Rules
2	**Examples include**: a) the settlement after the reporting period of a court case that confirms that the entity had a present obligation at the end of the reporting period. The entity adjusts any previously recognised provision related to this court case in accordance with IAS 37 Provisions, Contingent Liabilities and Contingent Assets or recognises a new provision. b) the receipt of information after the reporting period indicating that an asset was impaired at the end of the reporting period, or that the amount of a previously recognised impairment loss for that asset needs to be adjusted. For example: • the bankruptcy of a customer that occurs after the reporting period usually confirms that the customer was credit-impaired at the end of the reporting period; and • the sale of inventories after the reporting period may give evidence about their net realisable value at the end of the reporting period. c) the determination after the reporting period of the cost of assets purchased, or the proceeds from assets sold, before the end of the reporting period. d) the discovery of fraud or errors that show that the financial statements are incorrect. e) Deterioration in operating results and financial position after the reporting period may indicate a need to consider whether the going concern assumption is still appropriate. If the going concern assumption is no longer appropriate, the effect is so pervasive that this Standard requires a fundamental change in the basis of accounting, rather than an adjustment to the amounts recognised within the original basis of accounting. (IAS 10: para. 9 & 15)

8.5 *Non-Adjusting Event*

No.	Easy Rules
1	An event after the reporting period that is indicative of a condition that arose after the end of the reporting period.

No.	Easy Rules
2	**Examples include:** a) a major business combination after the reporting period (IFRS 3 Business Combinations requires specific disclosures in such cases) or disposing of a major subsidiary; b) announcing a plan to discontinue an operation; c) major purchases of assets, classification of assets as held for sale in accordance with IFRS 5 Non-current Assets Held for Sale and Discontinued Operations, other disposals of assets, or expropriation of major assets by government; d) the destruction of a major production plant by a fire after the reporting period; e) announcing, or commencing the implementation of, a major restructuring (see IAS 37); f) major ordinary share transactions and potential ordinary share transactions after the reporting period; g) abnormally large changes after the reporting period in asset prices or foreign exchange rates; h) changes in tax rates or tax laws enacted or announced after the reporting period that have a significant effect on current and deferred tax assets and liabilities; i) entering into significant commitments or contingent liabilities, for example, by issuing significant guarantees; and j) commencing major litigation arising solely out of events that occurred after the reporting period. k) If dividends are declared after the reporting period but before the financial statements are authorised for issue, the dividends are not recognised as a liability at the end of the reporting period because no obligation exists at that time. (IAS 10: para. 13 & 22)

Example:

After the reporting date a major credit customer of a company went bankrupt the company expected that little or none of the $12 million liabilities will be repaid. $10 million of the debt relates to sales made before the year end, $2 million relates to sales made in the first month after the reporting date.

The whole $12 million liabilities have been written off as irrecoverable debt expenses in the first year's Financial Statements. The finance director pointed out that, as the liquidation is an event after the reporting date, the liability should not in fact be written off, but disclosure should be made by note to first year's Financial Statements. The debt should be written off in the second year's Financial Statements.

Required: Whether the above accounting treatment is correct?

Answer:

Under IAS 10 an event after the reporting date is an event which occurs between the financial period end and the date on which the financial statements are approved by the board of directors.

$ 10m of the receivable existed at the reporting date and the liquidation of the major customer provides more information about that receivable. In accordance with IAS 10, this is an adjusting event which would require the debt existing at the reporting date to be written off in the first year's account.

The remaining receivable did not exist at the reporting date and should therefore be written off in the second year's financial account.

Chapter 9

IAS 33 Earnings Per Share (EPS)

Topic outline:

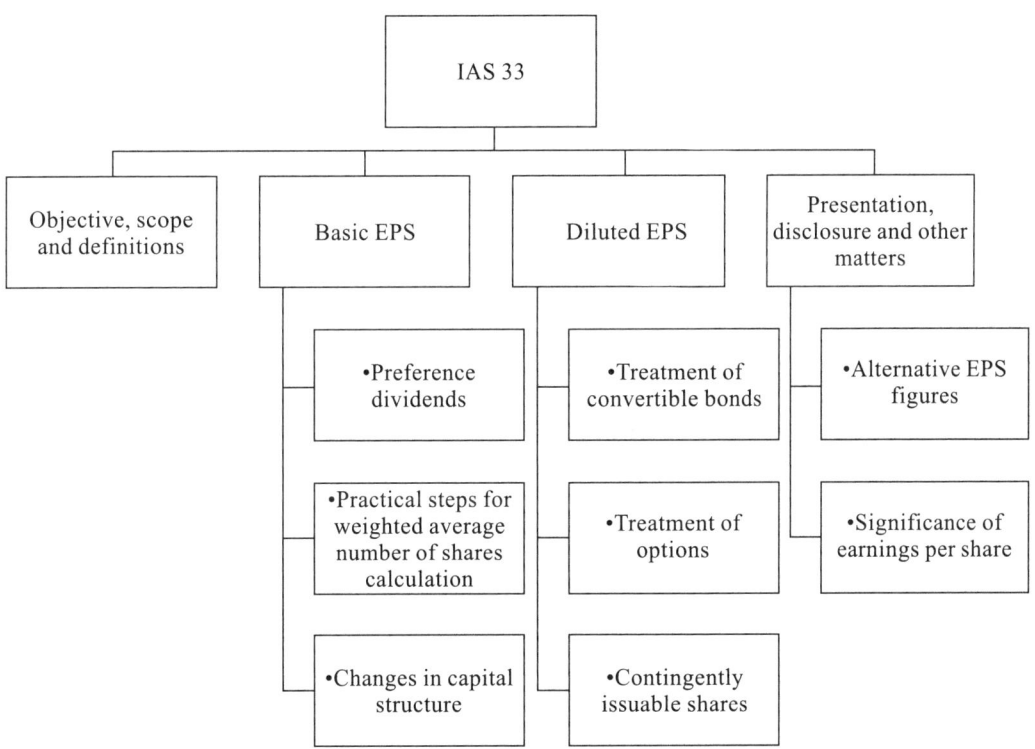

9.1 Objective

No.	Easy Rules
1	The objective of this Standard is to prescribe principles for the determination and presentation of earnings per share, so as to improve performance comparisons between different entities in the same reporting period and between different reporting periods for the same entity. Even though earnings per share data have limitations because of the different accounting policies that may be used for determining "earnings", a consistently determined denominator enhances financial reporting. The focus of this Standard is on the denominator of the earnings per share calculation. (IAS 33:para. 1)

9.2 Scope

No.	Easy Rules
1	This Standard shall apply to the individual or consolidated (with a parent) financial statements of an entity who shares are publicly traded; files or in the process of filling the accounts with a securities commission. In practice, if an entity prepares a prospectus for listing, EPS should be calculated. When an entity presents both consolidated and separate accounts, EPS need only be presented on the basis of consolidated results. EPS in the separate accounts should not be presented on the consolidated accounts. (IAS 33:para. 2-4)

9.3 Definitions

No.	Easy Rules
1	**Antidilution:** Antidilution is an increase in earnings per share or a reduction in loss per share resulting from the assumption that convertible instruments are converted, that options or warrants are exercised, or that ordinary shares are issued upon the satisfaction of specified conditions.

No.	Easy Rules
2	**Contingent share agreement:** A contingent share agreement is an agreement to issue shares that is dependent on the satisfaction of specified conditions.
3	**Contingently issuable ordinary shares:** Contingently issuable ordinary shares are ordinary shares issuable for little or no cash or other consideration upon the satisfaction of specified conditions in a contingent share agreement.
4	**Dilution:** Dilution is a reduction in earnings per share or an increase in loss per share resulting from the assumption that convertible instruments are converted, that options or warrants are exercised, or that ordinary shares are issued upon the satisfaction of specified conditions.
5	**Options, warrants and their equivalents:** • Options, warrants and their equivalents are financial instruments that give the holder the right to purchase ordinary shares. • Options and warrants are similar, and they give the shareholder a right but not an obligation to buy shares at an agreed price in the future. However, options are normally regulated in the traded market, i.e. the traded market sets limits, prices etc for those options whereas for warrants, they are more flexible since terms are set directly by the issuing company. • Equivalents may include employee plans where employees are granted a certain number of shares from the company as part of their remuneration. Another example is convertible bonds or convertible preference shares where the bond or preference shareholders are given a right to buy ordinary shares in the future. (IAS 33: para. 5)

9.4 *Basic Earnings Per Share (EPS)*

$$\text{Basic EPS} = \frac{\text{Net profit/(loss) attributable to ordinary shareholders}}{\text{Weighted average number of ordinary shares outstanding during the period}}$$

Numerator:

All items of income and expense attributable to ordinary equity holders of the parent entity that are recognised in a period, including tax expense and dividends on preference shares classified as liabilities are included in the determination of profit or loss for the period attributable to ordinary equity holders of the parent entity.

(IAS 33: para. 13)

This also includes redeemable preference shares dividends.

Denominator:

Weighted average number of ordinary shares on a time-weighted basis.

Examples to calculate earnings:

Example 1:

	$ m
Profit before tax	150
Tax	(30)
Profit after tax	120

Required: What are the earnings (numerator) to be included in the basic EPS calculation?

Answer: $ 120m

Example 2:

Extract from the statement of changes in equity:

	Retained earnings ($ m)
Opening balance	150
Profit for the year	120
Dividend paid	(15)
Closing balance	255

Required: What are the earnings (numerator) to be included in the basic EPS calculation?

Answer: $ 120m

Example 3:

Extract from the statement of changes in equity:

	Retained earnings
	$ m
Opening balance	150
Profit for the year	120
Dividend paid	(15)
Irredeemable preference share dividend	(10)
Closing balance	245

Required: What are the earnings (numerator) to be included in the basic EPS calculation?
Answer: $ 120m- $ 10m= $ 110m

9.5 *Treatment of Preference Dividends*

No.	Easy Rules
1	The after-tax amount of preference dividends that is deducted from profit or loss is: (a) the after-tax amount of any preference dividends on non-cumulative preference shares declared in respect of the period; and (b) the after-tax amount of the preference dividends for cumulative preference shares required for the period, whether or not the dividends have been declared. The amount of preference dividends for the period does not include the amount of any preference dividends for cumulative preference shares paid or declared during the current period in respect of previous periods. <div align="right">(IAS 33: para. 14)</div>

Example 4:

The gross profits of company A during the current year are $ 50,000. There are 30,000 10% redeemable preference shares of $ 1 each issued during the year where dividends are cumulative. The company decides to pay $ 1,200 preference shares dividends during the year.

In addition to that, there are two classes of redeemable preference shares:
Class A: 20,000 10% $ 1 each redeemable preference shares where dividends are non-cumulative. Dividends have not been declared during the year.
Class B: 10,000 5% $ 1 each redeemable preference shares where dividends are non-cumulative. Dividends have been declared during the year.

Required: Calculate the earnings to be included in the EPS calculation.
Answer:

	Gross profits	$ 50,000
	−Cumulative preference shares dividends (in full)	$ (3,000)—30,000×10%
	−Declared non-cumulative preference shares dividends	$ (500)—10,000×5%
	= Earnings	$ 46,500

Note:

Although the company pays $1,200 cumulative preference share dividends during the year, the earnings must subtract the full cumulative preference share dividends of $3,000. This means that the remaining $1,800 unpaid preference share dividends which are to be paid next year, should not be included in the next year's EPS calculation again because this has been included in the current year's EPS calculation.

The above $3,500 preference shares dividends are included in the finance costs section.

Example 5: Numerator (including NCI)

Company A owns 80% shares in company B (two years ago) and the profits after tax of company A are $100 million during the year, and the profits after tax of the company B are $30 million during the year.

Required: What are the earnings to be included in the basic RPS calculation?

Answer: $100m + 80% × $30m = $124m

This is because we need to show the profit or loss for the period attributable to ordinary equity holders of the parent entity.

(IAS 33: para. 13)

Examples to calculate the weighted average number of shares outstanding during the period:

Example 1:

On 1 January year one, the company has 100 million shares outstanding, and on 30 June year one, the business issued another 50 million shares at full market price. No further shares were issued until the year-end in year one.

Required: Calculate the weighted average number of shares outstanding in year one.

Answer:

Time	Issued shares (million)	Time portion	Total (million)
1 January–30 June	100	6/12	50
30 June–31 December	150	6/12	75
			125

Please note: the above-issued shares are assumed to be fully paid-up ordinary shares, i. e. cash is receivable when the shares are issued.

9.6 Practical Steps to Calculate the Weighted Average Number of Shares Outstanding

No.	Easy Rules
1	Ordinary shares issued as consideration for the acquisition of an asset other than cash are included as of the date on which the acquisition is recognised. [IAS 33:para. 21 (f)]

Example:

On 1 January year one, company A has 3 million ordinary shares outstanding. Company A acquired 80% shares by cash in company B on 30 June year one and agrees to exchange/issue additional 1 million shares to exchange shares in company B on 30 September year one.

Required: Calculate the weighted average number of shares outstanding in year one.

Answer:

Time	Issued shares (million)	Time portion	Total (million)
1 January–30 June	3	6/12	1.5
30 June–31 December	4 (3+1)	6/12	2
			3.5

Note: although shares will be issued on 30 September year one, we need to include the additional 1 million shares in the calculation from 30 June, i.e. at the date that the company A has control over company B.

No.	Easy Rules
2	If shares are issued but not fully paid, they are treated in the calculation of basic earnings per share as a fraction of a share, to the extent that they were entitled to participate in dividends, during the period relative to a fully-paid share. (IAS 33:Appendix A15)

Example:

On 1 January year one, a business as 1 million shares outstanding. On 1 October year one, it issued 400,000 shares and the issue price/call up price is $2 per share. However, investors only paid $0.5 per share. The balance will be paid next year.

Each partly paid share will be entitled to dividends in proportion to the percentage of the issue price paid up ($0.5/share) on the share.

Required: Calculate the weighted average number of shares outstanding.

Answer:

	Time	Issued shares (million)	Time portion	Total (million)
	1 January–1 October	1	9/12	0.75
	1 October–31 December	1.1 (1+0.1*)	3/12	0.275
				1.025

*400,000 shares × $0.5/$2 = 100,000 shares

No.	Easy Rules
3	Contingently issuable shares are treated as outstanding and are included in the calculation of basic earnings per share only from the date when all necessary conditions are satisfied (i.e. the events have occurred). Shares that are issuable solely after the passage of time are not contingently issuable shares, because the passage of time is a certainty. Outstanding ordinary shares that are contingently returnable (i.e. subject to recall) are not treated as outstanding and are excluded from the calculation of basic earnings per share until the date the shares are no longer subject to recall. Contingently issuable shares for diluted EPS calculation is different from the basic EPS calculation. For diluted EPS calculation, please see the example at the end of this chapter. (IAS 33: para. 24)

Example:

Company A operates a chain of fast food restaurants. On 1 January, the number of shares outstanding was 30,000 shares, and the year-end is 31 December.

To boost the performance, on 1 March, the board plans to issue additional 1,000 shares to senior management if the revenue growth from January to April is 5%. Additional 3,000 shares will be issued to senior management if 100 additional new restaurants are opened during the year. All these targets are met on 31 May year one.

On 31 October, the company issues 4,000 shares to senior management which are subject to recall if senior management does not serve the company during a three-year period. As at the year end, these shares are still subject to recall.

Required: Calculate the weighted average number of shares outstanding.

Answer:

Time	Issued shares	Time portion	Total
1 January–31 May	30,000	5/12	12,500
31 May–31 December	30,000+4,000=34,000	7/12	19,833
			32,333

Note:

1. Although the board agrees to the target on 1 March, those targets are met on 1 May, and therefore, we can only include the additional shares issued from 1 May onwards.

2. 4,000 shares are still subject to recall in the current year, and therefore, they should not be included in the basic EPS calculation.

9.7 Effects on EPS of Changes in Capital Structure

9.7.1 Without adjustments: A new issue of shares at full market price

No.	Easy Rules
1	If the new shares are issued at full market price, no further adjustments (fraction) are needed because in this case, the weighted average number of shares has risen and there has been a corresponding increase in resources, i.e. cash received at full market price.

Example:

At the end of August this year, the company made an issue at the full market price of 1 million ordinary shares. The year end is 31 December.

	Current year	Last year
Shares in issue as at 31 December	9 million	8 million
Earnings	$ 3.3 million	$ 3.28 million

Required: Calculate the EPS for the current and last year.

Answer:

	Current year	Last year
Earnings	$ 3.3 million	$ 3.28 million

Weighted average number of shares • Current year: 8 million × 8/12 + 9 million × 4/12 =	8.33 million	8 million
EPS	$ 0.39/share	$ 0.41/share

9.7.2 With adjustments

No.	Easy Rules
1	Further adjustments (fraction) are needed because in this case, the weighted average number of shares has risen and there has not been a corresponding increase in resources, i.e. cash is not received, or cash is received less than its full market price. Examples of these include: • Share split • Reverse share split • Bonus issue/stock dividend/capitalisation • Rights issue The number of ordinary shares outstanding before the event is adjusted for the proportionate change in the number of ordinary shares outstanding as if the event had occurred at the beginning of the earliest period presented. (IAS 33: para. 28)
2	**Share split and reverse share split:** Public limited companies may split the shares if their share prices are too high. A share split involves issuing more shares to current shareholders by increasing the number of shares outstanding. For instance, if the company currently has 2 million shares outstanding with $ 1 per share of its par value, a share split may increase the number of shares to 10 million with $ 0.2 per share of its par value. A reverse share split, on the other hand, means that if the share price of public limited companies is too low, companies may perform a reverse share split to reduce the number of shares outstanding and therefore, increase the share price. For example, if the company currently has 10 million with $ 0.2 per share of its par value perform a reverse share split to reduce the number of shares outstanding to 2 million shares with $ 1 per share of its par value. In financial accounting, there are no accounting entries needed to record a share split or a reverse share split transaction. A memorandum entry (not part of the double entry booking system) is needed to record the changes in par value and number of shares outstanding.

No.	Easy Rules
3	**Bonus issue/stock dividend/capitalisation:** This occurs when the business decides not to pay cash dividends to shareholders but give them free of charge shares instead. Accounting entry should be made regarding this transaction by reducing the share premium (if there is not enough share premium, we also need to reduce the retained earnings) and to increase the share capital. All the above transactions involve no changes to earnings during the year since the business receives no cash from the business and improve business performance. Therefore, whenever the transaction takes place, we will assume that the transaction/updated number of shares always exist at the beginning of the earliest period reported, i.e. in simple words, the updated number of shares should be used to calculate the EPS before and after the transaction date. If the number of ordinary or potential ordinary shares outstanding increases as a result of a capitalisation, bonus issue or share split, or decreases as a result of a reverse share split, the calculation of basic and diluted earnings per share for all periods presented shall be adjusted retrospectively. (IAS 33: para. 64)

Example:

Calculate the EPS for the current and last year if:

a. Outstanding number of shares this year is 2,000 shares from a stock split (1,000 shares before)

b. Outstanding number of shares this year is 1,000 shares from a reverse stock split (2,000 shares before)

c. Outstanding number of shares this year is 2,000 shares from a bonus issue of shares (1,000 shares before)

Suppose the above transactions took place in August this year.

	Current year	Last year		
Earnings	$ 1,000	$ 800		
Number of shares outstanding		a. 1,000	b. 2,000	c. 1,000
EPS		$ 0.8/share	$ 0.4/share	$ 0.8/share

Answer:

a.

	Current year	Last year
Earnings	$ 1,000	$ 800
Number of shares outstanding	2,000	2,000
EPS	$ 0.5/share	$ 0.4/share *

* An alternative way to restate the comparative EPS in last year is:

$$\frac{\$\ 0.8/\text{share} \times 1{,}000\ \text{shares (before)}}{2{,}000\ \text{shares (after)}} = \$\ 0.4/\text{share}$$

b.

	Current year	Last year
Earnings	$ 1,000	$ 800
Number of shares outstanding	1,000	1,000
EPS	$ 1/share	$ 0.8/share *

* An alternative way to restate the comparative EPS in last year is:

$$\frac{\$\ 0.4/\text{share} \times 2{,}000\ \text{shares (before)}}{1{,}000\ \text{shares (after)}} = \$\ 0.8/\text{share}$$

c.

	Current year	Last year
Earnings	$ 1,000	$ 800
Number of shares outstanding	2,000	2,000
EPS	$ 0.5/share	$ 0.4/share *

* An alternative way to restate the comparative EPS in last year is:

$$\frac{\$\ 0.8/\text{share} \times 1{,}000\ \text{shares (before)}}{2{,}000\ \text{shares (after)}} = \$\ 0.4/\text{share}$$

No.	Easy Rules
4	**Rights issue:** A rights issue of shares is an issue of new shares to existing shareholders at a price below the current market price. For instance, a company offers a 2 for 3 rights issue to existing shareholders where the current share price is $5 per share. A rights issue price may be set at $4 per share offered to existing shareholders. Therefore, in the EPS calculation, a bonus element $1 per share should be considered. Assume the business has 9,000 shares outstanding and after the rights issue, the number of issued shares would increase to 15,000 shares (9,000 shares + 9,000 shares×2/3). This means that the EPS would be further reduced because of an increase in the number of shares outstanding. Soon after the rights issue of shares takes place, the market price of each share may not reduce to $4 per share (rights issue price) given the effects of the current number of shares outstanding, additional shares issued and the current market price for each share is $5. Therefore, in the EPS calculation, we need to consider what would be the share price after the rights issue take place, and this is known as "theoretical ex-rights price". We do not use the actual ex-rights price in the calculation given the rights issue may take several months to complete. Unlike the previous share split/reverse share split/bonus issue, the rights issue of shares does enable the business to receive cash from shareholders and improve its earnings. Therefore, if the rights issue of shares takes place partway through the year, a time apportionment would be required, i.e. a bonus fraction should be calculated to divide the cum rights price into its ex-rights price, and this is illustrated later. The comparative EPS figure (last year) should also be restated.

Example: Theoretical ex-rights price:

A business has 1 million shares in issue and proposes to make a 2 for 3 rights issue at a price of $3/share. The market value of existing shares on the final day before the issue is made is $6/share (known as the "cum rights price", i.e. if investors buy a share at $6, investors will be entitled to a right ($3/share) reduction to buy new shares at $3/share).

*Please note, normally there will be a deadline that the shares will be traded with "rights", i.e. after this date, all the new shares traded will be "ex-rights".

Required: Calculate the theoretical ex-rights price per share after the rights issue take place.

Answer:

	Shares	Price	Total
New	2	$ 3/share	$ 6
Existing	3	$ 6/share	$ 18
	5		$ 24

Therefore, the theoretical ex-rights price = $ 24/5 = $ 4.8/share

Example: Fraction

From the previous example, the theoretical ex-rights price per share is $ 4.8/share, and the cum rights price per share is $ 6.

Required: Calculate the bonus fraction to be applied in the EPS calculation.

Answer:

$$\frac{\text{Cum rights price}}{\text{Ex-rights price}} = \frac{\$ 6/\text{share}}{\$ 4.8/\text{share}} = 1.25$$

This is to increase the current year's number of shares outstanding by 1.25 times (the denominator) so that the EPS would be reduced.

The last year's EPS should also be restated by reversing the bonus fraction, i.e. 1/1.25 to reduce the EPS figure in last year to enable figures more comparable.

Example: Rights issue of shares

The earnings to be used to calculate the basic EPS of company A are as follows:

Current year	$ 100,000
Last year	$ 90,000

Company A has 500,000 shares outstanding at the start of the current year and on 31 July (the year end is 31 December), it makes a 1 for 2 rights issue at a price of $ 5 per share. The market value of those shares on the final day before the issue is made is $ 8 per share.

Required: Calculate the basic EPS figures for both current and last year (restatement).

Answer: Without the rights issue, the basic EPS of the last period was:

$$\text{Basic EPS} = \frac{\text{Earnings}}{\text{Weighted average number of shares}} = \frac{\$ 90,000}{500,000 \text{ shares}} = \$ 0.18/\text{share}$$

Basic EPS this year:

Earnings = $ 100,000

Weighted average number of shares:

Time	Issued shares	Time portion	Fraction	Total
1 January–31 July	500,000	7/12	*8/7	333,333
31 July–31 December	500,000 + 500,000/2×1 = 750,000	5/12		312,500
				645,833

* Fraction = $\dfrac{\text{Cum rights price}}{\text{Ex-rights price} **} = \dfrac{8}{7}$

** Ex-rights price:

	Shares	Price	Total
New	1	$ 5	$ 5
Existing	2	$ 8	$ 16
	3		$ 21

Therefore, the theoretical ex-rights price = $ 21/3 = $ 7/share

The EPS for the current year = $ 100,000/645,833 = $ 0.15/share

The EPS for the last period (restated) = $ 0.18/share × inverse bonus fraction (7/8) = $ 0.16/share

Example: EPS after the rights issue

Continuing from the previous example, after the rights issue (year three), the earnings are $ 150,000. The number of shares outstanding after the rights issue is 750,000.

Required: Calculate the basic EPS.

Answer:

Basic EPS = $\dfrac{\text{Earnings}}{\text{Weighted average number of shares}}$ $\dfrac{\$\ 150,000}{750,000} = \$\ 0.2/\text{share}$

Please note, the weighted average number of shares to be used is the number of shares after the rights issue and in this case, 750,000 shares.

9.8 Diluted EPS

9.8.1 Treatment of convertible bonds

No.	Easy Rules
1	If a business has in issue some securities which do not currently have any claims to a share of equity earnings but may have future claims to a share of equity earnings, the EPS should be recalculated, i.e. the number of ordinary shares may increase in the future as a result of the holder converting those securities into ordinary shares. In this case, EPS is diluted, and this is known as "diluted EPS".
2	Examples of such securities: 1. **Convertible loan stock**: a business issues a convertible loan stock (normally, the coupon interest rate of such loan stocks is lower than the normal loan stocks without a conversion option in the market) which allows the holder to convert the loan stock into ordinary shares when the loan stock matures. 2. **Convertible preference shares**: a business issues a convertible preference share to investors which allows investors to convert those preference shares into ordinary shares in the future when it matures. 3. **Options or warrants**: a business issues options or warrants to investors or other stakeholders such as employees to buy its shares at an agreed price in the future, i.e. if those investors exercise options or warrants, they would then become shareholders in the business. 4. **A separate class of equity shares offered to employees which are not entitled to any dividends, but will be entitled to dividends in the future when those shares are vested**, i.e. if employees stay in business per the vesting period (say five years), then they can take those shares with them (vested shares) and leave the business (surely at this date, they are entitled to dividends). For unvested shares which are entitled to dividends, they should be considered when the diluted EPS is calculated.
3	**Adjustments to earnings**: For the purpose of calculating diluted earnings per share, an entity shall adjust profit or loss attributable to ordinary equity holders of the parent entity, by the after-tax effect of: (i) add back any dividends related to dilutive potential shares which have been deducted to calculate profits. (IAS 33: para. 33)

Example:

A business has $100,000 earnings during the year and $2 million convertible preference shares which allow the holders to convert into ordinary shares in the future. The dividends on those convertible preference shares are $9,000 before tax, and the tax rate is 30%. Those dividends are paid after tax.

Required: What is the adjusted earnings figure to be included in the dilutive EPS calculation?

Answer: Adjusted earnings = earnings + after tax dividends on convertible preference shares = $100,000 + 70% × $9,000 = $106,300.

The reason to add this back is because when those convertible preference shares are converted into ordinary shares in the future, the business could save those preference shares dividends.

No.	Easy Rules
4	**Adjustments to earnings continued:** (ii) add back any interest recognised in the period related to dilutive potential ordinary shares, i.e. interest on convertible loan stock. (IAS 33: para. 33)

Example:

A business has $200,000 earnings during the year and $50,000 8% convertible bonds which allow the bondholders to convert into ordinary shares in three years' time. The tax rate is 30%.

Required: What is the adjusted earnings figure to be included in the dilutive EPS calculation?

Answer: Adjusted earnings = earnings + after tax interest saved on those convertible bonds = $200,000 + 70% × (8% × $50,000) = $202,800

No.	Easy Rules
5	**Adjustments to earnings continued:** (iii) any other changes in income (or expense) that would result from the conversion of the dilutive potential shares. This normally takes place when a non-discretionary employee profit-sharing plan is offered. After the conversion of preference shares or bonds into ordinary shares, the profits would be adjusted (see above), and the shared profits will also be affected, i.e. it has a consequential effect. (IAS 33: para. 33)

Example:

A business has $200,000 earnings during the year and $50,000 8% convertible bonds which allow the bondholders to convert into ordinary shares in three years' time. The tax rate is 30%. A business also has a non-discretionary employee profit-sharing plan that pays 5% of its net profit annually to all eligible employees.

Required: What is the adjusted earnings figure to be included in the dilutive EPS calculation?
Answer: Adjusted earnings:

Earnings	$ 200,000
+ after tax interest saved on those convertible bonds 70%×(8%×$ 50,000) = 70%×$ 4,000 *	$ 2,800
- increase in employee sharing plan expense $ 4,000×5%×70% =	$ (140)
	$ 202,660

* A profit increase of $ 4,000 as a result of the interest saved (after tax) will increase the profits to be shared with employees.

9.8.2 Adjustments to the weighted average number of shares

No.	Easy Rules
1	The adjustment is the weighted average number of ordinary shares that would be issued on the conversion of all the dilutive potential ordinary shares (such as convertible preference shares and bonds, share options/warrants and a separate class of equity shares) into ordinary shares. It should be assumed that dilutive ordinary shares were converted into ordinary shares at the beginning of the period, or, if later, at the actual date of issue. In other words, if the dilutive ordinary shares scheme is available partway through the year, a time apportion adjustment is required. (IAS 33: para. 36)
2	If after the diluted EPS calculation, the EPS is not dilutive, i.e. it is higher than the basic EPS, the calculation is not needed/excluded. The computation assumes that most advantageous conversion rate or exercise rate from the standpoint of the holder of the potential ordinary shares. In other words, we need to show the maximum dilutive effect from the transaction. (IAS 33: para. 39)

Example: **Convertible bond (assumed the convertible bond is issued at the year end)**

A business has 6 million ordinary shares in issue, and during the year, the business also issued $ 2 million 10% convertible bonds which can be converted into ordinary shares in five years' time at a rate of five shares per $ 10 convertible bond. Earnings during the year are $ 1.2 million. Tax rate is 30%.

Required: Calculate the diluted EPS.

Answer:

Basic EPS = $\dfrac{\text{Earnings}}{\text{Weighted average number of shares}} = \dfrac{\$1.2m}{6m} = \$0.2/\text{share}$

Diluted EPS:

1. Adjustments to earnings: $\$2m \times 10\% \times 70\% = \$140,000$
2. Adjustments to weighted average number of shares: $\$2m/\$10 \times 5$ shares = 1 million shares

Diluted EPS = $\dfrac{\text{Earnings}}{\text{Weighted average number of shares}} = \dfrac{\$1.2m + \$0.14m}{6m + 1m} = \$0.19/\text{share}$

Example: EPS not diluted/Antidilution

A business has 6 million ordinary shares in issue, and during the year, the business also issued $2 million 10% convertible bonds which can be converted into ordinary shares in five years' time at a rate of three shares per $100 convertible bond. Earnings during the year are $1.2 million. Tax rate is 30%.

Required: Calculate the diluted EPS.

Answer:

Basic EPS = $\dfrac{\text{Earnings}}{\text{Weighted average number of shares}} = \dfrac{\$1.2m}{6m} = \$0.2/\text{share}$

Diluted EPS:

1. Adjustments to earnings: interest saved net of tax $\$2m \times 10\% \times 70\% = \$140,000$
2. Adjustments to weighted average number of shares: $\$2m/\$100 \times 3$ shares = 60,000 shares

Diluted EPS = $\dfrac{\text{Earnings}}{\text{Weighted average number of shares}} = \dfrac{\$1.2m + \$0.14m}{6m + 0.06m} = \$0.22/\text{share}$

Since after the calculation, the EPS is not diluted, i.e. $0.22/share is higher than the basic EPS $0.2/share (known as antidilutive) and therefore, this should be excluded from the diluted EPS calculation.

Example: Convertible bond part way through the year

Earnings during the year: $300,000

Weighted average number of shares outstanding = 1 million shares

The company issued $10,000 6% convertible bonds with each bond convertible into 20 shares of an ordinary share at par $10 on 31 August this year. The tax rate is 30%.

Required: Calculate the diluted EPS.

Answer:

Basic EPS = $\dfrac{\text{Earnings}}{\text{Weighted average number of shares}} = \dfrac{\$300,000}{1m} = \$0.3/\text{share}$

Diluted EPS:

Adjustment to earnings: interest saved net of tax = $\$100,000 \times 6\% \times 70\% \times 4/12 = \$1,400$

Adjustment to weighted average number of shares: $\$10,000/\$10 \times 20$ shares $\times 4/12 =$ 6,667 shares

$$\text{Diluted EPS} = \frac{\text{Earnings}}{\text{Weighted average number of shares}} = \frac{\$300,000 + \$1,400}{1\text{m} + 6,667} = \$0.29/\text{share}$$

Example: Most advantageous rate

The earnings of the business during the year after adjusting the interest saved net of tax of a convertible bond are $5 million.

In the basic EPS calculation, the weighted average number of shares is 1 million. The convertible bond contains the following conversion rights:

If the bond is converted in two year's time: 5 shares per $100 bond

If the bond is converted in three year's time: 3 shares per $100 bond

If the bond is converted in four year's time: 2 shares per $100 bond

Required: Calculate the diluted EPS.

Answer: Adjustment to weighted average number of shares: $5\text{m} / \$100 \times 5$ shares = 250,000 shares

Because the number of shares will be maximised if the calculation is based on the right "converted in two year's time".

$$\text{Diluted EPS} = \frac{\text{Earnings}}{\text{Weighted average number of shares}} = \frac{\$5\text{m}}{1\text{m} + 0.25\text{m}} = \$4/\text{share}$$

9.8.3 Treatment of options

No.	Easy Rules
1	Options and warrants are dilutive when they would result in the issue of ordinary shares for less than the average market price of ordinary shares during the period. The amount of dilution is the average market price of ordinary shares during the period minus the issue price. Therefore, to calculate diluted earnings per share, potential ordinary shares are treated as consisting of both the following: a) a contract to issue a certain number of the ordinary shares at their average market price during the period. Such ordinary shares are assumed to be fairly priced and to be neither dilutive (EPS is diluted if the exercise price/issue price is less than its fair value) nor antidilutive (because the issue price is up to the fair value). They are ignored in the calculation of diluted earnings per share. b) a contract to issue the remaining ordinary shares for no consideration. Such ordinary shares generate no proceeds and have no effect on profit or loss attributable to ordinary shares outstanding. Therefore, such shares are dilutive and are added to the number of ordinary shares outstanding in the calculation of diluted earnings per share. (IAS 33: para. 46)

No.	Easy Rules
2	**Adjustment to the denominator:** Number of options × $\dfrac{|\text{Exercise price (Issue price)} - \text{Fair value}|}{\text{Fair value}}$
3	**Time apportionment:** Similar to convertibles before, if the option is granted part way through the year, a time apportionment adjustment is needed.

Example: Share option

The following information relates to company A during the year:

Earnings: $ 1 million

Weighted average number of shares outstanding during the year: 2 million shares

Company A grants 200,000 options to employees to buy shares at an agreed price in the future with one option to buy one share.

The exercise price for shares under option during the year is $ 3 per share, where the average market price/fair value of each share during the year is $ 7 per share.

Required: Calculate the basic and diluted EPS.

Answer:

Basic EPS $= \dfrac{\text{Earnings}}{\text{Weighted average number of shares}} = \dfrac{\$\ 1m}{2m} = \$\ 0.5/\text{share}$

Diluted EPS $= \dfrac{\text{Earnings}}{\text{Weighted average number of shares}} = \dfrac{\$\ 1m}{2m + 114{,}286\ *} = \$\ 0.47/\text{share}$

* Adjustment:

Number of options × $\dfrac{\text{Exercise price (Issue price)} - \text{Fair value}}{\text{Fair value}} = 200{,}000 \times \dfrac{|\$\ 3 - \$\ 7|}{\$\ 7} = 114{,}286$

To explain:

200,000 options or shares should have been bought at $ 7 per share, i.e. $ 1.4 million in total, but now per the exercise price of $ 3/share, employees only need to spend $ 600,000 to buy those shares. In essence, employees can save $ 800,000 or can get 114,286 free shares ($ 800,000/$ 7 per share).

Example: Share option with time weighting adjustment

Taken from the previous example, suppose the business granted options to employees on 31 March during the year and the year end is 31 December.

Required: Calculate the diluted EPS.

Answer:

Diluted EPS $= \dfrac{\text{Earnings}}{\text{Weighted average number of shares}} = \dfrac{\$\ 1m}{2m + 114{,}286 \times 9/12} = \$\ 0.48/\text{share}$

Example: Share option with exercise price being the average fair value of each share

The following information relates to company A during the year:

Earnings: $ 1 million

Weighted average number of shares outstanding during the year: 2 million shares

Company A grants 200,000 options to employees to buy shares at an agreed price in the future with one option to buy one share.

The exercise price for shares under option during the year is $ 3 per share, where the average market price/fair value of each share during the year is $ 3 per share.

Required: Calculate the basic and diluted EPS.

Answer: The EPS is not diluted in this case because the exercise price of each share is the same as the market price.

9.8.4 Contingently issuable shares

No.	Easy Rules
1	As in the calculation of basic earnings per share, contingently issuable ordinary shares are treated as outstanding and included in the calculation of diluted earnings per share if the conditions are satisfied (i.e. the events have occurred).
2	Contingently issuable shares are included from the beginning of the period (or from the date of the contingent share agreement, if later).
3	If the conditions are not satisfied, the number of contingently issuable shares included in the diluted earnings per share calculation is based on the number of shares that would be issuable if the end of the period were the end of the contingency period.
4	Restatement is not permitted if the conditions are not met when the contingency period expires. (IAS 33: para. 52-57)

Example:

The earnings of the company A were $ 4 million with 3 million ordinary shares outstanding from 1 January year one.

In year 0, the company grants shares (potential ordinary shares) to its finance director that if at the end of the year two, the cumulative profits for the three years reach $ 7 million, additional 300,000 shares will be issued.

The net profits for the year 0 were $ 3.5 million. Therefore, the cumulative earnings for the first two years are $ 7.5 million.

Required: Calculate the dilutive EPS.

Answer: The contingently issuable ordinary shares, in this case, is not affecting basic EPS because these shares are potentially issuable.

When it becomes issuable? This is when the first two years result is available, i.e. $ 7.5 million cumulative earnings exceeding $ 7 million targets.

So the additional 300,000 shares should be included in the diluted EPS calculation from the beginning of the period, i.e. from 1 January year one:

$$\text{Diluted EPS} = \frac{\text{Earnings}}{\text{Weighted average number of shares}} = \frac{\$ 4m}{3m + 0.3m} = \$ 1.2/\text{share}$$

9.8.5 Presentation, disclosure and other matters

9.8.5.1 Presentation

No.	Easy Rules
1	An entity shall present in the statement of comprehensive income basic and diluted earnings per share for profit or loss from continuing operations attributable to the ordinary equity holders of the parent entity and for profit or loss attributable to the ordinary equity holders of the parent entity for the period for each class of ordinary shares that has a different right to share in profit for the period. An entity shall present basic and diluted earnings per share with equal prominence for all periods presented.
2	Earnings per share are presented for every period for which a statement of comprehensive income is presented. If diluted earnings per share is reported for at least one period, it shall be reported for all periods presented, even if it equals basic earnings per share. If basic and diluted earnings per share are equal, dual presentation can be accomplished in one line in the statement of comprehensive income.
3	An entity that reports a discontinued operation shall disclose the basic and diluted amounts per share for the discontinued operation either in the statement of comprehensive income or in the notes. An entity shall present basic and diluted earnings per share, even if the amounts are negative (i.e. a loss per share). <div align="right">(IAS 33: para. 66, 67, 68, 69)</div>

Example:

	Notes	52 weeks ended 23 February 2019			52 weeks ended 24 February 2018 (restated*)		
		Before exceptional items and amortisation of acquired intangibles £m	Exceptional Items and amortisation of acquired intangibles (Note 4) £m	Total £m	Before exceptional items and amortisation of acquired intangibles £m	Exceptional Items and amortisation of acquired intangibles (Note 4) £m	Total £m
Continuing operations							
Revenue	2	63,911	-	63,911	57,493	-	57,493
Cost of sales		(59,695)	(72)	(59,767)	(54,092)	(49)	(54,141)
Gross profit/(loss)		4,216	(72)	4,144	3,401	(49)	3,352
Administrative expenses		(1,989)	(86)	(2,076)	(1,786)	153	(1,633)
Profits/(losses) arising on property-related items		(21)	105	84	31	89	120
Operating profit/(loss)		2,206	(53)	2,152	1,646	193	1,839
Share of post-tax profits/(losses) of joint ventures and associates	13	24	11	35	(6)	-	(6)
Finance income	5	22	-	22	67	-	67
Finance costs	5	(536)	-	(536)	(562)	(38)	(600)
Profit/(loss) before tax		1,716	(42)	1,673	1,145	155	1,300
Taxation	6	(413)	59	(354)	(286)	(20)	(306)
Profit/(loss) for the year from continuing operations		1,303	17	1,319	859	135	994
Discontinued operations							
Profit/(loss) for the year from discontinued operations	7	-	-	-	-	216	216
Profit/(loss) for the year		1,303	17	1,319	859	351	1,210
Attributable to:							
Owners of the parent		1,305	17	1,322	859	359	1,208
Non-controlling interests		(2)	-	(3)	-	8	2
		1,303	17	1,319	859	351	1,210
Earnings/(losses) per share from continuing and discontinued operations							
Basic	9			13.65p			14.80p
Diluted	9			13.55p			17.75p
Earnings/(losses) per share from continuing operations							
Basic	9			13.65p			12.15p
Diluted	9			13.55p			12.11p

(Annual report from Tesco plc)

9.8.5.2 Disclosure

1	The amounts used as the numerators in calculating basic and diluted earnings per share, and a reconciliation of those amounts to profit or loss attributable to the parent entity for the period. The reconciliation shall include the individual effect of each class of instruments that affects earnings per share. (IAS 33: para. 70)
2	The weighted average number of ordinary shares used as the denominator in calculating basic and diluted earnings per share and a reconciliation of these denominators to each other. The reconciliation shall include the individual effect of each class of instruments that affects earnings per share. (IAS 33: para. 70)

Example:

Note 9 Earnings/(losses) per share and diluted earnings/(losses) per share
Basic earnings/(losses) per share amounts are calculated by dividing the profit/(loss) attributable to owner's of the parent by the weighted average number of ordinary shares in issue during the financial year.
Diluted earnings/(losses) per share amounts are calculated by dividing the profit/(loss) attributable to owners of the parent by the weighted average number of ordinary shares in issue during the financial year adjusted for the effects of potentially dilutive options. The dilutive effect is calculated on the full exercise of all potentially dilutive ordinary share options granted by the Group, including performance-based options which the Group considers to have been earned.
For the 52 weeks ended 23 February 2019 there were 72 million (2018: 27 million) potentially dilutive share options. As the Group has recognised a profit for the year from its continuing operations, dilutive effects have been considered in calculating diluted earnings per share.

	2019			2018 (restated)		
	Basic	Potentially dilutive share options	Diluted	Basic	Potentially dilutive share options	Diluted
Profit/(loss) (£m)						
Continuing operations*	1,322	-	1,322	992	-	992
Discontinued operations	-	-	-	216	-	216
Total	1,322	-	1,322	1,208	-	1,208
Weighted average number of shares (millions)	9,686	72	9,758	8,165	27	8,192
Earnings/(losses) per share (pence)						
Continuing operations	13.65	(0.10)	13.55	12.15	(0.04)	12.11
Discontinued operations	-	-	-	2.65	(0.01)	2.64
Total	13.65	(0.10)	13.55	14.80	(0.05)	14.75

* Excludes profits/(losses) from non-controlling interests of £(2)m (2018; £2m).

9.9 *Alternative EPS Figures*

No.	Easy Rules
1	If an entity discloses, in addition to basic and diluted earnings per share, amounts per share using a reported component of the statement of comprehensive income other than one required by this Standard, such amounts shall be calculated using the weighted average number of ordinary shares determined in accordance with this Standard. (IAS 33: para. 73)
2	Basic and diluted amounts per share relating to such a component shall be disclosed with equal prominence and presented in the notes. (IAS 33: para. 73)
3	An entity shall indicate the basis on which the numerator(s) is (are) determined, including whether amounts per share are before tax or after tax. (IAS 33: para. 73)

No.	Easy Rules
4	Examples can be: • EBITDA per share • Retained earnings per share • Operating cash flows per share

9.10 *Significance of Earnings Per Share*

No.	Easy Rules
1	EPS can be used to value a share. For instance, the EPS of a company can be used to multiply by its P/E ratio (price earnings ratio).
2	Reported and forecast EPS can have an impact on its share price. For instance, public limited companies would forecast its upcoming quarterly earnings per share figure in its interim Financial Statements, and such announcement has an impact on the share price (a low EPS may drag the share price down).
3	However, the EPS figure can be easily manipulated by the business. For instance, the earnings in the EPS calculation (numerator) can be manipulated by choice of accounting policies and estimates. The denominator (weighted average number of shares) can be affected by the business buying back shares or issuing additional shares (changes in capital structure such as bonus, rights issue of shares or issuing convertibles or options). Therefore, EPS in different companies are not directly comparable.
4	EPS can be used to assess the stewardship and management of the business by revealing its performance over the past periods. For instance, if the management remuneration is linked with the EPS figure, the management might distort results to achieve a favourable EPS. Alternatively, the management might hold back certain profitable projects by not reporting them in the forecast given the current quarterly EPS target is met, but to release the news or start the project only after the current reporting period.

Chapter 10

IAS 8 Accounting Policies, Changes in Accounting Estimates and Errors

Topic outline:

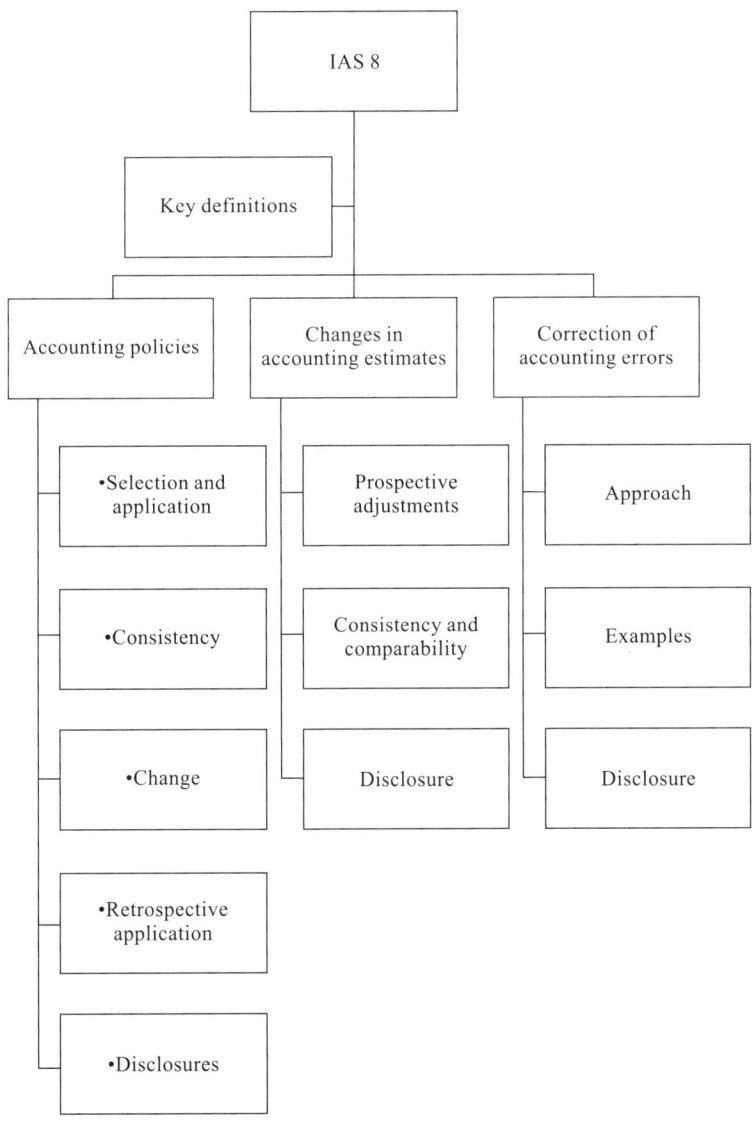

10.1 *Key Definitions*

No.	Easy Rules
1	**Accounting policies**: Accounting policies are the specific principles, bases, conventions, rules and practices applied by an entity in preparing and presenting financial statements.
2	**Principles**: These are generally accepted accounting principles (GAAP) or IFRS. For instance, per IAS 2 Inventories, inventories should be measured at the lower of cost and net realisable value. However, in some standards, such as in IAS 2 inventories, if items are interchangeable, the costs can be measured using FIFO or weighted average cost methods.
3	**Bases**: This refers to the measurement bases of items such as items measured at cost or fair value.
4	**Conventions**: In some cases, the GAAP/IFRS may not have specific guidance on how the transaction should be recorded. Therefore, it may be useful for the entity to refer to the conventions of other standard setting process of how the transaction should be dealt with. For instance, first class artwork accounting treatment is not covered in the IFRS, however, the entity can refer to the conventions adopted by other companies, i.e. UK GAAP FRS 30 Heritage Assets covers this area.
5	**Rules**: These are the rules or requirements the company must follow. For instance, Financial Statements are in accordance with the Companies Act 2006 in the UK.
6	**Practices**: These are the market practices that the company adopts. For instance: • The escalation clause in the lease contract includes inflation referring to the market rents. • Tobacco inventories which have an operating cycle that exceeds 12 months are classified as current assets, consistent with recognised industry practice • Pension increases, which allowed for, are generally assumed to be in line with inflation. Assumptions of life expectancy are in line with best practice in each territory. (IAS 8: para. 5)

10.2 *Selection and Application of Accounting Policies*

1	If a standard or interpretation (IAS, IFRS, IFRSIC (new term) and SIC (old term)) deals with a transaction, use that standard or interpretation. For instance, the treatment of the website cost is covered in detail in SIC 32 Intangible Assets-Web Site Costs.
2	If no standard or interpretation deals with a transaction, judgment should be applied by considering the following sources in descending order: • the requirements in IFRSs dealing with similar and related issues. • the definitions, recognition criteria and measurement concepts for assets, liabilities, income and expenses in the Framework. • the most recent pronouncements of other standard-setting bodies that use a similar conceptual framework to develop accounting standards, other accounting literature and accepted industry practices, to the extent that these do not conflict with the above sources. (IAS 8:para. 11)

10.3 *Consistency of Accounting Policies*

No.	Easy Rules
1	An entity shall select and apply its accounting policies consistently for similar transactions, other events and conditions, unless an IFRS specifically requires or permits categorisation of items for which different policies may be appropriate. If an IFRS requires or permits such categorisation, an appropriate accounting policy shall be selected and applied consistently to each category. For instance, all items in the same PP&E category adopt cost model whilst all items in another PP&E category adopt revaluation model per IAS 16. (IAS 8:para. 13)

10.4 Change in Accounting Policy

No.	Easy Rules
1	An entity shall change an accounting policy only if the change: a) is required by an IFRS; or (1) If change is due to new standard/interpretation, apply transitional provisions. (2) If no transitional provisions, apply retrospectively. • If it is impractical to determine period-specific effects or cumulative effects of the change, then retrospectively apply to the earliest period that is practicable. For instance, the change from the cost model to revaluation model to PP&E under IAS 16 does not require retrospective restatements. b) results in the financial statements providing reliable and more relevant information about the effects of transactions, other events or conditions on the entity's financial position, financial performance or cash flows. For instance, to match the physical flow of the sale of inventories, the business may change the measurement of the inventories cost flow from weighted average method to FIFO method.
2	**The following situations are not changes in accounting policies:** a) the application of an accounting policy for transactions, other events or conditions that differ in substance from those previously occurring (this means in substance, it is the first time that the transaction takes place. For instance, the reclassification of investment properties to inventories due to a change in purpose); and b) the application of a new accounting policy for transactions, other events or conditions that did not occur previously (transaction takes place for the first time) or were immaterial (does not involve a material change in the amount). (IAS 8: para. 16)

10.5 Retrospective Application

No.	Easy Rules
1	Retrospective application is applying a new accounting policy to transactions, other events and conditions as if that policy had always been applied. (IAS 8: para. 5)

No.	Easy Rules
2	A change in the measurement, presentation or recognition of an item in the Financial Statements would be seen as a change in accounting policy. • Measurement: 　-FIFO/Average cost of inventories; 　-Net off method or deferral method to account for government grant; 　-Cost or fair value model to measure investment properties. • Presentation: depreciation expense can either be presented in the costs of sales or administrative expense. • Recognition: adoption of IAS 23 borrowing costs to capitalise interest expenses as assets instead of expensing them if these costs meet with the criteria in the standard.

Example:

The company changes the inventory valuation method from FIFO to weighted average cost in year three because this provides reliable and more relevant information about the effects of transaction with the introduction of the new computerised system. Below are the statement of profit or loss before retrospective adjustments applied:

	Year three $ 000	Year two $ 000
Revenue	500	400
Costs of sales	(200)	(160)
Gross profit	300	240
Other expenses	(170)	(130)
Profits	130	110

The retained earnings as at the start of year two was $ 600,000, and the ending retained earnings balance was $ 710,000. The impact on inventory because of the change in accounting policy was calculated as follows:
- Inventory as at the end of year one: an increase of $ 20,000
- Inventory as at the end of year two: an increase of $ 30,000
- Inventory as at the end of year three: an increase of $ 40,000

Required: Show how the accounting policy change impacts on the year three and year two Financial Statements and prepare the comparative Financial Statements.

Answer:

Revised statement of profit or loss:

	Year three $ **000**	Year two $ **000**
Revenue	500	400
Costs of sales *	(190)	(150)
Gross profit	310	250
Other expenses	(170)	(130)
Profits	140	120

Please note: A retrospective application should be applied to all comparative Financial Statements before year three due to a change in accounting policy. In this example, we are only required to prepare comparative accounts in year two.

* Costs of sales:

	Year three $ **000**	Year two $ **000**
Per unadjusted P/L	200	160
Opening inventory adjustment	30	20
Closing inventory adjustment	(40)	(30)
Adjusted figures	190	150

Statement of changes in equity:

	Year three $ **000**	Year two $ **000**
Opening retained earnings	710	600
Retrospective application due to changes in accounting policy **	30	20
	740	620
Revised profits	140	120
Closing retained earnings	880	740

** Retrospective application:

	Year three $ 000	Year two $ 000
Increase in opening inventories	(20)	-
Increase in closing inventories	30	20
Cumulative increase in profits	10 − **30** (20+10)-adjustment in year three opening retained earnings	**20**-adjustment in year two opening retained earnings

10.6 Disclosures

No.	Easy Rules
1	(1) The title of the standard / interpretation that caused the change (2) Nature of the change in policy (3) Description of the transitional provisions (4) For the current period and each prior period presented, the amount of the adjustmentto: • Each line item affected • Earnings per share. (5) The amount of the adjustment relating to periods before those presented, to the extent practicable (6) If the retrospective application is impracticable, explain and describe how the change in policy was applied. Subsequent periods need not repeat these disclosures. (IAS 8: para. 28)

10.7 Comparability

No.	Easy Rules
1	Retrospective application mains the comparability principle enabling users of Financial Statements to assess the performance and position of the entity over time on a consistent basis.

10.8 *Changes in Accounting Estimates*

No.	Easy Rules
1	A change in an accounting estimate is an adjustment of the carrying amount of an asset or liability, or related expense, resulting from reassessing the expected future benefits and obligations associated with the asset or liability. Changes in accounting estimates result from new information or new developments and, accordingly, are not corrections of errors. (IAS 8:para.5)
2	Examples include: • Useful lives of depreciable assets • The residual value of PP&E • Depreciation methods of PP&E • Amortisation methods of intangible assets • Irrecoverable debts allowances • Determining the net realisable value of inventories • Warranty provisions • Changes in tax rates • Changes in fair value of financial assets or liabilities • Changes in foreign exchange rates

10.9 *Prospective Adjustments*

No.	Easy Rules
1	The effect of a change in an accounting estimate shall be recognised prospectively by including it in profit or loss in: a) the period of the change, if the change affects that period only (i.e. irrecoverable debt expense only affects the current year's statement of profit or loss); or b) the period of the change and future periods, if the change affects both (i.e. changes in depreciation method impacts both current year and future year's statement of profit or loss). (IAS 8:para.36)

10.10 *Consistency and Comparability*

No.	Easy Rules
1	The effect of a change in accounting estimates should be included in the same expense classification as was used previously for the estimate for consistency and comparability reasons.

10.11 *Disclosure*

No.	Easy Rules
1	Nature and amount of change that has an effect on the current period (or expected to have in future).
2	The fact that the effect of future periods is not disclosed because of impracticality. For instance, given the foreign exchange rate fluctuates significantly in recent periods, the estimate of the changes in exchange rate in the future periods are impractical to be disclosed.

(IAS 8: para. 39-40)

Example of changes in accounting estimate:

A business acquired a piece of PP&E three years ago for $ 200,000 with a useful economic life of 10 years. At the end of the third year, the directors determined that the remaining asset life should be revised to only 5 years.

Required: Accounting treatment for the change in accounting estimate in year four.

Answer:

At the end of the third year, the carrying value of the PP&E is:

$ 200,000 - $ 200,000 /10 years×3 years = $ 140,000

At the end of the third year, the useful economic life has been revised to 5 years and therefore, the depreciation charge per year should be:

$ 140,000/5 years = $ 28,000 from year 4 onwards.

Dr	Depreciation expense		$ 28,000
Cr	Accumulated depreciation		$ 28,000

10.12 Correction of Accounting Errors

No.	Easy Rules
1	Prior period errors are omissions from, and misstatements in, the entity's financial statements for one or more prior periods arising from a failure to use, or misuse of, reliable information that: a) was available when financial statements for those periods were authorised for issue; and b) could reasonably be expected to have been obtained and taken into account in the preparation and presentation of those financial statements (not a change in accounting estimate). (IAS 8: para. 5)
2	**Errors include:** • Mistakes of accounting policies application: i. e. not recognising sale revenue at the point of sale per IFRS 15 • Fraud: i. e. overstating sales revenue by issuing fake invoices before the reporting date • Misunderstanding of, or failure to notice, information at the time of preparation of financial statements/Misinterpretation of facts: i. e. not writing off a receivable from a credit customer who had announced as insolvent before the authorisation of financial statements • Mathematical errors • Omission of transactions and events from the financial statements
3	**Approach:** Retrospective restatement: correcting the recognition, measurement and disclosure of amounts of elements of financial statements as if a prior period error had never occurred. (IAS 8: para. 5) Restate the comparative amounts for prior periods in which error occurred or if the error occurred before that date-restate opening balance of assets, liabilities and equity for the earliest period presented. When it is impracticable to determine the period-specific effects of an error on comparative information for one or more prior periods presented, the entity shall restate the opening balances of assets, liabilities and equity for the earliest period for which retrospective restatement is practicable (which may be the current period). (IAS 8: para. 44) For instance, the fair value of the land may be wrongly stated in two years ago due to management fraud, and it is impractical to determine what is the correct fair value amount for that land when the error is found. In this case, an entity can correct an error prospectively.

10.13 *Disclosure*

No.	Easy Rules
1	1. Nature of the prior period error. 2. For each prior period presented, if practicable, disclose the correction to. 3. Each line item affected. 4. Earnings per share (EPS). • Amount of the correction at the beginning of the earliest period presented • If a retrospective application is impracticable, explain and describe how the error was corrected 5. Subsequent periods need not repeat these disclosures. (IAS 8: para. 49)

Example:

During year two, the business found out that certain inventories have been sold in year one, but they have been incorrectly included in as inventories in year one at $6,500.

The statement of profit or loss for year one and two are as follows:

	Year two $ 000	Year one $ 000
Revenue	104,000	73,500
Costs of sales	(86,500)	(53,500)
Profits before tax	17,500	20,000
Tax expenses	(5,250)	(6,000)
Profits after tax	12,250	14,000

In year one, the opening retained earnings was $20,000 and closing retained earnings were $34,000. The corporation tax rate is 30%.

Required: Show how the retrospective restatement (correcting period errors) should be recorded in the accounts in year two with comparatives prepared.

Answer:

Statement of profit or loss:

	Year two $ 000	Year one $ 000
Revenue	104,000	73,500
Costs of sales	(80,000)	(60,000)
Profits before tax	24,000	13,500
Tax expenses	(7,200)	(4,050)
Profits after tax	16,800	9,450

Statement of changes in equity:

	Year two $ 000	Year one $ 000
Opening retained earnings	34,000	20,000
Retrospective restatement • profits after tax difference (net of tax): $ 14,000 – $ 9,450	(4,550)	—
	29,450	20,000
Profits after tax	16,800	9,450
Closing retained earnings	46,250	29,450

The journal entry to correct the accounting error:

Dr	Costs of sales	$ 6,500
Cr	Inventories	$ 6,500

The adjustment to the year two opening retained earnings is net of tax.

Chapter 11

Taxation

Topic outline:

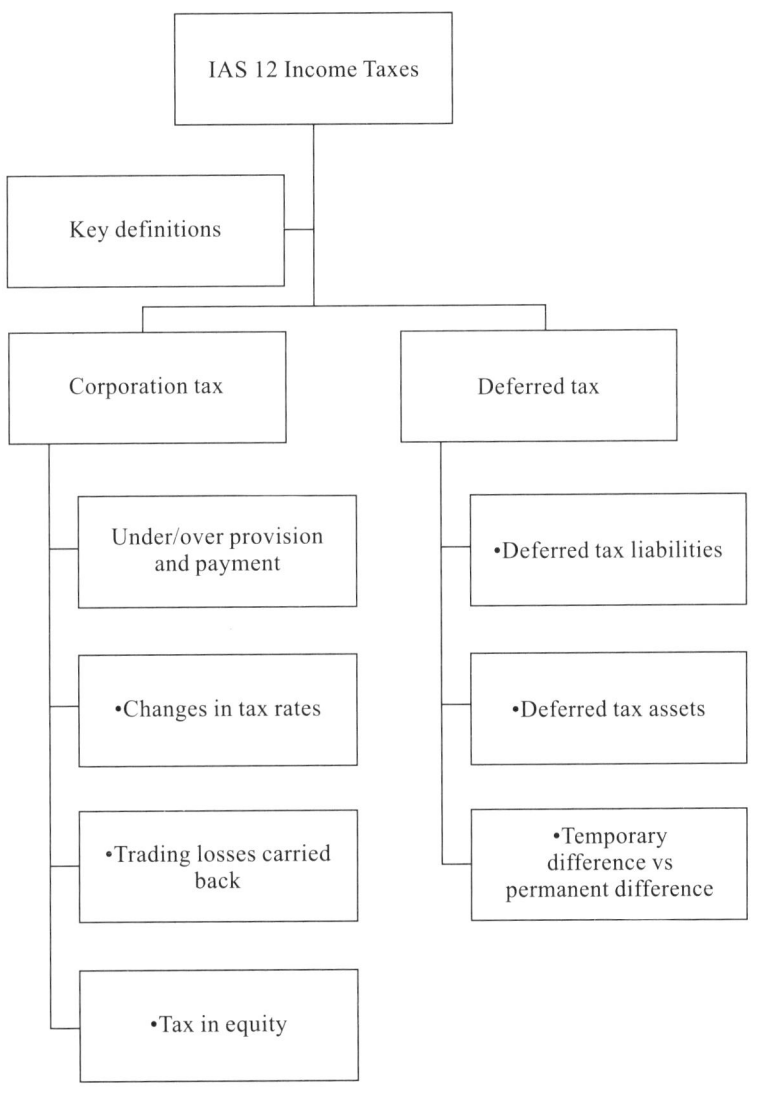

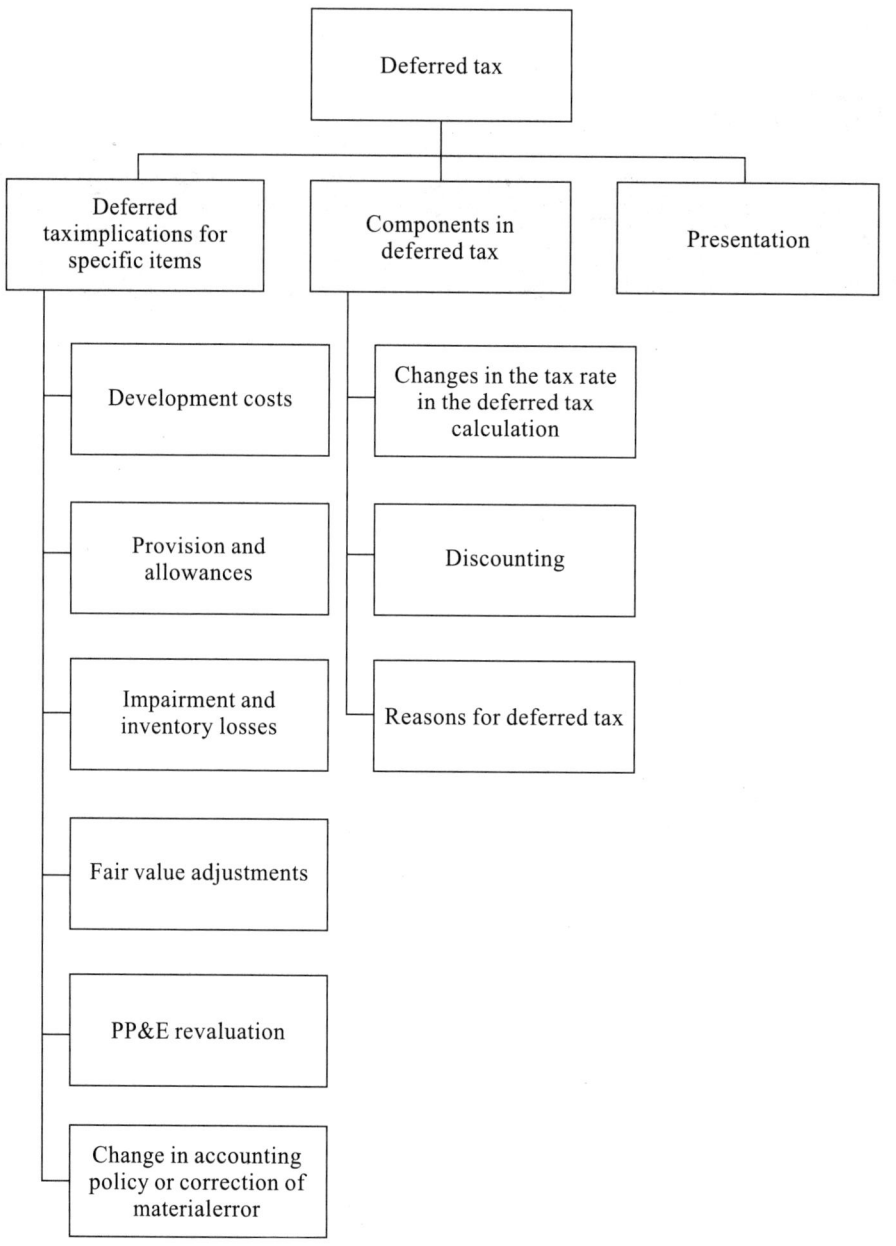

11.1 *Key Definitions*

No.	Easy Rules
1	**Current tax:** This is the amount of income taxes payable or recoverable in respect of the taxable profits or losses for a period. (IAS 12:para. 5)
2	**Taxable Profits Calculation** Taxable profit (tax loss) is the profit (loss) for a period, determined in accordance with the rules established by the taxation authorities, upon which income taxes are payable (recoverable). (IAS 12:para. 5) In other words, taxable profits are calculated based on the accounting profit, i.e. the profit before tax figure. To calculate the taxable profit, businesses need to start with the profit before tax, and adjust any income exempt from tax, as well as expenses disallowed for tax purposes.

11.2 *Accounting Treatment for Corporation Tax*

No.	Easy Rules
1	As at the year end, the business needs to estimate what will be the total tax due or owed to the tax authority. The business may have a tax accountant who computes the corporation tax to be paid in the form of the tax return, and the financial accountant then needs to record this transaction in the Financial Statements. For instance, the estimated corporation tax to be paid to the tax authority is $58,900. The journal entry is as follows: **Dr** Corporation income tax expense (P/L) $58,900 **Cr** Current tax payable (SFP) $58,900

11.3 *Underpayment of Corporation Tax*

No.	Easy Rules
1	Suppose the tax authority checks the company's tax return and finds out that the company has underpaid $500 in respect of the last year's profit. The business should then make the following journal entry in the current year's Financial Statements: **Dr** Corporation income tax expense (P/L)　　$500 **Cr** Current tax payable (SFP)　　$500

11.4 *Over Payment of Corporation Tax*

No.	Easy Rules
1	Suppose the business has overpaid $500 tax regarding the last year's profit. The journal entry is as follows: **Dr** Current tax payable (SFP)　　$500 **Cr** Corporation income tax expense (P/L)　　$500 The overpayment of tax results in a decrease in the tax liability and expense by $500. Current tax for current and prior periods shall, to the extent unpaid, be recognised as a liability. If the amount already paid in respect of current and prior periods exceeds the amount due for those periods, the excess shall be recognised as an asset. (IAS 12: para. 12)

11.5 *Payment to the Tax Authority*

No.	Easy Rules
1	When the $59,400 tax payment is settled, the following entry should be made: **Dr** Current tax payable (SFP)　　$59,400 **Cr** Bank (SFP)　　$59,400 This is to reduce the tax liability due and the bank asset by $59,400. In the UK, payment to the tax authority could be made by online or telephone banking, BACS transfer or direct debit.

11.6 Tax Rates or Tax Laws Which Are Enacted or Substantively Enacted

No.	Easy Rules
1	Current/Deferred tax liabilities (assets) for the current and prior periods shall be measured at the amount expected to be paid to (recovered from) the taxation authorities, using the tax rates (and tax laws) that have been enacted or substantively enacted by the end of the reporting period. (IAS 12:para. 46–47)
2	Suppose from the above example, the accounting year end is 31st December, and on 30th September, the tax authority has announced that the new corporation tax rate is to be revised to 18% from 5th January next year onwards. Therefore, when estimating the total tax expense for the current period, the new tax rate of 18% should be used, because the new tax rate has been substantively enacted or announced by the end of the reporting period. In the UK, the tax rate is set for each year from 1 April, in the Finance Act usually prior to this date.

11.7 Trading Losses Carried Back

No.	Easy Rules
1	The benefit relating to a tax loss that can be carried back to recover current tax of a previous period shall be recognised as an asset. (IAS 12:para. 13)

Example: Trading losses carried back

In the current year, the business incurred $ 30,000 trading losses. According to the tax law, trading losses can be carried back to offset against the previous year's trading profit. Assume the last year trading profit was $ 50,000 and the corporation tax rate 20%; the tax benefit can be calculated by using the current year's trading losses of $ 30,000 and multiplying this by 20%, to give $ 6,000.

Required: Explain the accounting treatment.

Answer: The following journal for the tax benefit is made:

Dr	Current tax receivable (SFP)	$ 6,000
Cr	Current tax payable (SFP)	$ 6,000

The debit side represents the current asset, i. e. tax receivables asset in the statement of financial position. And this means that the company expects to collect the tax refund from the tax authority, normally within one year. The tax refund is based on the amount of tax the company has paid in the previous year's account. The business must have reduced its tax liability in the previous year's account when the tax liability was settled. Because the business now expects to collect the tax refund, this means that the liability should not exist in the first place. Therefore, we need to reverse or credit the current tax payable liability of $ 6,000.

When the tax benefit is received, the following accounting journal entry should be made:

Dr	Bank (SFP)	$ 6,000
Cr	Current tax receivable (SFP)	$ 6,000

11.8 *Trial Balance Where the Under or Over Provision of Corporation Tax Is Shown*

	Dr	Cr
Taxation	Under provision	(Over) provision

Example:

As at the end of year one, the business estimates its tax liability to be $ 1 million. The trial balance below shows the amount of corporation tax under or over provided relating to profits in the last period.

	Dr	Cr
Taxation		$ 300,000

Required: Accounting treatment.
Answer:
As at the year end:

Dr	Income tax expense	$ 1m
Cr	Current tax payable	$ 1m

Over provision:

Dr	Current tax payable	$ 0.3m
Cr	Income tax expense	$ 0.3m

11.9 Tax Directly in Equity

No.	Easy Rules
1	The item to be charged directly to equity includes an adjustment to the opening balance of retained earnings resulting from either a change in accounting policy that is applied retrospectively or the correction of an error. (IAS 12:para 62 A)

Example:

In year two, the business changed its accounting policy regarding the treatment of borrowing costs that are directly attributable to the construction of a self-construction asset. In year one, the business expensed such costs, following the allowed treatment in IAS 23 Borrowing Costs. IAS 23 now states the business must capitalise these costs.

The business had borrowing costs in year two to be $ 2,600 and $ 5,200 in prior periods. The business's accounting records for year two and year one show:

	Year two $	Year one $
Operating profits	30,000	18,000
Finance costs	—	(2,600)
Profit before tax	30,000	15,400
Income tax	(9,000)	(4,620)
Profit after tax	21,000	10,780

In year one, opening retained earnings were $ 20,000 and closing retained earnings were $ 30,780. The income tax rate is 30%.

Required: Show how a change in accounting policy would impact on the Financial Statements.

Answer:

Statement of profit or loss:

	Year two $	Year one $
Operating profits	30,000	18,000
Finance costs	—	—
Profit before tax	30,000	18,000
Income tax	(9,000)	(5,400)
Profit after tax	21,000	12,600

Statement of changes in equity:

	Year two $	Year one $
Opening retained earnings	30,780	20,000
Restatement (change in accounting policy) Year 1: $ 5,200×(1−30%: net of tax) = $ 3,640 Year 2: ($ 2,600+ $ 5,200)×(1−30%: net of tax) = $ 5,460	5,460	3,640
	36,240	23,640
Profit for the year	21,000	12,600
Closing retained earnings	57,240	36,240

11.10 Deferred Tax

No.	Easy Rules
1	Deferred tax is an accounting measure to match the transaction's tax effect with its accounting impact.

No.	Easy Rules
2	**Tax base of assets:** The tax base of an asset is the amount that will be deductible for tax purposes against any taxable economic benefits that will flow to an entity when it recovers the carrying amount of the asset. If those economic benefits will not be taxable, the tax base of the asset is equal to its carrying amount. (IAS 12: para. 7)

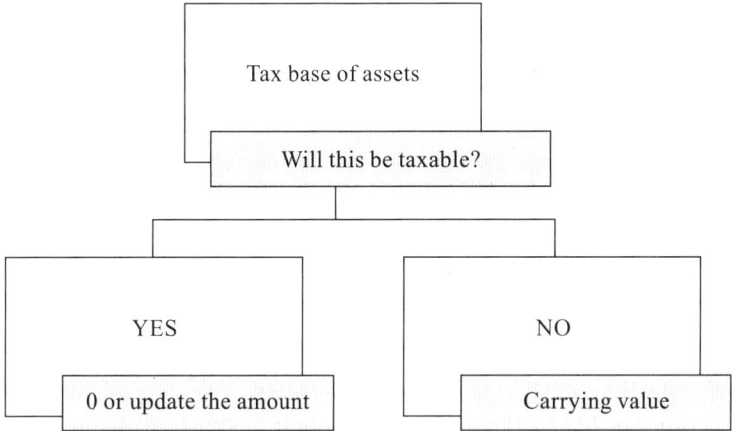

No.	Easy Rules
3	**Tax base of liabilities:** The tax base of a liability is its carrying amount, less any amount that will be deductible for tax purposes in respect of that liability in future periods. In the case of revenue which is received in advance, the tax base of the resulting liability is its carrying amount, less any amount of the revenue that will not be taxable in future periods. (IAS 12: para. 8)

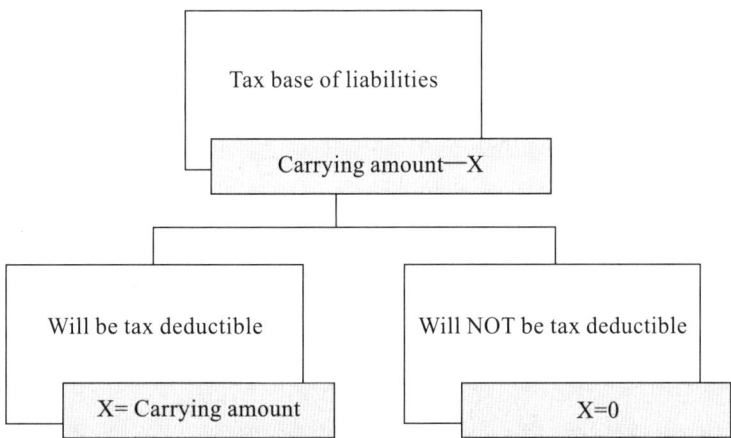

No.	Easy Rules
4	**Temporary differences**: Temporary differences are differences between the carrying amount of an asset or liability in the statement of financial position and its tax base (The tax base of an asset or liability is the amount attributed to that asset or liability for tax purposes.). a) **taxable temporary differences**, which are temporary differences that will result in taxable amounts in determining taxable profit (tax loss) of future periods when the carrying amount of the asset or liability is recovered or settled; or b) **deductible temporary differences**, which are temporary differences that will result in amounts that are deductible in determining taxable profit (tax loss) of future periods when the carrying amount of the asset or liability is recovered or settled. (IAS 12: para. 5)

Example:

Required: Calculate the carrying amount, tax base and the temporary differences for each of the transaction below:

1. The cost of the PP&E is $ 1 million. Accounting depreciation during the year is $ 300,000 and the tax depreciation (capital allowance or tax depreciation) is $ 400,000.

2. The interest receivable is $ 500. However, the tax rule states that the interest will be tax when the interest is received in cash.

3. The accrued interest is $ 500. However, the tax rule states that the interest is taxed on an accrual basis, i.e. when the interest becomes an interest receivable.

4. The provision liability is $ 600. However, the tax rule states that the tax relief is obtained if the provision is settled in cash.

5. The provision liability is $ 600. However, the tax rule states that the tax relief is obtained if the provision is on an accrual basis.

6. Income received in advance is $ 700. The tax rule states that this will be taxed on a cash basis, i.e. when the interest is received.

Answer:

1.

Carrying value = $ 1m − $ 300,000 = $ 700,000

Tax base = $ 1m − $ 400,000 = $ 600,000

This means that when the asset is sold (when it recovers the carrying amount of the PP&E) in the future, the proceeds from the sale (as taxable economic benefits) will be reduced by the amount of the PP&E, i.e. $ 600,000 (tax base of the PP&E will be deductible for tax purposes). In short, this is taxable in the future, and the tax base is updated by including the tax depreciation.

If those economic benefits will not be taxable, the tax base of the asset is equal to its carrying amount. For instance, if the tax rule in this country states that the proceeds from the sale of PP&E is not taxable (economic benefits will not be taxable), the tax base of the asset is equal to its carrying amount of $600,000.

Alternatively, there are $100,000 more depreciation expenses to be deducted from the taxable profits and hence the business can save tax on these $100,000. Therefore, in the future, when the asset is sold, the business must repay the tax saved on the $100,000 back to the tax authority.

Temporary difference = $700,000 − $600,000 = $100,000 (taxable temporary difference).

2.

Carrying value of the interest receivable asset = $500

Tax base = 0-the amount is taxable in the future and therefore, nil.

Temporary difference = $500 − 0 = $500 (taxable temporary difference)

3.

Carrying value of the interest receivable asset = $500

Tax base = $500-the amount is not taxable in the future, hence it equals to the carrying value.

Temporary difference = $500 − $500 = 0

4.

Carrying value of the provision liability = $600

The tax base of a liability is its carrying amount $600, less any amount that will be deductible for tax purposes in respect of that liability in future periods: in the future, $600 will be tax deductible.

Tax base = $600 − $600 = 0

Temporary difference = $600 − $0 = $600 (deductible temporary difference)

5.

Carrying value of the provision liability = $600

The tax base of a liability is its carrying amount $600, less any amount that will be deductible for tax purposes in respect of that liability in future periods: 0 because the amount has been included when it is accrued.

Tax base = $600

Temporary difference = $600 − $600 = 0

6.

For revenue received in advance, the tax base of the resulting liability is its carrying amount $700 less any amount of the revenue that will not be taxable in future periods: $700 because the $700 has already been taxed when cash is received.

Carrying value of the interest received in advance liability = $700

Tax base = 0 ($700 − $700)

Temporary difference = $ 700−0 = $ 700 (deductible temporary difference)

11.11 *Deferred Tax Liabilities*

No.	Easy Rules
5	**Deferred tax liabilities**: Deferred tax liabilities are the amounts of income taxes payable in future periods in respect of taxable temporary differences. (IAS 12:para. 5)

Example:

The temporary difference on the PP&E of company A is $ 5 million and the corporation tax rate is 30% this year. Assume there are no opening deferred tax liabilities.

Required: Calculate the deferred tax liability and its accounting treatment.

Answer: Deferred tax liability = temporary difference × tax rate = $ 5m×30% = $ 1.5m

Dr	Income tax expense	$ 1.5m
Cr	Deferred tax liability	$ 1.5m

11.12 *Deferred Tax Assets*

No.	Easy Rules
6	Deferred tax assets are the amounts of income taxes recoverable in future periods in respect of: a) deductible temporary differences; b) the carryforward of unused tax losses; and c) the carryforward of unused tax credits. (IAS 12:para. 5)
7	For deferred tax asset to be recognised, sufficient future taxable profits must be available against which the deductible difference can be utilised. Deferred tax assets are only recognised to the extent that it is probable that taxable profits will be available against which the deductible temporary difference can be utilised. (IAS 12:para. 28)

Example:
Case A:

The deductible temporary difference of the company B in terms of the warranty provision liability to be $ 3 million. And the corporation tax rate is 30%. Assume there are no opening deferred tax assets.

Case B:

Company C incurred $ 40 million operating losses in prior periods which can be utilised to offset future operating profits. The tax rate is 30%. Assume there are no opening deferred tax assets.

In year two, the business made $ 15 million trading profits. Therefore the unused tax losses now become $ 25 million. Company C is confident that future trading profits can be generated.

Case C:

To encourage investment in the area, the local government offers tax credits of $ 6 million if the business invests $ 100 million in this area. Company D is entitled to these tax credits and as at the year end, the unused tax credits ($ 6m can be offset directly against the taxable expense) are still $ 6 million.

Required: Journal entries for the above transactions.

Answer:

Case A:

Deferred tax asset = deductible temporary difference×tax rate = $ 3m×30% = $ 0.9m

Dr Deferred tax asset $ 0.9m

Cr Income tax expense $ 0.9m

Case B:

In year one:

Deferred tax asset = operating losses×tax rate = $ 40m×30% = $ 12m

Dr Deferred tax asset $ 12m

Cr Income tax expense $ 12m

In year two:

The deferred tax assets should be reduced by $ 15m × 30% = $ 4.5m.

Dr Income tax expense $ 4.5m

Cr Deferred tax asset $ 4.5m

Case C:

Deferred tax asset is the tax credit of $ 6 million offered by government.

Dr Deferred tax asset $ 6m

Cr Income tax expense $ 6m

11.13 Difference Between Temporary/Timing Difference and Permanent Differences

No.	Easy Rules
1	Temporary or timing difference between the carrying amount of the asset or liability in the statement of financial position and the tax base gives rise to deferred tax liabilities or assets.
2	Permanent difference between accounting and taxable profit is the difference in accounting and tax requirements, i.e. in most countries, entertaining expense and political donations are not allowed for tax purposes and therefore, they should never be included in the taxable profits.
3	The key to identifying whether the difference is temporary or permanent depends on whether this item will be subject to tax in the future. If it is subject to tax in the future, this is a temporary difference giving rise to deferred tax liability or asset. If not, this is a permanent difference and it does not give rise to deferred tax liability or asset.

11.14 Deferred Tax Implications for Specific Items

1. Development costs:

The carrying amount of the capitalised development costs is $ 2 million (after charging amortisation expense during the year). The development cost was fully deductible against taxable profits when it was incurred. The corporation tax rate is 30%.

Required: Deferred tax accounting treatment.

Answer:

Carrying value	−Tax base	=Temporary difference	×tax rate	=Deferred tax
$ 2m	−[CV $ 2m− $ 2m (will not be tax deductible)]	= $ 2m (taxable)	×30%	$ 0.6m

Dr	Income tax expense	$ 0.6m
Cr	Deferred tax liability	$ 0.6m

2. Provision and allowances:

A business recognised $ 7 million warranty provision liability and $ 3 million irrecoverable debt allowance. The corporation tax rate is 30%.

Required: Deferred tax accounting treatment:

1. If it is probable that the entity will earn sufficient taxable profit in future periods to benefit from a reduction in tax payments.

2. If it is not probable that the entity will earn sufficient taxable profit in future periods to benefit from a reduction in tax payments and the business expects only $ 1.8 million deferred tax can be recovered from future taxable profits.

Answer:1:

Carrying value	−Tax base	=Temporary difference	×tax rate	=Deferred tax
$ (7) m	− $ (7m−7m) = 0	$ (7) m	×30%	$ (2.1) m
$ (3) m	− $ (3m−3m) = 0	$ (3) m	×30%	$ (0.9) m
				$ (3) m

Dr	Deferred tax asset	$ 3m
Cr	Income tax expense	$ 3m

2: Deferred tax asset should only be recognised to the extent of $ 1.8m:

Dr	Deferred tax asset	$ 1.8m
Cr	Income tax expense	$ 1.8m

3. Impairment and inventory losses:

1	If the tax relief on the asset loss (inventory or other non-current assets such as PP&E) is only granted when the asset is sold, the reduction in asset value is ignored for tax purposes until the sale.

Example: PP&E impairment

The carrying value of the PP&E is $ 50 million and there is a $ 20 million impairment loss recognised by the entity during the year. The tax rule states that the tax relief on the PP&E asset loss is only granted when the PP&E is sold in the future. The corporation tax rate is 30%.

Required: Deferred tax accounting treatment.

Answer:

	Carrying value	−Tax base	=Temporary difference	×tax rate	=Deferred tax
	$ 30m	− $ 50m	$ (20)m	×30%	$ (6)m

Dr	Deferred tax asset		$ 6m
Cr	Income tax expense		$ 6m

Example: Inventory impairment

The cost of a piece of inventory is $ 3 million, however, as at the reporting date, the management estimated that its net realisable value to only be $ 2.1 million. In other words, the inventory has been impaired by $ 0.9 million. The tax rule states that the tax relief on the inventory asset loss is only granted when the inventory is sold in the future. The corporation tax rate is 30%.

Required: Deferred tax accounting treatment.

Answer:

	Carrying value	−Tax base	=Temporary difference	×tax rate	=Deferred tax
	$ 2.1m	− $ 3m	$ (0.9)m	×30%	$ (0.27)m

Dr	Deferred tax asset		$ 0.27m
Cr	Income tax expense		$ 0.27m

4. Fair value adjustments:

1	When a subsidiary is acquired, its net assets are measured at fair value. The fair value adjustments such as the recognition of additional intangible asset which has not been shown in the single company's Financial Statements. However, there will be no deductions available against taxable profits when these hidden assets are recovered (in simple words, the acquired business did not have an invoice for the internally generated goodwill, therefore, the tax authority will not allow this to be expensed when calculating the taxable profits), the tax base is therefore nil. But these assets relate to the subsidiary, the carrying value will be recovered through that subsidiary making future taxable profits and taxed at the subsidiary's corporation tax rate. The deferred tax amount is then used to update the goodwill figure (if the cost of the investment exceeds its fair value of net assets acquired). (IAS 12: para. 19-21)

Example: Fair value adjustment

Company A acquired company B and the fair value adjustment relating to the internally generated goodwill of company B is $ 5 million. The corporation tax rate in company B's jurisdiction is 30%. The recognised intangible asset for the internally generated goodwill has a tax base of nil because there will be no deductions against taxable profits when the asset is disposed/recovered.

Required: Deferred tax accounting treatment.

Answer:

Carrying value	−Tax base	=Temporary difference	×tax rate	=Deferred tax
$ 5m	−0	$ 5m	30%	$ 1.5m

Dr	Subsidiary's equity (Working 2 in consolidated account)		$ 1.5m
Cr	Deferred tax liability		$ 1.5m

The debit side of the entry is then taken to the goodwill calculation to reduce the goodwill figure:

Goodwill calculation:

Fair value of consideration	x
+NCI	x
−Subsidiary's net assets at the date of acquisition using fair value (+ $ 1.5m deferred tax liability here to reduce the overall goodwill)	(x)
= Goodwill at the date of acquisition	x

5. PP&E revaluation:

No.	Easy Rules
1	**Under IAS 16:** IFRSs permit or require certain assets to be carried at fair value or to be revalued (see, for example, IAS 16 Property, Plant and Equipment, IAS 38 Intangible Assets, IAS 40 Investment Property, IFRS 9 Financial Instruments and IFRS 16 Leases). In some jurisdictions, the revaluation or other restatement of an asset to fair value affects taxable profit (tax loss) for the current period. As a result, the tax base of the asset is adjusted and no temporary difference arises. In other jurisdictions, the revaluation or restatement of an asset does not affect taxable profit in the period of the revaluation or restatement and, consequently, the tax base of the asset is not adjusted. (IAS 12: para. 20)
2	Please note, in the professional qualification exam, the tax base of the PP&E is never adjusted for the revaluation gain.
3	**Certain items can be directly charged to equity include:** Revaluations of PP&E (IAS 16) The effect of a change in accounting policy or correction of a material error (IAS 8) (IAS 12: para. 61)

Example: Revaluation of PP&E

A business acquired a piece of land for $6 million and this has been revalued to $9 million by the independent valuer as at the reporting date. The tax rule states that revaluations do not affect the tax base of the asset or taxable profits (no deductions will be available against taxable profit as this asset is recovered). The corporation tax rate is 30%.

Required: Deferred tax accounting treatment.

Answer:

Carrying value	−Tax base	=Temporary difference	×tax rate	=Deferred tax
$9m	−$6m	=$3m (taxable)	30%	$0.9m

Dr		Other comprehensive income (and revaluation reserve)	$ 0.9m *
	Cr	Deferred tax liability	$ 0.9m

(IAS 12:para.61)

*This is because when the piece of land is revalued, the journal entry for this would be:

Dr		PP&E	$ 3m
	Cr	Revaluation reserve	$ 3m

We therefore need to treat the deferred tax adjustment of $ 0.9m as a reduction in revaluation reserve per IAS 12:para.61.

Please note, even though the business has no intentions to dispose of the asset, the business will generate cash flows from the use of the asset (i.e. to recover its $ 9m carrying value) which exceeds its tax depreciation in total, i.e. $ 6m. The excess gain will be subject to tax.

(IAS 12:para.20 (a))

To prepare a trial balance:

	Dr	**Cr**	
PP&E increase	$ 3m		PP&E increase
Deferred tax liability		$ 0.9m	Deferred tax liability
Revaluation reserve		$ 3m- $ 0.9m = $ 2.1m	Revaluation reserve
	$ 3m	$ 3m	

6. The effect of a change in accounting policy or material error

During year two, a material error was found regarding the year one's Financial Statements worth of $ 5 million. To correct this error, a $ 5 million reduction in the opening retained earnings in year two's statement of changes in equity and a $ 5 million decrease in PP&E are needed. As a result of the error correction, a $ 0.2 million decrease in deferred tax liability is needed.

Required: Accounting entries.

Answer:
Correction of error:

Dr	Retained earnings in year two	$ 5m
Cr	PP&E	$ 5m

Deferred tax:

Dr	Deferred tax liability	$ 0.2m
Cr	Retained earnings (directly to equity)	$ 0.2m

The above entry would be the same if a change in accounting policy is enforced. However, for changes in accounting policy, all the prior periods Financial Statements should be restated using the latest accounting policy for comparison purposes. For material errors found in the prior year's Financial Account, only prior period error should be adjusted.

11.15 Components in Deferred Tax

No.	Easy Rules
1	There are two components in the deferred tax: 1. Deferred tax relating to timing differences 2. Changes in deferred tax liability or asset.

Example:

In year one, the temporary difference for the item of PP&E was $ 1 million.

In year two, the carrying value of the deferred tax liability arises to $ 0.5 million.

Corporation tax rate is 30%.

Required: Accounting treatment for the above deferred tax liability in both year one and year two.

Answer:

Year one:

Deferred tax liability = Temporary difference × corporation tax rate = $ 1m×30% = $ 0.3m

Year two:

Deferred tax liability = $ 0.5m

Hence:

Dr	Income tax expense (suppose this is not related to revaluation)	$ 0.2m
Cr	Deferred tax liability	$ 0.2m

11.16 *Changes in the Tax Rate in the Deferred Tax Calculation*

No.	Easy Rules
1	Current/Deferred tax liabilities (assets) for the current and prior periods shall be measured at the amount expected to be paid to (recovered from) the taxation authorities, using the tax rates (and tax laws) that have been enacted or substantively enacted by the end of the reporting period. (IAS 12: para. 46–47)
2	For instance, the tax rate for the current year is 30%. However, the tax authority has announced that the new corporation tax rate is to be revised to 18% from 5th January next year onwards. Therefore, the current year's deferred tax calculation should be based on the 18% tax rate instead of the 30% because the 18% corporation tax rate has been substantively enacted by the end of the reporting period.

11.17 *Discounting for Deferred Tax*

No.	Easy Rules
1	Deferred tax assets and liabilities should not be discounted. The reliable determination of deferred tax assets and liabilities on a discounted basis requires detailed scheduling of the timing of the reversal of each temporary difference. In many cases such scheduling is impracticable or highly complex. Therefore, it is inappropriate to require discounting of deferred tax assets and liabilities. To permit, but not to require, discounting would result in deferred tax assets and liabilities which would not be comparable between entities. Therefore, this Standard does not require or permit the discounting of deferred tax assets and liabilities. (IAS 12. para. 53 and 54)

11.18 Presentation in P/L

The income tax components to be included in the statement of profit or loss includes:

current tax payable	x
+under/(over) provision of income tax relating to last year's profits	x
+increase/(decrease) in deferred tax liabilities	x/(x)
−increase/+decrease in deferred tax assets	(x)/x
Income tax =	x

Example:

The tax on trading profits and capital gain of a business for the year one is $ 5 million. The opening deferred tax liability of this business is $ 0.6 million and the carrying value of the deferred tax liability is $ 0.2 million. The following trial balance extract of the business shows the under or over provision of its income tax relating to the last year's profits:

	Dr	Cr
Income tax		$ 0.8 million

Required: Accounting treatment for the current tax payable liability, over provision of income tax and the deferred tax implication.

Answer:

1. Current tax payable liability:

Dr	Income tax expense	$ 5m
Cr	Current tax payable	$ 5m

2. Over provision of income tax:

Dr	Current tax payable	$ 0.8m
Cr	Income tax expense	$ 0.8m

3. Deferred tax liability reduction:

Dr	Deferred tax liability ($ 0.6m– $ 0.2m)	
Cr	Income tax expense	$ 0.4m

Therefore, the total amount to be included in the income tax (P/L):

Current tax payable	$ 5m
(Over) provision of income tax relating to last year's profits	$ 0.8m
+Increase in deferred tax liabilities	$ (0.4)m
Income tax =	$ 5.4m

In the statement of financial position:

Current tax payable	$ 4.2m
Deferred tax liability (non-current liability)	x– $ 0.4m

11.19 *The Reason to Calculate the Deferred Tax*

No.	Easy Rules
1	Deferred tax is not the actual amount of tax paid to the tax authority and this is an accounting term.

To illustrate this, let's have a look at the following example:

Example:

The following information relates to the business (m)

Profit before Tax	$ 10	$ 10
Accounting profit before tax	$ 10	$ 10
+Accounting depreciation	$ 3	$ 3
–Capital Allowance	($ 5)	($ 4)
= Taxable profit	$ 8	$ 9
×corporation tax rate @ 30%	($ 2.4)	($ 2.7)

Required: Calculate the income tax expense where:
1. Without deferred tax
2. With deferred tax

Answer:

1. Without deferred tax:

Profit before Tax	$ 10	$ 10
−Tax Expense @ 30%	($ 2.4)	($ 2.7)
Profit after Tax	$ 7.6	$ 7.3

Profit after tax figures for year one and two are not the same even though profits before tax in year one and two are exactly the same with the same tax rate applied and this confuses shareholders.

2. With deferred tax:

Profit before Tax	$ 10	$ 10
−Tax Expense @ 30% *	($ 3)	($ 3)
Profit after Tax	$ 7	$ 7

* Tax Expense

Tax Expense above	$ 2.4	$ 2.7
+ Deferred Tax Movement **	$ 0.6	$ 0.3
	$ 3	$ 3

** Deferred Tax Movement:

	Carrying Value	Tax Base	Temporary Difference x % =	Deferred Tax
1st year:	$ 12− $ 3 = $ 9	$ 12− $ 5 = $ 7	$ 2×30%	$ 0.6
2nd Year:	$ 9− $ 3 = $ 6	$ 7− $ 4 = $ 3	$ 3×30% =	$ 0.9

Profit after tax in year one and two are exactly the same if those profits before tax figures are the same with the same corporation tax rate applied. This is because by including the deferred tax movements in the calculation, the timing difference between the carrying value and the tax base of the item in the statement of financial position is considered.

11.20 Presentation of Current Tax and Deferred Tax

No.	Easy Rules
1	Deferred tax assets or liabilities are presented in the non-current asset or non-current liability section of the statement of financial position.
2	An entity shall offset current tax assets and current tax liabilities if, and only if, the entity meets with the following conditions: a) has a legally enforceable right to set off the recognised amounts. An entity will normally have a legally enforceable right to set off a current tax asset against a current tax liability when they relate to income taxes levied by the same taxation authority and the taxation authority permits the entity to make or receive a single net payment. b) intends either to settle on a net basis, or to realise the asset and settle the liability simultaneously. (IAS 12:para. 71-72)

References

[1] Abbas A. Mirza, G. H. (2010). *International Financial Reporting Standards (IFRS) Workbook and Guide*. Wiley.

[2] Adler, R. M. (2012). *Teaching IFRS*. London.

[3] Barry J. Epstein, E. K. (2008). *IFRS Policies and Procedures*. USA: Wiley.

[4] BDO. (2011). Blind Freddy-Common Errors in Accounting for Impairment-Part 5-Testing Goodwill for Impairment. Australia.

[5] BDO. (2013). *Ifrs in Practice*. UK.

[6] BPP. (2018). *ACCA Financial Reporting*. London: BPP Learning Media.

[7] Brüggemann, U. (2011). *Essays on the Economic Consequences of Mandatory IFRS Reporting around the world*. Germany: GABLER.

[8] Canada, C. (2013). *Guide to International Financial Reporting Standards in Canada IAS 36 Impairment of Assets*. Canada.

[9] Chen, S. (2019). *IFRS 16 Leases A comical yet practical journey into the world of IFRS Leases*. Hong Kong: International Economic Press.

[10] Chen, S. (2019). *The No. 1 No-Nonsense Basic Financial Accounting Theory Handbook*. Hong Kong: International Economic Press.

[11] Deloitte. (2019). *IAS 20 Accounting for Government Grants and Disclosure of Government Assistance*. Retrieved from IAS 20 Accounting for Government Grants and Disclosure of Government Assistance: https://www.iasplus.com/en/standards/ias/ias20

[12] EY. (2017). *Worldwide Capital and Fixed Assets Guide*.

[13] Foundation, I. (2018). *Conceptual Framework for Financial Reporting*. IFRS Foundation.

[14] IFRS Foundation. (2019). *IFRS Blue Book*. London.

[15] International Financial Reporting Standards Foundation. (2019). *IFRS Red Book*. London: IFRS.

[16] Kaplan Financial. (2018). *CIMA F2 Advanced Financial Accounting*. London: Kaplan publishing.

[17] KPMG. (2014). *IAS 33 Earnings per Share*. KPMG.

[18] PWC. (2008). *Top 10 tips for impairment testing*. PWC.

[19] Seraphim, C. (2015). *IFRS update*. BIBLIOGRAPHY

[20] Kirk, R. (2008). *IFRS: A Quick Reference Guide*. Elsevier.

[21] Walton, P. (2009). An Executive's Guide for Moving from US GAAP to IFRS. New York: Businessexpert.